KU-122-340

PARENTAL INVOLVEMENT IN CHILDREN'S READING

Parental Involvement in Children's Reading

Edited by Keith Topping and Sheila Wolfendale

CROOM HELM
London & Sydney

NICHOLS PUBLISHING COMPANY
New York

Croom Helm Ltd, Provident House, Burrell Row,
Beckenham, Kent BR3 1AT

Croom Helm Australia Pty Ltd, Suite 4, 6th Floor, 64-76 Kippax Street,
Surry Hills, NSW 2010, Australia

British Library Cataloguing in Publication Data

Parental involvement in children's reading.
1. Reading (Elementary) 2. Parent-teacher
relationships
I. Topping, Keith J. II. Wolfendale, Sheila
372.4 LB1573

ISBN 0-7099-2487-9
ISBN 0-7099-2488-7 Pbk

First published in the United States of America 1985 by
Nichols Publishing Company, Post Office Box 96
New York, NY 10024

Library of Congress Cataloging in Publication Data
Main entry under title:

Parental involvement in children's reading.

Includes index.
1. Reading—Great Britain—Parent participation—
Addresses, essays, lectures. 2. Reading—Great Britain—
Remedial teaching—Addresses, essays, lectures.
I. Topping, Keith J. II. Wolfendale, Sheila, 1939-

LB1050.P3243 1985 372.4'0941 85-13704
ISBN 0-89397-230-4

Printed and bound in Great Britain
by Billing & Sons Limited, Worcester.

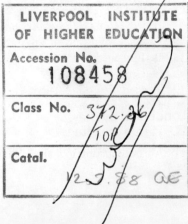

CONTENTS

PREFACE

This book has been written by practising teachers, university academics and educational psychologists. It is about parental involvement in reading projects of very various scale and method. Some contributions are very practical and descriptive, others are more analytical and include evaluative evidence. Many of the contributions incorporate both aspects, bridging the gap between practice and research.

Readers from a variety of backgrounds should thus find something useful within the pages that follow: teachers, parents, researchers, education administrators, school psychologists, teacher trainers and reading advisers, to name but a few. Naturally, different readers will find different parts of the book especially appealing.

Parental involvement in children's reading is an area of very rapid growth in education. This volume offers an overview of a changing world, in which practice is constantly developing and improving. It is hoped that the availability of this book will further the dissemination of good practice.

A brief word here about the structure of the book may help the reader to use it with greater ease and efficiency.

In Part 1, the general introduction, the first chapter describes the context of modern international trends in the involvement of parents in their children's education generally. The second chapter briefly considers models of the reading process and offers an analysis of why parental involvement in children's reading works.

Part 2 is the largest part of the book, and is divided into four subsections. Each subsection is concerned with a particular type of project, viz. 'Parent Listening', 'Paired Reading', 'Behavioural Methods' and 'Variations'. Each subsection starts with an introductory chapter providing a straightforward description of the techniques and processes included in the subsection.

Part 3 comprises three chapters concerned with the implementation of projects to promote parental involvement in children's reading. The first chapter in this part reviews the story so far, draws some conclusions, and speculates about prospects for the future. The second chapter considers how to plan and carry out projects. The third chapter gives details of useful resources and their availability.

Given this structure, readers should be able to dip into the book at different places, to suit their level of background knowledge, current professional requirements, and mood of the moment.

In any event, the co-editors would welcome readers' comments on the format of the book, and views about the optimal structure for further editions. They would also be very pleased to hear from readers who are undertaking interesting work in this exciting area of development.

In the meantime, have a good read.

1 OVERVIEW OF PARENTAL PARTICIPATION IN CHILDREN'S EDUCATION

Sheila Wolfendale

Introduction

The contributions in this volume form a significant representation and reflection of a phenomenon in comtemporary education. Of the various forms of parental involvement, parental involvement in children's reading is to date the most explored and fullest expression of a working relationship between parents and professionals.

Readers of this book will discern differences in reading-theory rationale and in research base; differing techniques, scale of operations and quite different genesis of and impetus for each project described. What the contributors have in common is the premiss that

(1) promotion of home–school links via curriculum focus, that of reading in particular, is a desirable aim;
(2) in words taken from the Plowden Report (para. 114, 1967) 'by involving the parents, the children may be helped'.

Broader Perspectives to the Involvement of Parents

The story of the American Head Start and Follow-through ventures has been extensively documented (Lazar, 1979) and summarised (Curtis and Blatchford, 1981) and the particular relationship between 'disadvantage' and compensatory education, especially within the British context, chronicled (Woodhead, 1976; Mortimore and Blackstone, 1982; also see Chapter 2). This author (Wolfendale, 1983) considers the foundations for intervening — that is, for making educational provision over and above or complementary to existing curriculum. Children from allegedly 'depriving' backgrounds have been the recipients of 'compensatory' intervention approaches. These are characterised by: extra input in the way of resources, including staff, equipment and in-service; special curricula, language programmes, cognitively oriented approaches; fostering of home–school–community links.

In recent years, the inherently negative approach of directing intervention mainly to those children who are deemed to be 'at risk', who apparently need the inoculation of special programmes, has been transformed. Intervention can be defined as an intentional match between carefully articulated education and curricular aims and the necessary objectives towards realisation of these. In recent years this has broadened to encompass all children. People working in compensatory milieux have transmitted such knowledge and experience about effective ways of matching teaching methods, task analyses and learning sequences with short- and longer-term objectives.

Pedagogic principles of optimising human potential become applicable then to all children. Broadening the conceptual base of intervention does not mean reverting to the notion of an undifferentiated curriculum. On the contrary, the variety of approaches, rooted within a number of differing theoretical foundations, which are now available means that content and method can be selectively targeted to meet the learning needs of all specific children.

A logical extension of this line of argument is that it is not necessary (and indeed may be invidious) to apply labels to groups of children to whom we direct a particular approach. It can be seen that some of the work reported in this book has been with children who traditionally have been ascribed to categories depending upon the way in which their 'problems' have been assessed and diagnosed. Accounts are also included of work that makes no distinction between the special needs of some children and the learning needs and requirements of all children. Thus, this formulation of intervention is demonstrated as being robust enough to be applied to children with transient or enduring special educational needs in ordinary and special schools, and to children whose learning in and adjustment to school have never caused concern.

What has also been in recent times amply demonstrated is the fact that parents are actively interested in their children's development and educational progress. Even the minority of parents with whom teachers find contact difficult, turn out to have well-founded reasons for not responding to schools' overtures. There is, therefore, no philosophical justification to preclude the potential involvement in children's education by parents. There is every justification for taking the view that parents are entitled to have knowledge of and access to educational decision-making. To create a structure for the provision and manifestation of these rights would be one formal way of ensuring support and encouragement for parents whose enthusiasm and activation are sapped by adverse support and encouragement for circumstances (Wilson and Herbert, 1978).

The willingness of a significant number of parents to participate in parental involvement in reading programmes instigated by schools will hopefully attest to the strength and viability of policies aimed at fostering home–school links. The 'ethics of intrusion' are seen to be positive where parents see the collaboration as fruitful.

Areas of Involvement by Parents in their Children's Development and Education: A Review of Recent Developments

Government Reports and the Place of Parents

Each of the reports on education and child servics from Plowden to Warnock on special education in Britain and equivalent legislation in the USA has drawn attention to and emphasised the potential of collaboration between professionals and parents to enhance children's development and learning. Each report has invoked and relied upon 'evidence' from many intervention projects that indicates that parental involvement in educational and community-based programmes is an entirely positive influence upon the child. The reports include Plowden (1967), Bullock (1975), Court (1976), Taylor (1977) and Warnock (1978), while equivalent American legislation is enshrined in Public Law 94-142, The Education for All Handicapped Children Act, passed by the US Congress in 1975.

The recommendations in these reports cover a spectrum of areas of collaboration between parents and professionals working with children in a number of fields. The last two decades have seen an increasing parental presence in educational institutions and at the interface of school and community. In the area of special educational needs, in legislative processes, in decision-making and in provision, parental representation is increasing. Several areas will now be briefly reviewed.

Parents and Preschool

Several studies have set out to explore the parameters of involving parents (usually mothers) in the preschool years and in various types of early childhood experience. Smith (1984) in reporting her earlier study (Smith, 1980) summarises a variety of attitudes by preschool staff to parental involvement in these words: 'the strongest feeling was the importance of continuity and shared experience between home and school, of access to the group and to the child's experience there' (p. 282). The study of Tizard *et al*. (1981) was a practical demonstration of the activities in which parents can participate, as well as of the constraints upon co-operation. In a later book (Tizard and Hughes, 1984) Tizard argues for a reappraisal of the contribution of the home to children's development, to cognitive and learning processes, and urges a match between the respective provisions of the home and of preschool.

A major influence has undoubtedly been the growth of the preschool playgroups, the majority of which are managed by a parent committee and run largely by parents. The original impetus in the 1960s was the insufficiency of nurseries and day-care facilities — as a model of parent initiation and parent power, the playgroups have been hugely influential.

There are now a number of different sorts of initiative in the preschool arena which seek to explore a variety of ways in which parents and staff can work together. A current DHSS-funded project entitled 'Services for Families with Young Children' is based at the National Children's Bureau. The main aims are:

(i) To explore the extent to which services for families with children under five are planned, implemented and delivered in partnership with those families for whom they are intended.
(ii) To identify and examine a number of initiatives in which a working partnership is achieved between parents and workers in the health, education, social service and voluntary sectors.
(iii) To disseminate information and promote discussion of parent–professional partnerships.

The area of preschool and early childhood education has been a pacesetter for educational innovation for many years, and latterly this honourable tradition is extending to a rapprochement between home, community and preschool provision. As to whether or not the outcomes from programmes of parental involvement vindicate the setting up of such programmes, in terms of measurable gains, there are clearly broader criteria by which to gauge the success of the ventures. As Smith (1984) makes clear in her discussion, we cannot and should not regard only 'gains' as the index; less tangible factors to do with parental confidence-building, teachers' positive perceptions, the manifest spin-off to children, probable enhanced competence in managing and teaching children by the adult care-givers, and so on, are equally important. The reader will see that in the accounts of parental involvement in reading which follow that the postulated benefits which underlie the hypothesis in each case are seen to be wider than 'just' hoped-for gains on test/retest measures of reading attainment.

The School, the Home and the Community

A conceptual starting-point for viewing the child in the family, at school and within the community is that of the ecological approach (Hobbs, 1978; Bronfenbrenner, 1979) and the notion of mapping out the ecosystem for each child, so that one can see the juxtaposition of that child to his or her parents (care-givers), siblings, relatives, locality, friends, clubs, even shops, amenities — and, of course, the school network with relation to teachers and peers. Such an approach enables us, too, to analyse the systems of which each child is a part, and use this as a basis for problem-definition and problem-resolution (Apter, 1982).

The Educational Priority Area projects (Halsey, 1972) explored in practice the possibilities for making accessible the provisions of educational institutions (schools, adult education) to parents and other adults in the wider community, and also of creating opportunities for group support and 'self-help' groups to be generated and sustained by the local community, adults and children. Much of this work was and remains seminal; Wolfendale (1983) provides a view of a number of well-known earlier and current initiatives.

Several programmes have now become fixtures of the local and regional scene, being funded by the Local Education Authority (LEA) and/or government, by voluntary organisations, and even by the EEC. Some examples: the Coventry Community Education Development Centre is LEA-funded (see Chapter 9 in this book; Widlake and Macleod, 1984) as in Home–School Link in Milton Keynes and the Liverpool Parent Support Programme (Davis, 1984). The Newham Parents' Centre receives funds from the LEA, the EEC and other sources — now that the London Borough of Newham has initiated a 'Going Community' policy, the links between the voluntary Newham Parents' Centre and the LEA are strengthened and the groundwork of the NCP as a ginger group, which has initiated a number of projects over a period of several years, has borne fruit (e.g. Crisp *et al.*, 1983). The Southampton-based organisation SCOPE (Poulton and Poulton, 1979) incorporates parent education groups and helps prepare children for school. Among other sources, SCOPE has received grants from a bank.

These and other examples attest to the effectiveness, as judged by the organisers and participants, of drawing together, within local networks, the people who most significantly impinge upon and affect the lives and well-being of children.

Children, Parents and Schools

A number of studies have chronicled the 1970s trend towards increased parental representation and presence in schools, covering aspects such as parental assistance to teachers in hearing children read, helping in other activities, participating in outings and membership of parent–teacher associations (Cyster *et al.*, 1979; HMI Survey, 1978). During the 1970s and the present decade, exploration into the potential and the dimensions of home–school relationships has continued. The area of parental involvement in reading, which forms the subject-matter of this book, is the largest 'growth area'.

However, there are a number of significant initiatives, some of which are mirrored by the public pronouncements of people with influence in education and in policy-making circles.

All political parties have endorsed the provisions within the 1980 Education Act for greater parental representation on schools' governing bodies; undoubtedly over time, parents will, as a corporate force, build up collective expertise on relevant matters of school policy, curriculum and organisation, and will acquire skills of questioning, bargaining, negotiating and decision-making within the governing body.

A number of LEAs and other organisations have commissioned reports into the viability of home–school policies (Hills, 1984; Woods, 1984) which may be paralleled by concurrent pilot projects within the Inner London Education Authority (ILEA). The members of ILEA commissioned a committee of enquiry into the authority's secondary schools. In the report of the enquiry (Hargreaves, 1984) a significant amount of attention was given to parental involvement and a number of recommendations were made for implementing home–school policies. There followed, within ILEA, a period of consultation between the authority, schools, parents and the community.

Within a number of localities parental involvement and the promotion of home–school policies has been the subject of in-service for teachers. Booklets have been prepared (cf. Hertfordshire, undated; Atherton, 1982; COPE, undated) and in several parts of the country there is a tie-up between a local institution of higher education and schools, for example, the Development of Effective Home/School Programme (Atkin and Goode, 1982; Day, 1984).

International Perspectives

There is an international backcloth to the growing preoccupation with developing effective home–school partnership. The Americans and Canadians are well advanced in this whole topic area, conceptually and practically; books and manuals stream out of publishing houses, full of guidance, tasks and exercises (for just one example, see Berger, 1983). In at least one Canadian province, parental involvement is mandatory by law. North American experience is ahead of ours in some respects, so it is not surprising to come across a book (Pizzo, 1983) which tells parents 'how self-help and child advocacy groups can help you get: better schools, improved health care, safer highways, more responsive government services'. The Institute for Responsive Education (IRE) in Boston, Massachusetts, based at Boston University, has over the last few years carried out a comprehensive programme of parental involvement in schools and community. Founded on the premiss that citizen participation is an essential ingredient in school improvement and that citizens' access to information is indispensable for effective participation, IRE has produced more than 30 reports, handbooks, bibliographies and other publications (see p. 15 for examples).

Nearer to British shores, there is an increasing amount of information on family–school relations in European countries (Macbeth, 1984). The European Commission is backing a newly formed European Parents' Association, whose central aim to 'achieve a better understanding in Europe of what parents expect from schools'. The Council of Europe organised a major week-long conference in Norway in the summer of 1984 on teacher–parent collaboration. The final talk, Reflections on Home–School Links in the Future, was delivered by the Norwegian Parliamentary Secretary to the Minister of Church and Education.

Parents and Special Educational Needs

A number of the principles underlying conjoint parent–professional ventures which have been referred to in this chapter and which form the basis for parental involvement in reading programmes also apply to the considerable amount of work that has taken place during the 1970s and now the 1980s in the area of special educational needs. The work of the teams at the Hester Adrian Research Centre, University of Manchester, has been seminal in demonstrating how effective joint parent–professional assessment and teaching can be for children with severe learning difficulties and handicapping conditions (Cunningham and Sloper, 1984; Mittler and McConachie, 1983). Likewise, the clinical work of the Newsons and colleagues which has included direct parental participation in assessment and diagnosis (Newson and Hipgrave, 1982) is highly relevant in showing what is possible. The Warnock Report had commended the Portage Scheme as constituting good practice and for being the epitome, as we know it in the UK, of an effective, multidisciplinary parent and professional partnership, in which all participants co-operate in devising and carrying out teaching programmes for young (but also school-age) children with learning difficulties and handicaps. The take-up of Portage in the UK has been impressive (Cameron, 1982; Dessent, 1984; Daly *et al.*,

1985).

The premiss on which this work is based are:

- parents are expert on their own children;
- their skills complement professional skills (for the concept of 'equivalent expertise' (see Wolfendale, 1983, Chapter 2);
- parents can impart vital information and make informed observations;
- parents have the right to be involved;
- parents should contribute to decision-making;
- parents can be highly effective teachers of their own children.

This author is currently involved in an exercise which is founded on these principles and designed to test them out. This is the idea of parental profiling in which parents construct a 'child at home' profile which complements professional assessment. A related venture is a national piloting exercise which is exploring effective ways in which parents can make their written contribution to the 1981 Education Act, Section 5 of Assessment and Statementing Procedures, which it is their legal right to do so (Wolfendale, 1984) along with the extension of other parental rights under this Act.

Paralleling these developments has been the publication of books written mainly for parents on aspects of rearing and managing children and dealing with particular problems and learning situations (Westmacott and Cameron, 1981; Carr, 1980), but which can also be used for workshops with parents, teachers and other workers (Harris, 1983; Twiford, 1984).

Parents and Teachers: Common Concerns

Having outlined the rationale of involving parents in their children's schooling and provided a brief review of recent developments in a number of related areas, it may be timely now to examine issues pertaining to the adults with prime daily responsibility for children. It is inevitable that in the section that follows, somewhat more attention is given to the realities of the parental role than to teachers' role, for this is a book which claims to explore a phenomenon that is still regarded as novel in many quarters.

The educational literature abounds with treaties and tomes on educational philosophy, teaching method, curriculum matters and so on. Traditionally, little scrutiny has been given to the dimensions of parents' position *vis-à-vis* their children's education.

Over millennia and in most societies, the overwhelming majority of parents have demonstrated to a greater or lesser extent concern over their progeny's welfare, interest in and commitment to their progress. Their involvement may be demonstrated unconsciously or intentionally; that is, parents may act as role model, may transmit the culture to their offspring, may interpret the moral and social code, may carry out the necessary daily caretaking functions 'instinctively' without necessarily appraising these tasks — or, they may have a thought-out and articulated approach, and ascribe purpose to their actions. The exhortations to parents to 'bathe children in language' from the earliest moments represents this call to intentionality in the child-rearing process.

The view can be taken that children are 'learning' all the time, that is, using their sensory equipment, receiving, storing, processing information, outputting on a selective, decision-making basis (Davie *et al.*, 1984). It follows that, by and large, their adult care-givers are 'teaching' all or most of the time, in the ways listed in the previous paragraph.

With these premisses in mind, then, the bifurcation of home and school activity becomes less tenable. Advocates of parental involvement in reading and related home- and school-based learning programmes hold that

(i) parents and teachers have in common a pedagogic role which incorporates a protective, nurturing aspect into the training one;
(ii) parents and teachers share responsibility for maximising the learning potential of their charges and for creating opportunities for enjoyable and enhancing experiences;
(iii) parents and teachers have some shared aspirations for children's progress and successful coping in a variety of life situations.

The movement towards greater parental involvement represents a profound shift in attitudes on the part of teachers, or to put it another way, successive cohorts of teachers believe in or accept a philosophy they are keen to put into practice. Parents who have not traditionally been in a position to instigate contact, let alone sustain involvement are responding positively. Their co-operation is a tangible manifestation of an otherwise tacit acknowledgement of the underlying principles. This author has outlined elsewhere (Wolfendale, 1983, Chapter 10) what the benefits of collaboration might be for children, their parents and tecahers, and refers to 'equivalent expertise' — that is, the notion that parents and professionals both bring to the enterprise their own highly relevant experience of children and their skills, honed over time, of rearing or teaching them.

In the case of teachers, they bring knowledge of child development and of theories of learning and teaching and have the advantage of an accumulating store of professional wisdom as the backcloth to their practice. They can appraise individual differences in learning receptivity, rate of learning, etc., and can match each child's learning needs to the provision on offer.

Parents contribute their life experience as well as accumulating knowledge of their own child's (or children's) development and individual characteristics, and have the advantage of experiencing minute-by-minute child contact in a variety of situations. They, too, can appraise their child's learning responsiveness; they can make predictions as to outcomes and make a match between what the child needs (in the sense of primary as well as, of course, secondary needs) with whatever resources and support the home and family have to offer.

This complementarity of 'role' is less a neat formula than it is perceived to constitute a framework for co-operative working.

The Significance of Parental Involvement in Reading

The advent of parents on to the educational scene is a recent phenomenon, as we have charted, and the dimensions of their involvement are under scrutiny (Craft *et al.*, 1980). Parental involvement in reading, whether school-focused (Stierer, 1984) or home-based is to date the major sphere of activity, as this book will amply testify. The contributors view the value of the exercise as being of significance in terms not only of measurable performance, but of other 'spin-offs' — these are not incidental or tangential but actually central to the enterprise. They have to be, to validate the main hypothesis concerning parental participation.

Parental involvement in children's reading can therefore be regarded as a vehicle for the realisation of a number of aims to do with children's learning in particular, and with home–school relations in general. Among the former we can list:

(i) acquisition of reading skills from beginning reading to higher-order literacy skills;
(ii) familiarity with and enjoyment of reading for information and meaning;
(iii) fostering learning skills and applying enquiry and search strategies in home and school settings;
(iv) preparation for adult competence in these areas in a society which is increasingly using information technology — communication competence must remain a prime goal.

Among the latter (home–school relations) we can list:

(i) parents gaining knowledge about contemporary education, their child's learning in school, about intricate processes involved in learning to read and about teaching methods that teachers employ, some of which parents are 'trained' and encouraged to use;
(ii) parents having some say in educational decision-making;
(iii) parents getting to know teachers;
(iv) teachers getting to know parents and the family contexts of children;
(v) teachers gaining support and endorsement for their endeavours;
(vi) within-home and within-school benefits: parental involvement in reading programmes have been known to facilitate communication and co-operation between teachers, and to foster co-operation between siblings and other family members.

The Dimensions of Parental Involvement

Embedded within the preceding discussion are notions to do with parameters of parental involvement and the ways in which this has been defined. A perusal of the literature reveals that often the term is used synonymously with 'participation' and even with 'partnership'. Recent developments do exemplify that not only has the frequency of parent–teacher contact increased dramatically over the last decade but the type of contact has and is still changing. That is, from the minimal contact that characterised pre-1970 — parental attendance at school concerts, plays, annual open evenings — we can chart, on a chronological continuum, the continuation of these traditional activities alongside the introduction of a qualitatively different form of parent–teacher, home–school linkage. 'Involvement' is an active noun and is rightly used to denote the range of activities.

For the purpose of this book, the term 'parental involvement' is chosen, for the work described therein represents the gamut of those activities. Within that range, however, we can discern differences. In some, parents have been passive, albeit enthusiastic, recipients of others' suggestions; in others, the parents would say that they had been consulted at points; in yet others, they would perceive that they had helped to shape and influence developments and outcomes. The dichotomy 'teachers teach, parents rear' becomes blurred and involvement is equal, if what we mean by that is that all the adults participate and we may not be concerned about the relativities (the 'amount' being done by each adult participant). Despite the assertion that has just been made, the reality is that there must remain a demarcation in definition, as well as in practice, between teachers' responsibilities and the maintenance of professionalism, and parents' own rightful territory and responsibilities. Thus, the checks and balances to maintain the status quo are inbuilt. Involvement by parents can certainly take a variety of forms and in fact can be extensive.

But this author is cautious about the free-and-easy way in which some writers confuse 'involvement' with 'partnership'. For each term differs in semantic and in executive senses. There have been recent attempts to define partnership between parents and professionals in education and other child-focused services (Mittler and McConachie, 1983). This author has written elsewhere (Wolfendale, 1983) about partnership concepts and has enumerated a list of 'partner' characteristics, which include:

parents are active and central in decision-making and its implementation;
parents are perceived as having equal strengths and equivalent expertise;
parents are able to contribute to, as well as receive, services;
parents share responsibility, thus they and professionals are mutually accountable.

Perhaps partnership is a desired and feasible end-state, an attainable aspiration, one end of the continuum — or it may turn out to be unworkable and unrealistic. The responsibility upon those of us who are engaged upon the pursuance of viable models of parental involvement is that we should ensure that the current momentum can be sustained by all parties and the manifest enthusiasm be harnessed to meet the learning needs of all children.

References

Apter, S. (1982), *Troubled Children, Troubled Systems*, Pergamon, Oxford

Atkin, J. and Goode, J. (1982), 'Learning at Home and at School', *Education*, vol. 10, no. 1, 3–13, Spring

Atherton, G. (1982), *The Book of the School: A Study of Handbooks for Parents Issued by Schools in Scotland*, issued by the Scottish Consumer Council

Berger, E. (1983), *Beyond the Classroom, Parents as Partners in Education*, C.V. Mosby Company, St Louis, Missouri

Bronfenbrenner, V. (1979), *The Ecology of Human Development*, Harvard University Press, Cambridge, Mass.

Bullock, Lord A. (Chairman) (1975), *A Language for Life*, report of the Committee of Inquiry, HMSO, London

Cameron, R.J. (ed.) (1982), *Working Together: Portage in the UK*, NFER-Nelson, Windsor

Carr, J. (1980), *Helping Your Handicapped Child*, Penguin, Harmondsworth, Middlesex

COPE (undated), *School–Home–Community Relations*, Committee on Primary Education

Court, D. (Chairman) (1976), *Fit for the Future*, report of the Committee on Child Health Services, vol. 1, HMSO, London

Craft, M., Raynor, J. and Cohen, L. (eds) (1980), *Linking Home and School*, 3rd edn, Harper and Row, London

Crisp, A., Cockburn, P., Eversley, J. and Phillips, R. (1983), *Books, Schools and an Urban Committee*, Newham Parents Centre, 747 Barking Road, London, E13

Cunningham, C. and Sloper, P. (1984), 'The Relationship between Maternal Ratings of First Word Vocabulary and Reynell Language Series', *British Journal of Educational Psychology*, 54, 160–7

Curtis, A. and Blatchford, C. (1981), *Meeting the Needs of Socially Handicapped Children*, NFER-Nelson, Windsor

Cyster, R., Clift, P.S. and Battle, S. (1979), *Parental Involvement in Primary Schools*, NFER, Windsor

Daly, B., Addington, J., Kerfoot, S. and Sigston, A. (eds) (1985), *Portage: The Importance of Parents*, NFER-Nelson, Windsor

Davie, C., Hutt, S.J., Vincent, C. and Mason, M. (1984), *The Young Child at Home*, NFER-Nelson, Windsor

Davis, J. (1984), *Evaluation Reports, Liverpool Parent Support Programme*, School of Education, Liverpool University

Day, C. (1984), *External Consultancy: Supporting School-based Curriculum Development*, School of Education, Nottingham University

Dessent, T. (ed.) (1984), *What Is Important about Portage?*, NFER-Nelson, Windsor

Halsey, A.H. (ed.) (1972), *Educational Priority: EPA Problems and Policies*, vol. 1, HMSO, London

Hargreaves Report (1984), *Improving London Schools*, Inner London Education Authority

Harris, S. (1983), *Families of the Developmentally Disabled: A Guide to Behavioural Intervention*, Pergamon, Oxford

Hills, R. (1984), *Parental Participation in the Education of Young Children*, project reports, Centre for Educational Research and Development, Lancaster University

HMI Survey (1978), *Primary Education in England: A Survey*, HMSO, London

Hobbs, N. (1978), 'Families, Schools and Communities: An Ecosystem for Children', *Teachers' College Record*, vol. 79, no. 4, May

Institute for Responsive Education, 605 Commonwealth Ave., Boston, Mass. 02215, Davies, D. (ed.), *Schools where Parents Make a Difference*

—— Clasby, M., *Community Perspectives on the Role of the School in the Community*, IRE Report no. 3

—— Collins, C., Noles, O. and Cross, M. (1982), *The Home–School Connection, Selected Partnership Programme in Large Cities*

Lazar, I. (ed.) (1979), *Lasting Effects after the School*, US Printing Office, Washington

Macbeth, A. (1984), *The Child Between*, HMSO, London

Mittler, P. and McConachie, H. (eds) (1983), *Parents, Professionals and Mentally Handicapped People*, Croom Helm, London

Mortimore, J. and Blackstone, T. (1982), *Disadvantage and Education*, Heinemann, London

Newsom, E. and Hipgrave, T. (1982), *Getting Through to Your Handicapped Child*, Cambridge University Press, Cambridge

Pizzo, P. (1983), *Parent to Parent*, Beacon Press, Boston, Mass.

Plowden, B. (chairman) (1967), *Children and their Primary Schools*, HMSO, London

Poulton, L. and Poulton, G. (1979), 'Neighbourhood Support for Young Families', *Early Child Development and Care*, vol. 6, nos 1 and 2

Smith, T. (1980), *Parents and Preschool*, Grant McIntyre, London
Smith, T. (1984), 'Teachers and Parents Working Together', in Fontana, D. (ed.), *The Education of the Young Child*, 2nd edn, Blackwell, Oxford
South West Hertfordshire (undated), *Parents and School*, Teachers' Centre
Stierer, B. (1984), 'Parental Help with Reading in Schools', Project, University of London Institute of Education
Taylor, T. (chairman) (1977), *A New Partnership for Our Schools*, report of the Committee on School Management and Government, HMSO, London
Tizard, B., Martimore, J. and Burchell, B. (1981), *Involving Parents in Nursery and Infant School*, Grant McIntyre, London
Tizard, B. and Hughes, M. (1984), *Young Children Learning*, Fontana, London
Twiford, J. Rainer (1984), *Managing Children's Behaviour*, Prentice-Hall, Englewood Cliffs, New Jersey
Warnock, M. (chairman) (1978), *Special Educational Needs*, report of the Committee of Inquiry into the Education of Handicapped Children and Young People, HMSO, London
Westmacott, S. and Cameron, R.J. (1981), *Behaviour Can Change*, Globe Education, Basingstoke, Hants
Widlake, P. and Macleod, F. (1984), *Raising Standards: Parental Involvement Programmes and the Language Performance of Children*, Coventry Education Development Centre
Wilson, H. and Herbert, G. (1978), *Parents and Children in the Inner City*, Routledge & Kegan Paul, London
Wolfendale, S. (1983), *Parental Participation in Children's Development and Education*, Gordon & Breach Science Publishers, London
Wolfendale, S. (1984), 'Parental Profiling and the Parental Contribution to Section 5 (1981 Education Act) Assessment and Statementing', available from author, Psychology Department, North East London Polytechnic
Woodhead, M. (1976), *Intervening in Disadvantage*, NFER, Windsor
Woods, P. (1984), *Parents and School*, Welsh Consumer Council, Cardiff

2 PARENTAL INVOLVEMENT IN READING: THEORETICAL AND EMPIRICAL BACKGROUND

Keith Topping

During the last quarter-century theories of learning have become less charming but more useful. The influence on education of Jean Piaget, Jerome Bruner and B.F. Skinner has waxed and waned in turn. The star currently rising in the west seems to be the work of Norris Haring and his associates (Haring *et al.*, 1978). This lacks nothing in utility, but whether that will prove sufficient for it to be taken unto the bosom of the teaching profession remains to be seen.

Set against this wider context, much of the academic research into the processes of reading seems fragmentary, circular and trivial. A preoccupation with the dissection of thc skill of reading has left many researchers carving their names on a tree but unable to find a way out of the wood. Just as the Snark is being pounced upon, it persists in turning into a Boojum.

The medical model of human functioning, with its emphasis on a plethora of pseudo-explanatory categories and its preoccupation with purported intra-cranial events, is gradually being flushed out of education by more sophisticated and practical ideas, which have much more relevance to life in the classroom and the actual business of teaching children to read. In the field of reading, attempts to 'diagnose' deficits in mysterious subskills which are hypothesised to form the infrastructure of the reading process are becoming less and less frequent — no doubt extinguishing owing to the lack of success of programmes of remediation derived therefrom. Learning to read is aptly compared by Young and Tyre (1983) to learning to ride a bicycle — even if the *obvious* subskills can be learned independently, until you can perform them all *simultaneously*, you still fall off the bicycle. The 'bottom-up' approach to reading is being rapidly usurped by the 'top-down' perspective — which takes the surface features of children's reading behaviour (i.e. observed reality) as its starting-point, and goes on from there.

Research on Reading

Research into neurological correlates of reading failure presents a confused picture. Peculiarities of cerebral laterality have been found in some small clinical groups of poor readers, but not in more substantial surveys of larger populations. The vast majority of children with aberrant laterality show no reading problems, and reading problems are not more common among children with aberrant laterality. The evidence concerning a link between directionality and reading problems is inconclusive. Some studies have reported a high incidence of pre- and peri-natal complications in samples of children with reading difficulties, while other studies have failed to replicate this finding, irrespective of the degree of control of other variables. There is some evidence (of variable quality) of eccentric electro-encephalograph (EEG) findings with small groups of children with reading failure, but the implications of this are unclear. The notion of brain damage or dysfunction as a cause of reading failure is virtually impossible to prove and of negligible educational relevance.

There is no doubt that a family history of reading failure is common among children with reading problems, but it is extremely difficult to disentangle the effects of heredity and family environment. It seems likely that a genetic factor is implicated, however. Girls seem to perform more uniformly well on average at reading than boys, whose reading abilities are considerably more variable; but there is no conclusive evidence that this reflects genetic factors, except in so far as the latter may determine general rate of maturational development or a predisposition to conforming behaviour in school.

Problems of visual and auditory perception were very important in the 'sub-skills diagnosis' school of reading failure analysis. Many studies have shown that children with reading difficulties do badly on tests of visual perception (including discrimination and memory), particularly of a sequential nature, although a minority of studies have not found this to be the case. Much the same applies to auditory perception. However, it is difficult to establish whether such difficulties are the cause or effect of reading failure, or merely a parallel phenomenon, particularly as they are by no means present in all cases. In any event, it has been suggested that they are more relevant in the early stages of reading failure than in the later.

Eye movements have recently again been a focus of research effort, and there is now considerable evidence that children with reading difficulties exhibit a variety of eccentric eye movements while reading. However, whether these are cause or effect of reading failure is open to question, as is the matter of whether these aberrations are physiological, emotional or behavioural in origin. A majority of the various studies on the integration of visual and auditory perception find children with reading failure worse than controls, but again this is not a uniform outcome, and the validity of some of the measures and their relevance to the reading process must be in doubt. There is some evidence that poor readers also tend to be poorly co-ordinated, but there is a small amount of contradictory evidence and the causative linkages and/or remedial implications are unclear. There is no satisfactory evidence that physical or 'body-image awareness' exercises improve reading abilities.

A recent growth area has been research based on an information-processing model of reading failure, wherein the child with reading difficulty is seen as having dysfunctions in naming, labelling and/or information storage facility and capacity, which has implications for visual and auditory sequencing.

Readers may be forgiven for thinking that what initially sounds frightfully up-to-date is actually the dear old medical model surfacing again. A number of (mostly small-scale) studies have been carried out into various isolated aspects of frequently dissimilar models of information processing, all of which seem to have remarkably little relevance to teaching children how to read.

The research begins (finally) to show a degree of utility when it turns to consider reading as a developmental process, carrying the implication that at different ages and stages different types of failure might occur. There is some evidence that reading delay is often accompanied by language delay, but only longitudinal research could illuminate which was causative, if either. Several studies have noted the difficulties poor readers often have in phonic analysis and synthesis, and how easily they become confused between similar letters, digraphs and words, but the conclusions drawn have often been contradictory. Other studies have suggested breakdowns in encoding or decoding, but this takes us back into positing theoretical 'black box' artefacts. A number of workers have explored the semantic aspects of reading, rapidly becoming entangled in the association with language development. Currently popular with many teachers is the psycholinguistic model of the reading process (see Smith, 1978; Clay, 1979), which postulates that good readers operate by strategies of anticipation and problem-solving largely based on contextual information. Linguistic and cognitive knowledge is meshed with semantic and syntactic cues from the text to enable prediction and search to confirm or reject semantic hypotheses.

Readers wishing to pursue these avenues of enquiry further are referred to useful reviews in Moseley (1975), Layton (1979), Tansley and Panckhurst (1981), Pavlidis and Miles (1981), Friedlander (1981), Jorm (1983) and Beech (1985).

Emotional and Behavioural Factors in Reading Failure

There are a number of studies demonstrating a correlation between reading failure and various emotional difficulties or 'disorders', but it is problematic to determine which is cause and which effect, or whether both are caused by other factors. Although failing readers often show low self-esteem, even here it is impossible to be sure that the former has caused the latter, and some writers propose that a small number of children cling to their disability to fulfil deep emotional needs. Certainly more than one study has noted high levels of anxiety and insecurity in some failing readers, and it is well established that excessive anxiety levels interfere with learning. Perhaps here we have the first hint of what teachers have always known but researchers have usually disregarded — that reading failure is not only multiply but cumulatively caused.

Certainly teachers will be familiar with cases where children are unable to organise themselves to learn to read because life at home is totally disorganised or totally preoccupying, or where a child retreats from reading as part of a learned helplessness designed to solicit sympathy, attention and constant support, or where a child refuses to learn to read as a last-ditch stand against over-demanding parents or as a manipulative ploy with over-protective parents.

On the whole, however, teachers probably encounter as many failing readers with too *little* anxiety about reading progress as those with too much, and generally the research evidence supports the view that emotional problems are present in a minority of children with reading problems, and in those cases, the reading failure seems more likely to have caused the emotional problems than vice versa.

Worthy of note is some scattered work on variables of what might be termed 'cognitive style' or learning behaviour. There is some evidence that failing readers are more likely to be 'field-dependent' (i.e. distractable) in style, while other studies suggest learning disabled children lack foresight and tend to choose short-term tasks. Physiological correlates of these phenomena have been measured. However, a child's capacity to attend to one set of stimuli in one situation need not tell us anything about attentional capacity for different stimuli in another, and here again there is also the old chicken-and-egg problem concerning direction of causation. Many of the studies have used stimuli and experimental conditions alien to those of the classroom and any implications for teaching have not been spelled out.

Past evaluative studies of attempts to intervene in the emotional and behavioural correlates of reading failure make uninspiring reading.

Counselling, non-directive 'talking cures' and play therapy from professionals have a poor track record. The exception is the work of Lawrence (1971, 1972, 1974), who demonstrated that individual counselling and attention from non-professionals resulted in substantial gains in reading test scores.

The Relative Influence of Home and School on Educational Outcomes

Environmental factors are of course significant in the aetiology of reading failure, but researchers have by and large chosen to ignore the possible relevance of incompetent teaching, frequent changes of school or teacher, lack of suitable materials, poor staffing ratios, and so on, apparently preferring to scrutinise the pupils' home environment for reasons for lack of attainment.

There are regional variations in attainment in the UK which do not match the broad pattern of wealth distribution, but within specific regions there is no doubt that reading failure is more prevalent in the lower socio-economic orders, who also tend to score less well on intelligence tests, although these latter correlate only weakly with reading ability. There is no strong correlation between 'broken homes' and reading delay, although specific family crises can affect children's capacity to learn for the duration, and social class V families suffer more than their fair share of these. (Birth complications are also more common in this class.) Reading difficulties are commoner in children from large families. There is some evidence that as children grow older the influence of home variables on attainment becomes stronger in relation to school variables.

There is evidence of a link between parental interest/encouragement and educational outcomes, but there are problems in satisfactorily measuring the former. The Plowden Report data suggested that schools in working-class areas gave parents less *opportunity* to contact school, while it was just such parents who expressed the strongest desire for more information. Low levels of literacy in the home tend to predispose children to reading failure, and such children often show low levels of 'academic' motivation, but the direction of causation is debatable.

Reviews of the available evidence conclude virtually unanimously that the influence of home on school performance is considerably greater than that of the school, although this is methodologically very difficult to prove. There is evidence that teachers tend to underestimate the ability of pupils from lower-class homes. However, there can be very marked differences in attainment levels between schools in socially homogeneous areas, and the importance of school variables, which arguably can be more easily manipulated than home variables, should not be under-rated.

Factors in the Effectiveness of Parental Involvement on Children's Reading Behaviour

If home factors are so powerful an influence, why has the education world been so slow to attempt to mobilise this power? In the hurry to put together 'compensatory' programmes (which served only to give disadvantaged children more of the same and knock them deeper into the hole they were already in), parents tended to get overlooked — at least till recently. Having considered the research on what a handicap parents can be to children (the deficit model of parenthood), perhaps we can now look at something more positive and useful — the mediatory processes which seem to operate when parents effectively involve themselves in their children's reading development. The factors probably involved can be considered in turn.

Practice

Children who read at home regularly simply get more practice at reading than those who don't. It is well established that practice consolidates a skill, promotes fluency and minimises forgetting. However, it is important that the practice is *positive* — i.e. is practice at reading *successfully*. Practice at making a lot of errors will have the opposite effect. Teachers have typically tried to keep error rates in check by using carefully structured and graded reading schemes. The techniques described later in this volume tend to rely as much, if not more, on carefully articulated support and correction procedures, utilised by parents, for this purpose. Some of them *also* include controlled reading materials, while others eschew this 'artificiality'.

Feedback

In a busy classroom the opportunities for a child to receive temporally relevant feedback about the correctness of attempts to decode a particular word or deduce the semantic implications of a section of text are severely limited. In the luxury of a one-to-one situation with a parent, feedback can be immediate, preventing the compounding of error upon error into increasing confusion.

However, while we may safely assume that a lack of *early* feedback is a handicap to the failing reader, it does not necessarily follow that *immediate* feedback is advantageous. As McNaughton and Glynn (1981) point out, feedback can vary not only in its timing, frequency and contingencies, but also in the level of informational or instructional content and in its motivational effects. Many willing and well-meaning parents, hearing their children read at home, pounce on error words and use phonic-analysis and synthesis correction procedures which are at best time-consuming and at worst catastrophic, producing despair in the child and tension in the relationship. Feedback about single-word errors which is too immediate can inhibit the child's use of contextual clues, impede development of self-correction strategies, and impair comprehension of the text. Feedback about semantic deductions (comprehension) tends to be offered much less frequently by parents. So while parental involvement offers valuable opportunities for increased feedback, unless it is guided feedback it could do more harm than good.

These first two factors apply to any adult offering 'one-to-one' listening to a failing reader. One-to-one tutoring *per se* has other advantages: it enables teaching procedures to be individually tailored and paced to particular needs and speeds, it promotes a high percentage of on-task behaviour, and it enables a highly interactive, participative, activity-based style of teaching and learning.

Other factors to be detailed apply more particularly to the *parent* 'listener'. A relevant variable here may be the level of *expectancies*. There is substantial research documentation of the way teachers' academic expectations of pupils of low socio-economic status tend to be depressed, subsequently creating a self-fulfilling prophecy. In some cases, at least, it would be safe to assume that parents had higher as well as fonder expectations of their children than the teachers, and that parental involvement projects might partially operate by children's abilities rising at home to meet higher and suddenly more clearly articulated parental expectations. The plausibility of this theory is unfortunately tarnished by the fact that most parental involvement projects start from the premiss that the target children have problems — i.e. are below average — so parents are informed of the school's views on this at an early stage, and their expectations are lowered, or at least confused. Unless a parental motivation to prove the school wrong is a major factor in parental involvement projects, caution is necessary in imputing a causative role to the factor of parental expectation. But in two other areas we are on safer ground. Two fairly basic desires in children are: to be like, and to be liked by, their parents.

Reinforcement

To be liked, approved of, smiled at, praised, patted on the back, rewarded with indulgences or treats — very little of this falls to the lot of the failing reader in school. But teachers are task-masters (not really people), and how much more valuable these goodies would be coming from those who are really significant in your life — your family. While families vary in their degree of organisation, coherence and emotional tone, a little more social reinforcement costs nothing and can only improve the situation. Children can dismiss as insignificant a teacher who figures in their lives for less than a year, but not so the responses of a parent whom they're stuck with for ever. Parents also have the advantage of being able to use tangible rewards, if necessary, much more easily than teachers.

So the social reinforcement a parent dispenses for success at reading, word by word if necessary, is often infinitely more powerful than the teacher's attempts in the same direction, and can be given more frequently and regularly (if required) than a teacher can manage. However, neither teachers nor parents tend to be very good at praising frequently spontaneously, and if left to their own devices both groups make negative, corrective utterances much more frequently, so guidance and training in this can form a valuable aspect of a parental involvement project.

It might be argued that the children's progress was merely a result of having extra 'attention', and indeed Lawrence's (1971, 1972, 1974) work would appear to support this contention. Unfortunately, 'attention' in this context is a very fuzzy, undifferentiated concept, and difficult to integrate in an analysis of any thoroughness. A suggestion to parents merely to 'give extra attention' is likely to prove difficult to translate into specific practice and could cover a multitude of sins. If parents commit themselves to listening regularly to their child read, this may increase the total amount of attention the child receives, or may mean that the limited amount of adult attention available is only accessible via reading activity. While this latter may raise the status of reading activity in the child's eyes, it will not necessarily result in progress unless reinforcement is also present.

Modelling

Modelling is the demonstration of a behaviour by one person and the copying of it by another (consciously or otherwise). Many children want to 'be like' grown-ups, particularly the most significant grown-ups in their life, their parents. The modelling is likely to be more powerful the more the child feels emotionally involved with, and wants to be like, the model. (Or, if we dare slip into psychoanalytical jargon, the more the child 'identifies' with the model.) The enthusiasm for and interest in reading that the parents express is likely to be crucial in developing the child's motivation, via the modelling process. It follows that the father's role in this could be particularly crucial for boys, and one might assume that the greater incidence of reading failure in boys is partially a result of the majority of primary teachers being female (but see Thompson, 1975). It may rather be because boys tend to identify more with the peer group and less with adults than do girls.

If parental modelling of enthusiasm and interest in reading is an important factor in the success of parent involvement projects, it follows that the materials supplied need to be attractive enough to facilitate this. It also follows that guidelines about techniques should be seen by the parents as straightforward and sensible, so that parents can accommodate them to their existing conceptual frameworks. A technique which is seen by parents as complex, incomprehensible, alien and little more than a burden foisted on them by the school will not promote the establishment of the kind of positive modelling needed.

The four major factors common to all parent involvement projects are summarised in Figure 2.1. Other factors may operate with those projects where a particular technique is specified. The sheer novelty of a technique may elicit a response in both parents and child (so long as they see it as sensible as well as novel). This could be castigated as mere 'Hawthorne effect', but if it can be maintained it is none the less valuable.

Figure 2.1: Main Factors in Effectiveness of Parental Involvement

Compared to teacher input, parental:

M	Modelling — is more powerful
P	Practice — is more regular
F	Feedback — is more immediate
R	Reinforcement — is more valuable

The powerful effects of parental modelling are carried beyond merely a good example of enthusiasm and interest in those techniques which ask parents for considerable personal involvement in the reading process in addition to just monitoring. Where parents model correct reading or self-correction procedures, a parental demonstration is likely to be worth many minutes of a teacher's verbal instruction.

Another major advantage of specifying a parental involvement technique may well lie in the incompatibility of the technique with previous parental 'teaching' behaviours. Negative spontaneous parental behaviours (e.g. excess attention to errors, critical comments) are more likely to be effectively eliminated by training in an incompatible technique than by exhortations to desist.

A final factor which can come into play in parental involvement projects organised on a group training and feedback basis is that a group ethos can develop among parents and/or children. This may move towards group solidarity or group competitiveness, or move in one way among the parents and another among the children, but will be an influence to be reckoned with whatever happens.

Changes in Parental Behaviour during Parental Involvement in Reading

While the focus of the previous section was on factors directly affecting the children's reading behaviour, various implications for parental behaviour were drawn therein, and it is worthwhile for project planners to consider in greater detail how effectively to manage parental behaviour (secure full parental co-operation).

Reference has already been made to the value of training in specific techniques for eliminating previous unhelpful parental practices, like shouting and phonics-bashing. For many parents, anxiety about their children's progress is accompanied by feelings of inadequacy, frustration and tension. They don't know how to help, and these emotions often spill out into family conflict during abortive home 'tutoring' sessions. When a parent involvement project finally gives parents concrete guidance, the sense of relief can be considerable. What is seen in school as an increase in parental confidence could be equally well described as a reduction in parental anxiety and frustration.

In the longer run, there are more subtle considerations affecting the kind of guidance that is given. Initially, if parents feel they are being 'allowed' into school and given a fragment of mystical (teachers') skill, *some* parents will feel honoured. Later, the parents will realise the skills are really quite simple and might draw unfortunate conclusions. For long-term change, the parents must take the skills on board as truly *theirs*, not borrowed clothes. Parents should be involved in a partnership with school in which it is acknowledged from the start that the parents are the major influence. Parents must not be left to feel that they are parasites upon the education system, but an integral part of the educative process. There are implications here for school policy in all curriculum areas. There are also implications for dialogue — parents are to be listened to, and not just talked at.

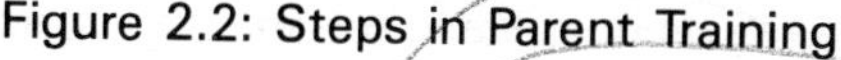

Figure 2.2: Steps in Parent Training

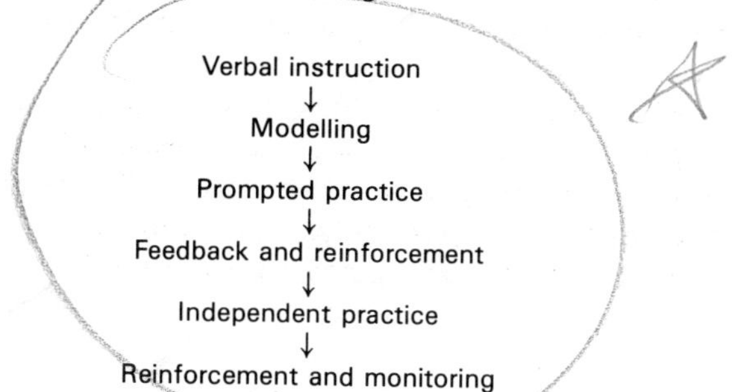

Returning to the more immediate concerns of getting a parent involvement project off the ground, it is worth repeating that it is pointless to tell parents what you *don't* want them to do without telling them what you *do* want them to do. Providing clear guidelines is a step forward, but it will be more effective to provide proper training. This is likely to consist of the processes specified in Figure 2.2.

Even then many parents will not adhere completely to the instructions. (Rate of praising often proves a particular problem, for example.) There is always a conflict between wanting perfect practice to maximise success and allowing parents to modify procedures idiosyncratically to make the techniques really 'theirs'. Unfortunately, what degree of compromise works best varies from family to family and can ultimately only be determined empirically.

Finally, the importance of reinforcement for the *parents* should not be underestimated. In the early stages of a project, the parents will need generous social reinforcement, both individual and group, from school. In the longer run, there will be the reward of seeing their children progress, which will maintain their 'tutoring' behaviour as necessary.

But a reinforcement hiatus between these two can sabotage a project. As with any other learner, parents need early success, small steps in difficulty, and care to avoid over-burdening with information. Only a small time commitment should be requested. If the tuition activities prescribed are varied and entertaining in themselves, this ancillary reward should sustain parental momentum over any reinforcement hiatus.

Notwithstanding these cautions, as with all other areas of work, there is a case for trying the 'lightest', least time-consuming intervention first and only proceeding to 'heavier' interventions for those children still with difficulties. While parental involvement projects need to be thorough and carefully planned, there is no need to take a sledgehammer to crack a nut.

Additional Factors in the Effectiveness of Four Specific Techniques

Descriptions of the techniques themselves are given in the introduction to the subsections on 'Paired Reading' and 'Behavioural Methods'. Readers who are less than omniscient may prefer to return to the rest of this chapter after reading these introductions, particularly as what follows is largely in abbreviated and diagrammatic form.

Paired Reading

Positive factors:

(1) Provides a very strong model.
(2) Provides a continuous prompt.
(3) Errors greatly de-emphasised.
(4) Emphasises continuity and fluency.
(5) Emphasises contextual clues and comprehension.
(6) Child chooses ungraded self-motivating books.
(7) Very simple and requires no special materials.

Disadvantages:

(1) No check on frequent error words.
(2) No further specific teaching techniques.
(3) Does not promote independent self-correction of errors.

Direct Instruction

Positive factors:

(1) Provides a very strong model.
(2) Provides a very strong graduated prompt.
(3) Structured in small steps.
(4) Checks and rechecks mastery.
(5) Very detailed (often scripted).
(6) Builds in generalisation.

Disadvantages:

(1) Commercial materials are usually expensive.
(2) They also tend to be structured for a homogeneous group.

Precision Teaching

(More a system of evaluating teaching than actually a teaching method itself.)

Positive factors:

(1) Carefully structured.
(2) Small task-analysed steps.
(3) Checks and re-checks mastery.
(4) Checks accuracy *and* fluency.
(5) Visual record of success.

} for the *individual*

Disadvantages:

(1) Teaching *methods* not specified.

Pause, Prompt and Praise (Glynn)

Positive factors:

(1) Reduced emphasis on errors.
(2) Provides contingent, discriminatory prompts.
(3) Promotes independent self-correction of errors.
(4) Emphasises contextual clues and comprehension.
(5) Relatively simple.

Disadvantage:

(1) Usually requires controlled material.

The Relationship Between Different Techniques

As the subsection of this book entitled 'Variations' demonstrates, different techniques of parental involvement in reading are not necessarily mutually exclusive. In Figure 2.3, an attempt has been made to show the interrelationships between different techniques. Almost all methods place some emphasis on reinforcement, so this has not been included separately. The latter stages of 'Paired Reading' refer to one possible elaboration (Topping, 1984). The 'Direct Instruction' channel refers to one particular commercial scheme, and others could be substituted, e.g. 'Corrective Reading A, B, and C', or 'Metra Beginning Reading I and II'. The heavy arrows in the diagram indicate procedural steps in use of technique and the lighter ones possible points of interchange between techniques.

Figure 2.3: Parental Involvement in Reading: The Options and their Interaction

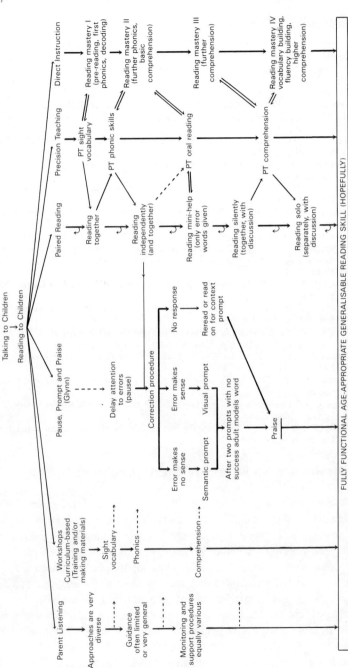

References

Beech, J. (1985), *Learning to Read: A Cognitive Approach to Reading and Poor Reading*, Croom Helm, London/College-Hill Press, San Diego, California.

Clay, M.M. (1979), *Reading: The Patterning of Complex Behaviour*, 2nd edn, Heinemann Educational, Auckland

Friedlander, J. (1981), *Early Reading Development: A Bibliography*, Harper & Row, London

Haring, N.G. *et al*. (1978), *The Fourth 'R': Research in the Classroom*, Charles E. Merrill, Columbus, Ohio

Jorm, A.F. (1983), *The Psychology of Reading and Spelling Disabilities*, Routledge and Kegan Paul, London

Lawrence, D. (1971), 'The Effects of Counselling on Retarded Readers', *Educational Research*, vol. 13, 119–24

Lawrence, D. (1972), 'Counselling of Retarded Readers by Non-professionals', *Educational Research*, vol. 15, 48–51

Lawrence, D. and Blagg, N. (1974), 'Improved Reading Through Self-initiated Learning and Counselling', *Remedial Education*, vol. 9, 61–3

Layton, J.R. (1979), *The Psychology of Learning to Read*, Academic Press, New York

McNaughton, S. and Glynn, T. (1981), 'Delayed versus Immediate Attention to Oral Reading Errors: Effects on Accuracy and Self-correction', *Educational Psychology*, vol. 1 (1), 57–65

Moseley, D. (1975), *Special Provision for Reading: When Will They Ever Learn?*, NFER, Windsor

Pavlidis, G.T. and Miles, T.R. (eds) (1981), *Dyslexia Research and its Applications to Education*, Wiley, Chichester

Smith, F. (1978), *Understanding Reading: A Psycholinguistic Analysis of Reading and Learning to Read*, 2nd edn, Holt, Rinehart and Winston, New York

Tansley, P. and Panckhurst, J. (1981), *Children with Specific Learning Difficulties*, NFER-Nelson, Windsor

Thompson, G.B. (1975), 'Sex Differences in Reading Attainments', *Educational Research*, vol. 18 (1), 16–23

Topping, K.J. (1984), *The Kirklees Paired Reading Training Pack*, Kirklees Psychological Service, Huddersfield

Young, P. and Tyre, C. (1983), *Dyslexia or Illiteracy? Realizing the Right to Read*, Open University Press, Milton Keynes

PART 2:

PARENTAL INVOLVEMENT IN READING IN ACTION

A. PARENT LISTENING

3 AN INTRODUCTION TO PARENT LISTENING

Sheila Wolfendale

From time to time in the past there has been acknowledgement that parents play a part at least in their children's development and education. For example, Savanarola (1452–98) wrote this advice for mothers on teaching their children to talk:

> Around the age of 2, when the infant begins to talk and to have some knowledge, one should skilfully and alluringly encourage the child to utter different words, while saying 'My little baby' and calling him by name; and at that time you should have a certain thing that he likes and say 'I will give you this if you repeat what I say' and then similarly vary from one word to another.

Echoes of this advice can be heard in contemporary articles, in parental involvement in language programmes for preschool children (Beveridge and Jerrams, 1981). Froebel, whose influence upon kindergartens and nurseries was immense, recognised the importance of maternal involvement in early language development, and devised programmes of speaking and singing rhymes and games for parent and child. Interaction via verbal and play activities has always been an intrinsic part of the parent–child relationship, and the desire by parents to participate in some small way in their children's learning in the first years at school is common. To them, it seems a logical extension of singing nursery rhymes or telling stories (Wade, 1984) that they should share in the process of teaching and learning reading skills.

The time-honoured means of parents helping their children to learn to read is by listening to them reading. Some teachers have frowned upon parental 'interference' on the grounds that parents use teaching and correction methods that run counter to a school's methods; countless other teachers endorse and participate in the tradition of parents listening to their children reading, and willingly send the reading book home, with a request that parents mark which pages have been read.

This practice varies, too — ranging from an expectation by teachers that parents will play a passive, listening role, with just a murmured correction, to encouragement to parents that they can discuss the teaching content, the story and the pictures. Informally, teachers can go further than this, even, to suggest that a particular method being employed in school to teach reading could be followed through at home. This author recollects that her oldest child's reception class teacher was an advocate and user of the phonic approach and so encouraged her to use this method when listening to her son 'build up' his words, and to correct accordingly (it worked!).

We saw in Chapter 1 that during the 1970s and following the Plowden Report, that there has been a dramatically increasing parental presence in schools, and that surveys have confirmed that one major activity in which schools are keen to involve parents is in helping with reading (Stierer, 1985).

The objectives of Stierer's research are: to appraise the scale of the practice of using parents as reading helpers in the classroom; to examine the significance for teachers and parents; and to describe schemes. In his survey of practice in 381 schools, Stierer reports that 'hearing children read' is the predominant, but not exclusive, parent volunteer activity and that it is more common for them to work with better readers. He identifies a number of emerging professional and educational issues of which the most relevant for the purposes of this book are: the expertise brought to the enterprise, and 'the special status of *reading* in the relationship between home and school'. (See also Volunteer Reading Help, 1983.)

Because of the premium placed upon literacy in this society, it is not surprising that involvement in reading by parents has been and is used as a medium for boosting children's progress, and for promoting home–school links. The relevance of reading as a vehicle, a means to an end (as well as being that 'end') was discussed in Chapter 1.

Books written for parents on how to 'teach' reading attest to continuing absorption in the notion of parents being their own children's educators (Baker, 1980; Kusnetz, 1980; Taylor, 1984; Thatcher, 1984).

Listening to Children Read

As a practice of long standing, 'hearing children read' remains the pre-eminent reading activity between adult and child. As a means of assessing reading attainment, it is for the teacher the most direct and accessible way of gaining progress, reading strategies and error-type. It is not of course the only method and in some ways it is a blunt one (unless it is used as part of a repertoire of other assessment techniques), but its importance has long been acknowledged in reading texts.

For example, Moyle (1968) lists seven reasons why hearing children read is valuable, and adds 'hearing children read regularly is an admirable pursuit in its own right but its effectiveness is greatly increased if it is looked upon as a teaching situation, and full records are kept and made use of in the future' (p. 119). He gives guidelines for this activity.

Several years later Bullock (1975) also discussed the value of teachers listening to children reading and observed that 'it should be an essential part of the diagnostic process' (p. 252, para. 17.18). The Bullock Committee members further noted that as most teachers set a premium on a quick, confident and unhesitating delivery of the words, they may lose opportunities in what is a teaching–learning situation. 'The technique of hearing children read is at its most effective when errors are seen as miscues which provide a "continuous window into the reading process" ' (p. 253, para. 17.18).

Reading aloud is presumed to be a precursor to later skill stages, including that of silent reading. However, as Clay observes (1972), it is not just a dispensable stage along the way to fully functional reading — it provides, in its own right, self-stimulation, and gives opportunity for self-correction (see Chapter 21 in this book).

The research of Southgate *et al.* (1981) focusing on the lower junior age range confirms the predominance of the 'listening to children read' practice of teachers: 'it was clearly regarded by all teachers as the backbone of their teaching and monitoring of reading' (p. 126).

Parents Listening to Children

The educational function of hearing children read is therefore well established. We can perhaps regard the supremacy of this approach within parental involvement in reading programmes as being entirely consistent with widespread educational practice, pervading as it does behavioural frameworks (Chapters 18–23 in this book) and paired reading (Chapters 11–17). Its potential and actual value is that it can be used as a low-key routine reading activity for parent and child, or highly systematically, with precise teaching, correction and reinforcement techniques built into the programme.

For teachers, too, the 'parents' listening to their children' approach can be dovetailed into and run parallel to a school's reading scheme; it can be comfortably absorbed into routine provision which is simply extended 'outwards' to home. Yet equally, the approach can form the central plank of an exploratory study with pre- and post-testing and monitoring techniques as essential features. This section of the book includes examples of all kinds, and these in turn are representative of other current work (Sigston *et al.*, 1984) or have provided the exemplar to others' work — e.g. Friend (1983), who explicitly acknowledges the Haringey Reading Project (see Chapter 4).

Whatever the nature or extent of the parental involvement in reading schemes, reliance upon the parents listening (with or without prompting, correcting, reinforcing) can be quite compatible with the theoretical basis of the school's reading policy, depending upon the stage of a child's acquisition of reading skills.

Hearing children read can be applicable to look-and-say, key words, sentence methods and language experience models. For a mainly phonic approach, care might need to be taken to introduce 'parent listening' at the appropriate time when synthesising skills are being consolidated.

Keith Topping makes similar general points in his introduction to Paired Reading (of which listening is a component) which is not surprising, given the intrinsic robustness of both approaches.

Pupils Reading to their Parents: which Pupils?

The contributions to this section are primary-focused. This is a reflection of the fact that the bulk of parent reading programmes have been concentrated on the early years at school, with reading beginners, or with older 'remedial' juniors. Less frequently have secondary school schemes been reported — there are some examples, using other methods, in this book (also see Ebbutt and Barber, 1979). Secondary school involvement is in fact increasing (Gryce, 1984).

The first wave of enthusiasm for a novel approach is passing and is giving way to a more sober and realistic appraisal of method matched to pupil. *Pace* the sentiments expressed in Chapter 1 about meeting the learning needs of all children, we are hopefully entering a phase when we can discriminate between methods — and, within methods, we can vary the instruction in an attempt to optimise the learning.

The bearing that these remarks have on the applicability of parent (or other adult) listening is that we are now at a stage when we can prescribe a process that begins with careful prior analysis (by the class teacher, advisory teacher or educational psychologist) of a child's task approach, reading strategy, 'sticking points', learning style, pace and rate of learning. The method and the content (reading book, pre-prepared take-home sheets) can then be selected on these individual criteria. Pre-training of teachers and parents (and children) as well as the recording system adopted constitute a crucial part of this differential approach. The merit of parent listening is that it provides the core around which a programme (for example, nightly, thrice-weekly) can be constructed for children at any level of reading competence.

Characteristics of Parent Listening Programmes

First, we must consider what distinguishes recent and current work from what has been referred to earlier in this chapter as the time-honoured tradition of teachers sending books home for children to read to their parents.

Simply, the degree of structure and specificity that goes into designing and executing what is discernibly a *programme* and not *ad hoc* practice characterises contemporary work, much of which is described in this book.

The 'recipe for success' of intervention programmes has been described elsewhere (Wolfendale and Bryans, 1979) and all the work brought together in this book includes the requisites that are meant to guarantee successful outcomes — and indeed each project reports significant results, on a number of dimensions.

In common with the other contributors, when this author is talking to and working with teachers, planning guidelines are outlined which include the following considerations:

Roles: what part will psychologist, teacher(s), parent(s), child agree to play, and what will be the areas of responsibility?

Recipients: initial learners (infant school) or older children with reading difficulties (junior middle, secondary)?

Material: school book, library loan, remedial/resource centre loan, pre-prepared cards and sheets, storage and access?

Type of programme: Paired Reading, child reading, parent reading, language experience approach? What kind of correction and reinforcement will be built in?

Training: for teacher(s) and parents? Workshop, meeting, visits? One or more sessions? Use of video/role play to make points?

Measurement and recording: selection criteria, samples, controls and comparisons, pre- and post-assessment measures, monitoring and probing, record-keeping for teachers and parents, when and where to see parents?

Time-span: decide at planning stage length of reading programme. Build in renewable option.

Criteria for evaluation: result of pre- and post- and any other assessment (teachers', parents'). Children's views, follow-up, cost-effectiveness criteria, repeatability and generalisability. If renewed, does the provision become part of school's home–school policy?

These planning considerations, which constitute an *aide memoire* rather than a prescription, apply to all parental involvement programmes, irrespective of method. Their inclusion in and relevance to this section is the result of their adoption within parent listening programmes representing a significant departure from traditional laissez-faire practice. A parental involvement in a reading programme is now defined as one which contains most if not all of these elements. Thus, success is less an incidental bonus than a planned-for goal.

Some of the chapters in this section describe work that has been regarded as seminal and the model for minor and major replications, some of which themselves are proving influential, and which are routinely part of school or Local Education Authority provision.

The reader will discern how each project has in common with the others the planning requisites, and one or more sessions of teacher and parent training. The latter includes teaching points, strategies for prompting, correcting, praising — in general, the promotion of positive responses and the setting of conducive learning conditions. Recording systems feature centrally, perceived as the basis for two-way communication as well as a vehicle for modifying the programme.

Summary

Each article reports and discusses the outcomes, the evident success, which is attributable in retrospect in part to those prerequisite factors, in part to the manifest, even infectious, enthusiasm of all the participants. Does the halo-effect matter? Does its presence diminish the value and validity of the exercise?

The purity of experimental procedures is bound, in the 'real' world of educational research, to be 'contaminated' by many variables outside the experimenter's control. Besides which, it is arguable if teachers see themselves routinely as researchers — innovation is another matter defined in less stringent terms, and may legitimately be part of educational practice. What matters at this point in time is that workers in the parent listening area are building up bodies of knowledge about success- as well as failure-governing factors. In turn, this experience will provide the building blocks to further knowledge concerning the nature of the reading process in school and at home, the part that parents can play in the process, and the contribution of this tripartite activity (of teacher, parent and child) to the rest of the curriculum.

References

Baker, C. (1980), *Reading Through Play*, Macdonald Education, London

Beveridge, M. and Jerrams, A. (1981), 'Parental Involvement in Language Development: An Evaluation of a School-based Parental Assistance Plan', *British Journal of Educational Psychology*, 51, 259–69

Bullock, A. (Chairman) (1975), *A Language for Life*, HMSO, London

Clay, M. (1972), *Reading: The Patterning of Complex Behaviour*, Heinemann Educational Books, London

Ebbutt, C.M. and Barber, E.J. (1979), *A Description of a Homework Reading Scheme*, Inner London Education Authority

Friend, P. (1983), 'Reading and the Parent: After the Haringey Reading Project', *Reading*, vol. 17, no. 1, 7–12, United Kingdom Reading Association

Gryce, P. (1984), 'Practice in a Secondary School: Reading Together', in Griffiths, A. and Hamilton, D. (eds), *Parent, Teacher, Child*, Methuen, London

Kusnetz, L. (1980), *Your Child Can Be a Super Reader*, Learning House, New York

Moyle, D. (1968), *The Teaching of Reading*, Ward Lock Educational, London

Sigston, A., Addington, J., Banks, V. and Striesow, M. (1984), 'Progress with Parents: An Account and Evaluation of a Home Reading Project for Poor Readers', *Remedial Education*, vol. 19, no. 4

Southgate, V., Arnold, H. and Johnson, S. (1981), *Extending Beginning Reading*, Heinemann Educational Books Ltd, London

Stierer, B.M. (1985), 'School Reading Volunteers: Results of a Postal Survery of Primary School Head Teachers in England', *Journal of Research in Reading*, 3 (1), 21–31

Taylor, G. (1984), *Be Your Child's Natural Teacher*, Impact Books, London

Thatcher, J. (1984), *Teaching Reading to Mentally Handicapped Children*, Croom Helm, London

Volunteer Reading Help (1983), *The First Ten Years, 1973–1983*, ILEA Centre for Language in Primary Education, Sutherland Street, London, SW1

Wade, B. (1984), *Story at Home and School*, Educational Publication, no. 10, University of Birmingham

Wolfendale, S. and Bryans, T. (1979), *Identification of Learning Difficulties — A Model for Intervention*, National Association for Remedial Education, Lichfield

4 PARENTAL INVOLVEMENT AND READING ATTAINMENT: IMPLICATIONS OF RESEARCH IN DAGENHAM AND HARINGEY

Jenny Hewison

The topic of parental involvement in reading has, for some years now, aroused strong reactions amongst teachers, ranging from the bitingly hostile to the glowingly enthusiastic. Recently, however, another response has emerged: the scathingly cynical. Parent involvement, according to this last point of view, is nothing but the latest educational fashion, destined before too long to join its predecessors in oblivion. A recent article in the *Times Educational Supplement* (Ireland, 1984) captured this sentiment with witty accuracy:

> Then out it all came. We were obviously jumping on the latest bandwagon, PI — parental involvement. She bet a pound to the proverbial we had some complicated scheme for parents to hear their children read, and a parents' room, and curriculum evenings, and bookshops and a toy library, and how could I possibly justify all this and me a union person too?

In the pages to follow, I am going to argue against the view that parental involvement in reading is 'just a fashion', and hence of no more than transient interest. From the very outset, however, I want to emphasise that the main arguments against transience, as far as I am concerned, consist not in simply heralding the effectiveness of special parent involvement projects (such as the Haringey project, with which I was associated), but rather in considering very carefully the reasons *why* such projects were successful.

Factors Influencing the Development of Reading

My argument begins with the very general question: what do we know about the reasons why some children learn to read satisfactorily, and others do not? More specifically — and therefore more helpfully — what, if anything, do the majority of poor readers have in common? Can we characterise them in any way? In what ways do they differ from children who learn to read successfully?

The answers to these questions have to be framed with care. Many, many factors have been shown to be associated with poor reading: vision and hearing problems, emotional maladjustment, language disabilities, difficulties in transferring information between sensory modalities, memory deficits — the list could go on and on. To this catalogue of impairments affecting individual children, it is customary to add factors such as the use of inappropriate teaching methods or materials, which are likely to diminish the quality of learning experiences for whole groups of children.

It is easy, amidst this wealth of information, to overlook the fact that we have not yet characterised most failing readers. Children with hearing problems do tend to be poor readers — but most poor readers do not have hearing problems. The difference in the form of the argument is exceedingly important, but overlooked or ignored by most authorities on the developing of reading. Textbooks for teachers, for example, usually just list 'factors associated with the development of reading', and give the student no idea whether the various factors listed affect one child in 10,000 or one child in ten.

Some research looking specifically at the relative importance of different influences on reading development — in the sense of the number of children affected — has, however, been carried out. It has revealed that what most poor readers have in common is not a particular sort of IQ profile, or a sensory deficit, or a history of poor teaching or exposure to unsuitable reading materials: what most poor readers have in common is a particular sort of home background (Douglas, 1964; Central Advisory Council for Education, 1967; Morris, 1966; Davie *et al.*, 1972).

The above research, published in the 1960s and early 1970s, revealed that children from homes where parents pursued manual occupations (particularly semi- and unskilled manual occupations) were much more likely than their 'non-manual' counterparts to be poor readers. Since social class itself cannot be regarded as an explanation of reading failure, it might be expected that reading researchers would have exercised themselves in the last ten or 15 years with searching investigations into the true causes of home-background-related reading failure. This has not happened. Instead, reading journals are full of reports of research into memory defects, abnormal eye movements, the design of reading materials, and so on, and so on.

By contrast with the continuing (and ever-expanding) volume of material directed to the study of teachers and teaching materials, and to the characteristics of individual children as learners, research into the mechanisms by which social background influences reading is sparse. It is preoccupied with only one or two preferred 'explanations' and, in terms of the research methods used, very unsophisticated. Lack of parental interest in education, an absence of 'reading models' in the home, and the inadequacy of family patterns of language-use have been widely, and quite uncritically, accepted as adequate explanations of reading failure in children from working-class backgrounds.

This is not the occasion to review in detail the research basis for these 'explanations'. Suffice it to say that the quality of the evidence is actually very poor, and that quite clearly we cannot as yet 'explain' the influence of social background on reading development. Quite clearly also, reading researchers and other authorities do not regard the subject as one deserving of their interest. Put another way, reading failure in those groups of children for whom it is most *expected* does not appear to arouse the curiosity of teachers or researchers, despite the fact that their *expectations* are based on no adequate *explanation* of the processes taking place.

Research in Dagenham

The research reported in this section was one attempt, on a very small scale, to find out more about the ways in which home background exerts its influence on reading performance. The research was stimulated by two pieces of information, both derived from the studies mentioned above: first, that the average reading performance of children from working-class backgrounds is substantially below that of their middle-class counterparts; and, second, that very great individual variation may be observed around that low average value. Put more simply, some working-class children become successful readers, while others — of course — do not. The Dagenham research asked the following questions: what factors, if any, characterise successful readers in a working-class area? Potential home environment influences were studied, but so also were the effects of IQ. (School influences were minimised by studying only children attending the same schools; but were in any case always checked as possible explanations of any reading differences observed.)

A detailed description of the Dagenham research is available elsewhere (Hewison, 1979; Hewison and Tizard, 1980). For present purposes, it is sufficient to give only a brief and quite selective account of the research, and to comment on its main findings.

Dagenham is a large council housing estate on the eastern outskirts of London. The sample of seven-year-old children studied there exhibited the low average reading attainments expected in such an area, but also the diversity of achievement levels referred to above. Some children were very good readers indeed. The project consisted in putting together reading and IQ test scores obtained on the children with information about their home backgrounds, gathered from interviews with their parents. When this was done, a number of highly revealing, but often quite unexpected, patterns emerged.

A large number of factors were found to be correlated with reading success in the sample of children studied, including parental attitudes and parental language, and also a variety of measures of the child's IQ. However, the factor which emerged as most strongly associated with reading success was whether or not the parents reported that they regularly heard the child read at home. Children whose parents did hear them read regularly tended to be much better readers than those whose parents did not.

The next stage in the analysis of the Dagenham data was to investigate further the important finding that some children had several reading 'advantages' — a high IQ, a favourable language environment, help with reading at home, parents who were themselves keen readers, and so on; other children had only one or two 'advantages'; and some had none at all. Attempts were therefore made to 'disentangle' this network of influences with, once again, very illuminating results. Two examples of these analyses are described below.

Help with reading at home, and a favourable home language atmosphere tended, as might be expected, to go together. Quite a few children had both 'advantages'; quite a few children had neither; but some children had one without the other. When the pattern of reading scores across the different groups were studied, it emerged that children in homes where the language atmosphere was apparently unfavourable, but where help with reading *was* given, still tended to be better readers. On the other hand, children in homes where the language atmosphere appeared to be favourable, but where help was *not* given, were not at any clear reading advantage. In other words, although a favourable language atmosphere and parental help did tend to go together, when the two characteristics were separated out, parental help was seen to confer by far the greater reading advantage.

The second example of 'disentanglement' which will be given refers to the interrelationships between parental help with reading, IQ, and reading performance. It was first observed that children with IQs below the sample average were somewhat less likely to be heard read at home than were children with above-average IQs. About 33 per cent of children in the first category were said to receive help, whereas this applied to

63 per cent of children in the second category. Turning to the average reading score of children in the four different groups (obtained by cross-clarifying the sample by IQ band *and* by help with reading), the average age-standardised reading score of children in the lower IQ band was 96 for those who did receive help with their reading, and 87 for those who did not. In the higher IQ band, children who received help obtained an average reading score of 105, while the figure for children not receiving help was 88.

In other words, if children did not receive help with their reading at home, then belonging to the higher or the lower IQ band made very little difference as far as reading performance was concerned. Among children who did receive help with their reading, the higher IQ group were the better readers, but both groups were considerably ahead of the higher as well as the lower IQ groups in the 'no help' part of the sample.

It must be stressed, before proceeding further, that the above research was carried out in only one area, and involved in total rather less than 300 children (and only 100 of these belonged to the sample for which it was possible to collect IQ data). The research findings are presented here, not because they provide *answers*, but rather because they raise *questions* — questions about the adequacy of accepted explanations of reading failure, and questions too about the direction of future research and policy in that area.

It will be obvious that it was important to exercise great care in interpreting the findings of the Dagenham research, even given the limitations of a small and very local study. All that had been established was that associations existed between certain reported kinds of parental behaviour, and the reading performance of children. These associations might have arisen for a variety of reasons: perhaps, to give just one example, only children who were good readers were prepared to read to their parents at home. None the less, the possibility existed that the association was indeed based on a cause-and-effect relationship, with parental help being the cause of improved reading performance. If this was so, then there were policy implications which could not be overlooked, since both the received wisdom and the prevailing practice of the time were based on discouraging parents from taking an active part in helping their children learn to read (Goodacre, 1968; Department of Education and Science, 1975).

Further research of a survey nature (i.e. looking at existing patterns of behaviour and performance) would not have thrown any additional light on the issues. It was therefore necessary to undertake instead an experiment, in which attempts would be made to *change* behavoiur. The outcome of that change would then be evaluated, and the findings interpreted in terms of whether or not they strengthened the case for a causal mechanism linking parental help with improved reading performance in children.

An experiment was therefore designed in which *all* parents of certain groups of children would be encouraged to hear their children read at home; and in which the reading development of those children would be evaluated, with reference to control groups, in a systematic and rigorous way.

The Haringey Reading Project

The research, directed by Professor Jack Tizard, and conducted with the active co-operation of the Local Education Authority, took place in the London Borough of Haringey, which is an Outer London Borough with many 'inner-city' problems. The Haringey Reading Project, as the study has come to be known, has been reported in detail elsewhere (Tizard, Schofield and Hewison, 1982). As with the Dagenham research, therefore, only a brief account of the research and its findings will be given here.

The experimental innovation in the Haringey project consisted in asking all parents of children in certain top infants' classes to listen to their children read aloud for a short period, several times a week, from reading material selected and sent home by the child's class teacher. Comparable children in other classes in the two schools taking part in the project acted as 'controls'; and the 'experimental' and 'control' classes were chosen at random. Both the schools housing the parent involvement project were situated in disadvantaged areas, and both had reading standards some way below the national average.

The project intervention ran for two years, while the children were in the last year of the infants, and the first year of the junior school. Standardised reading tests were used to assess the performance of project and control children before, during and after the intervention period.

In summarising the results of the project, I find it useful to think in terms of seeking answers to three broad questions. Were the parents *willing* helpers? Were they *able* helpers? And, finally were they *effective* helpers?

Taking the first of these questions, it was found that most parents did agree to help their children with reading, and were willing and prepared to provide that help for the duration of the project. Taking the second question, the great majority of parents provided constructive help and support for their children, and avoided counterproductive behaviour such as pushing their children too hard, or confusing them with inappropriate information. Lastly, the parents' help was highly effective. At the end of the intervention period, children from the 'experimental' classes were reading at a considerably higher level than their controls. Particularly striking was the observed reduction in the proportion of children performing at the very weakest level of all (a standardised score of 84 or below on the NFER test used): more than 17 per cent of control class children were found to be performing in this range, but only 6 per cent of children from the parent involvement classes were doing so. (The national figure is about 15 per cent.)

When the children were followed up one year after the intervention was over, the proportion of project children found to have age-standardised scores of 84 or less was still only about 9 per cent, compared to a national figure of about 15 per cent and a figure for the project control classes of between 25 and 30 per cent. (More recent information on the children's reading development, provided by courtesy of Haringey LEA, and as yet unpublished, confirms that the reading gains made by the project children had still not 'washed out' by the time they left the junior school.)

Implications for Understanding the Causes of Reading Failure

The results of the Haringey project have been quite widely publicised, and 'parent involvement' has won a measure of acceptance as an approach to the problem of reading failure. What has received less attention are the implications of the findings for our understanding of the *causes* of reading failure — reading failure, that is, in children unaffected by the activities of researchers running special projects. The results of the research in Haringey greatly strengthen the argument that parental help *leads to* improved reading performance, not only in special projects, but in ordinary schools and homes in Dagenham, and elsewhere too.

It canot be stated too strongly that, while parental involvement in reading might seem to be just another fashion as far as school policies are concerned, a great many parents have been quietly, and effectively, involving themselves in their children's reading for a long time now; and many will no doubt continue to do so, irrespective of schools' policy on the subject. One figure which is particularly noteworthy (but which does not in fact appear to have been noted) comes from the survey carried out for the Plowden Committee. In that survey, the parents of 73 per cent of children in the top infants said that they helped their children with homework. Given the age of the children, it is quite likely that much of this help was help with reading (Central Advisory Council for

Education, 1967.) As far as I can discover, reading professionals have exhibited no interest whatsoever in this finding — relating as it does to the activity of nearly three-quarters of parents — presumably because it was taken for granted, until very recently, that parental help had no beneficial effects. From this story, the lesson must be learnt that fashions for teachers, and for parents, do not necessarily correspond.

A Number of Unanswered Questions

Even if it were accepted that parental help with reading leads to improvements in reading performance, it is still not at all clear by what mechanisms this improvement is brought about. Two alternative possibilities were envisaged during the planning of the Haringey project: that reading gains were the result of extra practice, or that they were the result of enhanced motivation. A rather ill-thought-out attempt was made in Haringey to decide between these two alternatives by studying additional groups of children given help from someone who was not a parent. The intention was to provide these children with extra practice at reading, but without the motivational component which is present when the helper is a parent. As events turned out, it was not possible to run this part of the project as originally intended, and therefore no information was collected which could throw light on the question of causal mechanisms. (With hindsight, it seems likely that this was in any case the wrong approach, becuase it over-simplified the issues involved by reducing them to a straight choice between two alternatives.)

The need for further research into mechanisms has been recently highlighted by the growing popularity of another approacht to parental involvement in reading, known as 'Paired Reading'. This approach is described in detail elsewhere in this volume. For present purposes, it is sufficient to note that Paired Reading, and the Haringey project, derive from two very different approaches to the problem of reading failure. As described above, the latter was based on a rather atheoretical analysis of what the parents of successful readers were already doing. Paired Reading, in complete contrast, is based closely and explicitly on behaviour-modification principles, derived from psychological learning theory. In Haringey, the aim was to extend what many parents would do anyway. Consequently, parents were asked simply to listen to their children read; they were given a certain amount of advice, but no specific training, on how to do this. Paired Reading, on the other hand, is a highly structured activity which requires parents to be trained in its application by teachers or educational psychologists, prior to commencing helping their children.

A number of reports have recently been published, showing the gains made by problem readers after a period of parental help using the Paired Reading method (Bushell, Miller and Robson, 1982; Topping and McKnight, 1984; Chapter 14 of this book). Once again, however, the questions about mechanisms arise. *Why* does Paired Reading lead to performance gains? Is the mechanism essentially the same as that underlying the Haringey approach, despite surface dissimilarities in technique? Or are the highly structured elements of the Paired Reading approach essential to the method's success? Can the two methods be compared in effectiveness when applied to the same type of child? Is Paired Reading more suitable for older children already experiencing reading difficulties, and the Haringey approach more suitable for younger children 'at risk' of reading failure? Do the two methods, so different in rationale, converge in practice — i.e., do parents using the Paired Reading system tend to lapse after a time into Haringey-style 'listening'?

We do not yet have the answers to these questions. When answers do become available, however, as well as being of practical importance in guiding policy, they should also shed light on more theoretical questions — namely, on the nature of the mechanisms linking parental help with improved reading performance.

The Role of Practice

In the absence of proper research findings, it is only possible to speculate about the mechanisms linking parental help with reading gains. My own speculations, for what they are worth, centre on the role of practice. Analogies may be drawn here with acquiring other skills, such as the ability to do gymnastics, to play a musical instrument, or to speak a foreign language. In all these fields, the importance of proper instruction is unquestioned, as is the contribution of individual aptitude; but so also is the role of practice. Learning to read, it seems to me, is no exception to the general rules of skill-acquisition. Reading experts have overlooked an important source of differences between children, by failing to note and appreciate the differences in the quantity and quality of those children's opportunities for practice.

It may be noted in passing that reading professionals' attitude to the kind of practice provided by parents may well be coloured by their beliefs about the function of 'hearing children read'. Reading teachers, for example, may use the activity for teaching and assessment purposes, as well as for giving children practice. Considerable professional expertise may be drawn upon in the analysis of errors, the choice and timing of feedback, the seizing of opportunities for new teaching, and so on. It is, however, a mistake to assume that just because 'hearing children read' *can* be used for all these purposes, that on all occasions it *ought* to be. To make this second assumption implies that parents have no business engaging in an activity which requires a professional's skills. The more one thinks about it, the more absurd it is to propose that children should only read to an adult if that adult is going to use the episode for teaching or assessment purposes. Putting the argument this way illustrates very clearly the illogicalities which can result from an under-estimation of the role of practice.

In my speculation about the mechanisms by which parental help leads to reading gains, I have so far paid little attention to motivational factors. As was stated earlier, evidence on the question is still lacking, and all that I can offer is my personal opinion. The extreme form of the argument, that the *only* thing which parents provide is a boost to their child's motivation to learn, seems to me implausible. This amounts to saying that if children could be given an equal quantity of motivation by other means, then the act of reading aloud to parents would serve no additional educational purpose. This is an attractive option to teachers who feel their professionalism threatened by the contribution of parents. However, it suffers once again from the weakness of under-estimating the importance of 'the quantity and quality of children's opportunities for practice'.

In the absence of evidence to the contrary, the most plausible explanation seems to me to be that when parents hear their children read, they are providing them with a very special and very potent combination of benefits: namely, extra practice in a motivating context. On grounds both of common sense and psychological learning theory, this prescription for skill-acquisition has a lot to commend it.

New Developments

Research to answer some of the very many questions raised in this chapter is clearly required. As yet, however, very little research has been initiated on these topics. The new work which has been conducted since the Haringey project has instead been addressed to practical questions — such as the applicability of parent involvement schemes to different local conditions, or different age groups of child (Jackson and Hannon, 1981; Dyson and Swinson, 1982; Rennie, 1984; Griffiths and Hamilton, 1984; Sigston *et al.*, 1984; and Chapters 5, 6 and 8 of this book). New work arising from the Paired Reading tradition has followed a similar course (Spalding *et al.*, 1984; plus other work referred to in this volume).

Clearly, the above developments are very important. They offer information of great practical value to classroom teachers and to policymakers; they look to the future rather than the past. Reasonably enough, teachers tend to be more interested in *how* to apply a particular technique than in *why* that technique brings about the desired effect. I acknowledge these concerns, but choose, in concluding this chapter, to return to questions of 'why', because these questions — and, of course, their answers — lie at the heart of the most forcefully expressed criticisms of parental involvement in reading.

When teachers who reject parental involvement in reading are asked to give their reasons, many different types of reply are given (Hannon and Cuckle, 1984; Stierer, 1984). Many of these reasons are identifiably about questions of 'how' — how to maintain the interest of parents, how to cope with parents who do not read or speak English, how to make sure books do not get lost or damaged — but the more telling responses are about questions of 'why'. One of Stierer's respondents encapsulated these criticisms of parental involvement in reading by remarking: 'I should also refuse major surgery from a hospital porter'. Without a proven explanation of *why* parental help aids reading performance, there can be no adequate answer to criticisms of this kind. If parental help provides children with the invaluable combination of practice-plus-motivation suggested above, then this contribution deserves to be recognised, and the critics rebutted, in the interests of everybody concerned.

References

Bushell, R., Miller, A. and Robson, D. (1982), 'Parents as Remedial Teachers', *Journal of the Association of Educational Psychologists*, vol. 5, no. 9, 7–13

Central Advisory Council for Education (1967), *Children and their Primary Schools* (the Plowden Report), HMSO, London

Davie, R., Butler, N. and Goldstein, H. (1972), *From Birth to Seven*, Longman in association with the National Children's Bureau, London

Department of Education and Science (1975), *A Language for Life* (the Bullock Report), HMSO, London

Douglas, J.W.B. (1964), *The Home and the School*, McGibbon & Kee, London

Dyson, J. and Swinson, J. (1982), 'Involving Parents in the Teaching of Reading', *Journal of the Association of Educational Psychologists*, vol. 5, no. 9, 18–21

Goodacre, E.J. (1968), *Teachers and their Pupils' Home Background*, NFER, Windsor

Griffiths, A. and Hamilton, D. (1984), *Parent, Teacher, Child: Working Together in Children's Learning*, Methuen, London

Hannon, P.W. and Cuckle, P. (1984), 'Involving Parents in the Teaching of Reading: A Study of Current School Practice', *Educational Research*, vol. 26, no. 1, 7–13

Hewison, J. (1979), 'Home Environment and Reading Attainment: A Study of Children in a Working-class Community', unpublished PhD thesis, University of London

Hewison, J. and Tizard, J. (1980), 'Parental Involvement and Reading Attainment', *British Journal of Educational Psychology*, vol. 50, 209–15

Ireland, T. (1984), 'United We Stand', *Times Educational Supplement*, 21 September

Jackson, A. and Hannon, P. (1981), *The Belfield Reading Project*, Belfield Community Council, Rochdale

Morris, J.M. (1966), *Standards and Progress in Reading*, NFER, Windsor

Rennie, J. (1984), *Parental Involvement Schemes and the Reading, Writing and Spelling Skills of Primary School Children*, Community Education Development Centre, Coventry

Sigston, A., Addington, J., Banks, V. and Striesow, M. (1984), 'Progress with Parents: An Account and Evaluation of a Home Reading Project for Poor Readers', *Remedial Education*, vol. 18, 170–3

Spalding, B., Drew, R., Ellbeck, J., Livesey, J., Musset, M. and Wales, D. (1984), 'If You Want to Improve Your Reading, Ask Your Mum', *Remedial Education*, vol. 19, 157–61

Stierer, B. (1984), 'Home Helps', *Times Educational Supplement*, 29 June

Tizard, J., Schofield, W.N. and Hewison, J. (1982), 'Collaboration between Teachers and Parents in Assisting Children's Reading', *British Journal of Educational Psychology*, vol. 52, 1–15

Topping, K. and McKnight, G. (1984), 'Paired Reading — and Parent Power', *Special Education Forward Trends*, vol. 11, no. 3, 12–15

5 IMPLEMENTATION AND TAKE-UP OF A PROJECT TO INVOLVE PARENTS IN THE TEACHING OF READING

Peter Hannon, Angela Jackson and Beryl Page

Introduction

Among the recently developed approaches by which schools can involve parents more in the teaching of reading to young children, the simplest and most direct is that pioneered in the Haringey project (Tizard, Schofield and Hewison, 1982; and see Chapter 4 of this book). Just send school reading books home with children and encourage and support parents to 'hear' their own children read. A project based on this idea was carried out from 1978 to 1983 in a primary school in the north of England. Perhaps because it was an easily visible example of the practical application of the idea, the Belfield Reading Project became widely known. The project has yielded a considerable amount of interesting information, but here we would like to focus on just one aspect. How did the school set about turning the idea into practice and to what extent did parents respond? The more clearly and honestly this particular case can be documented, the better other schools will be placed to judge whether something similar would be feasible and desirable for them.

The Setting for the Project

The setting for Belfield Reading Project was a medium-sized primary school for children aged 4–10, which had 240 places and a part-time nursery class. From its opening in 1973 it had been designated a community school by the LEA. The building was typical of other modern semi-open-plan schools — except that it had a larger than usual hall, the equivalent of one extra classroom, and an adjoining public branch library. For most of its life the school had some extra staffing to enable it to function as a community school.

The children attending the project school were drawn almost exclusively from a catchment area, designated as a Social Priority Area (SPA). In 1983, 74 per cent of the children came from families whose income was sufficiently low for them to obtain free school meals (some of the remaining 26 per cent may have been eligible but did not claim). Information from the 1981 Census, relating to the enumeration districts which made up the school catchment area, provided a description of the population served by the school. It was overwhelmingly working class (91.2 per cent in social classes III-M to V; 51.5 per cent in classes IV or V). Two-thirds of households were in council accommodation. There was quite a high proportion of large families (14.4 per cent with three or more children) and the level of overcrowding was three times the national average. Various indicators of the number of immigrant families in the area suggested that the proportion was about 1.5 times the national average (and therefore relatively low). The level of unemployment was very high: a rate of 26. 6 per cent, nearly three times the national average. In summary, children in this project were drawn mainly from white, working-class families, many with low incomes.

Previous School Practice

From its opening, the school was strongly committed to its community role and to work with parents. This led to a wide range of initiatives (documented elsewhere, e.g. Hannon, 1979) which concentrated mainly on the development of community groups, community use of school premises, and preschool provision. Parents were very much in evidence in the school building during and outside school hours. They were invited to help in classrooms, too, although the proportion involved remained low.

In relation to the teaching of reading, the official school policy before the project was to encourage parental involvement at all stages. Detailed guidance, contained in a booklet distributed to all parents at school entry, included very specific suggestions for pre-reading and early reading activities at home (e.g. reading stories to children, making books). It was also clearly stated that children would be encouraged to take school books home and the hope was expressed that parents would hear their children read every night. As far as can be ascertained, individual class teachers were all in sympathy with this policy. None had reservations about allowing books home if requested, and on occasions most had initiated the practice with certain children and parents. Compared to other schools studied by Hannon and Cuckle (1984) the project school's practice in this respect was unusually positive towards parents. Nevertheless, there was never any systematic attempt to ensure that reading books were *regularly* taken home by all children and it is unlikely that it ever happened on such a scale.

Pre-existing Parental Involvement and Reading Attainment

An attempt was made to explore pre-project parental involvement in the teaching of reading. The parents of all children in the two cohorts which went through the school immediately before the project were interviewed as the children reached the end of the top infants' year and the children's reading was tested (NFER Reading Test A). Data were collected on 76 children aged six years eleven months to seven years eleven months. It was found that many parents had been heavily involved in helping their children learn to read. The proportion of children said to be heard to read at home 'almost daily' was 38 per cent; only 16 per cent had 'never' been heard. This is a high level of parental involvement, but probably not much higher than that found in working-class families studied by Newson and Newson (1977) and Hewison and Tizard (1980). The mean reading quotient of the children regularly heard to read ('almost daily') was, at 100.2, significantly higher than that of other children (90.3), in line with the findings of Hewison and Tizard (1980). It appears then that before the reading project began, parents were already involved, to varying extents, in hearing their children read at home and that children's reading attainment, as measured by a reading test, was strongly related to the extent of involvement.

Implementation

By 1978 teachers in the infants unit at the school were looking for ways of extending work with parents and, learning of the Haringey project then underway, decided to try something similar. The main differences were that it was decided to start with children at a younger age (five-year-olds rather than six-year-olds) and to mount a project using the school's own resources without direct assistance from outsiders. Parents were involved for three years (until the end of first-year juniors), rather than two years; over the five years of the project most class teachers worked in this way for up to three years, rather than just one year. Since many of the practical details of implementation have already been reported by Jackson and Hannon (1981), what follows is an outline.

The project began at the beginning of the 1978–9 school year with all second-year infants. The children were vertically grouped in four infant classes, for four class teachers were involved. The organisation of the project had to meet the needs of three groups of people — children, parents and teachers — without being a burden on any of them. This general principle is undoubtedly more important than the exact details of what was done, much of which is bound to depend on the particular circumstances of the project school. Reading cards were sent home and teachers wrote suggestions about what children could read to their parents. There was space for parents to mark the card if children did actually read, and a space for their comments, too, if they had any. Each morning children returned to school with their books and cards. The class teacher heard them read (either the same passage or a new one) and then wrote out the suggested reading for the next evening. The aim was to have this happen every school day, five nights a week, for every child in the target year group. This may seem rather too frequent, but it was felt that there were advantages in making reading at home a near-daily routine given that it was suggested for just a few minutes each time and that the 'little and often' formula had much to recommend it. Also, it fitted into existing infant classroom practice, which was for teachers to hear children of this age read every day. At first many of the reading books were from the Ladybird Key Words scheme but, early in the project and partly as a result of it, a larger and more eclectic stock of books was built up and children were given considerable freedom in choosing books within difficulty levels decided by teachers.

To meet the needs of class teachers careful thought was given to devising easy-to-work procedures for ensuring that children went home with their books, that they brought them back again, that they had read them at home, that new reading cards were ready each week, that parents needing help were spotted quickly, and so on. Various techniques were employed to encourage children to play their part — including, for example, plenty of advance explanation before the starting day and plastic wallets to carry books. As far as parents were concerned, their interest and co-operation was secured mainly by individual, personal contact. Letters were sent home, parents were spoken to when they brought their children to school or collected them, meetings were held in school, lists of what to do and what not to do were handed out and, later, an introductory video film was made. In addition, home visits were carried out, usually by the project co-ordinator who had two half-day sessions per week for project work. During the first term all parents were visited at home at least once, and some several times.

Two further cohorts of children were introduced to the project in much the same manner in its second and third years, bringing the total involved to well over 100. The first cohort had by then reached the first-year juniors level, and the number of class teachers participating had grown to seven. For this and other reasons, slight modifications were made to the project's organisation, particularly in relation to the older children.

It was recognised that there was no necessity for class teachers to hear some of the better readers daily and, although those children could still be encouraged to read at home every night, their parents were also advised to help in ways other than hearing reading (e.g. by talking about what the child had read). For children with continued difficulties in learning to read, the class teachers concerned felt that other reading-related activities (e.g. games) should sometimes be sent home instead of reading books. However, for the great majority of children in the project, nightly reading of a school book to their parents remained the aim. The project was considered to have reached an end after five years (in 1983), in which three successive cohorts of children had each completed three years in it. The school's practice continued to incorporate project methods, but they could no longer be considered innovative and were not monitored to the same extent.

Teachers

It is valuable to consider the implementation of the project from the class teacher's point of view. At the conclusion of the project, all eight class teachers who had ever been involved were interviewed about this and several other issues. They were asked about changes required in their classroom teaching. A majority (six) felt that the project had not required extra time from them, but two teachers felt that it had (in using reading cards and hearing readers). Three of the teachers felt that they were spending more time hearing readers; although the remaining teachers did not share this feeling, most did recognise that hearing reading had become more of a fixed point in their daily classroom organisation. Interaction with parents did not appear to have increased greatly overall, but surprisingly, more of it was concerned with children's reading.

Resources

One further issue remains to be considered here, namely the *resources* used to implement the project. The financial resources (required for stationery and extra books) did not amount to much in comparison, say, to general capitation expenditure. Extra money is welcome in this school activity as in many others, but it would be wrong to consider it vital. A more important resource, which might be a limiting factor in developing this form of parental involvement in other settings, is teaching staff. As already mentioned, the project school, as a community school, did have extra staff. However, the issue is complicated by the fact that the extra staff were deployed mainly to further what might be called 'non-school' community initiatives (e.g. support of community groups, adult education classes, preschool playgroup and toy library), and only to a limited extent on initiatives directly related to children in school (e.g. educational home visiting). Therefore, for each year of the project, a detailed analysis was carried out of the school staffing and of the number of pupils enrolled at the time of the annual DES returns. After allowing for 'non-school' staff deployment, it emerged that the average pupil:teacher ratio over the project period was 21.7:1. This is slightly more favourable than the average for all primary schools in England which, according to DES statistics, was 22.9:1 over exactly the same period. One might have expected an SPA school with a reception year of four-year-olds to be much more favourably staffed. Comparable ratios for some entire LEAs are better (e.g. Haringey, 20.4:1, ILEA, 18.2:1). From this it would appear that the Belfield Reading Project was implemented without significantly more teachers than might be found in many schools. Perhaps what really matter are staff attitudes and the way in which teachers are deployed within a school. In the project school there were well-established positive attitudes towards parents, and flexible timetabling and classroom organisation allowed teachers to be released for half-day or evening sessions in which home visiting and other project work could be undertaken.

Take-up

In assessing the take-up by parents of what was offered in the project the first source of information to consider is what parents themselves reported doing. As children in the three project cohorts reached the end of the top infants' year (i.e. when they had completed two out of three years in the project) interviews, similar to those reported earlier for pre-project children, were carried out. Of the 79 children who reached this stage of the project, interviews were satisfactorily completed for 77. By comparing data on pre-project and project children one can see the impact on levels of parental involvement. (All data reported below refer only to children who attended the project school from the beginning of second-year infants. Latecomers, whether in project or pre-project cohorts, are excluded.)

The aim of the project was to increase the frequency of children being heard to read at home to the 'almost daily' level for all children. Figure 5.1 shows a significant pre-project to project change in the proportions of children said to be heard to read at different frequencies. All but two of the project children were said to read at least 'several times a week', and 90 per cent were said to read 'almost daily' to someone. Most of

Figure 5.1: Proportions (%) of Children Said to be Heard to Read at Different Frequencies before and after Project (from Interviews of Parents)

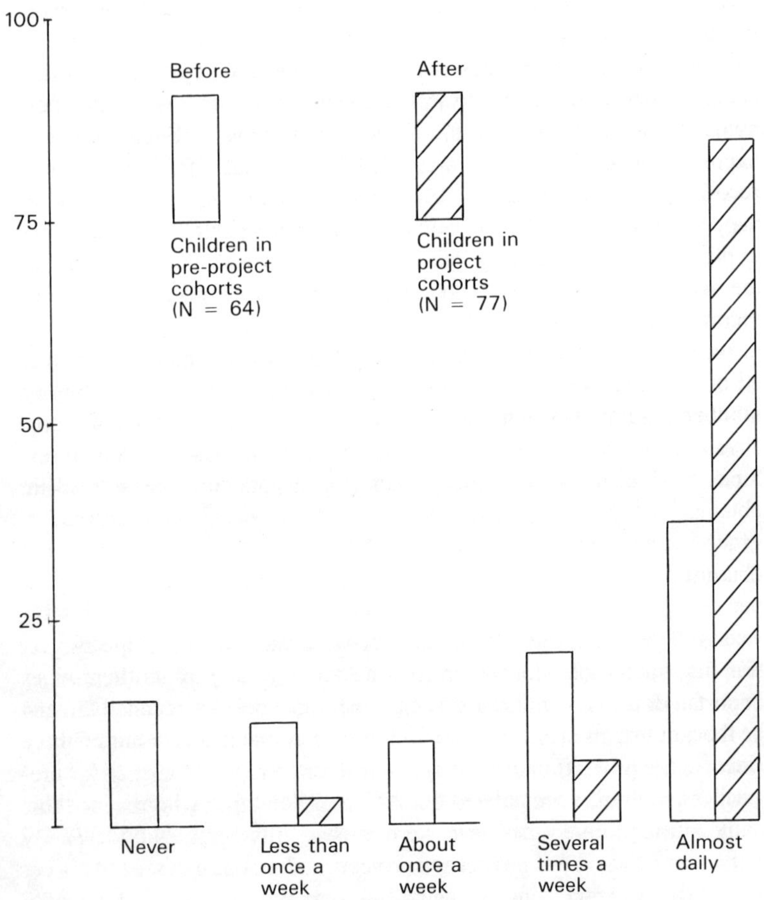

the children (88 per cent) were said to read to their mothers, about half to fathers (52 per cent), and a significant number to grandparents, siblings or other members of the household (46 per cent). The balance between these three groups was similar to that for pre-project children although, overall, more people were involved in hearing reading. There were predictable differences in the children's reading materials. Use of school reading books, at least sometimes, had been reported for 61 per cent of pre-project children but had increased to 100 per cent for project children. The use of other materials (other books in the home, 46 per cent; library books, 35 per cent; other materials including comics, newspapers, encyclopaedias, 25 per cent) had also increased, but not as much.

A basic difficulty in measuring take-up in this kind of project is that one is concerned with an activity which takes place in the privacy of the home. Asking parents is the most obvious way to discover what has been happening, but what they report may be misleading. For example, their recollection may owe more to what they wanted to happen than what did happen, or their replies to an interviewer may be influenced by the desire to please. A second implementation measure was therefore devised. All the weekly reading cards for children in the project were collected and records were kept (by teachers, using a microcomputer) of the number of *recorded* home-reading sessions (i.e. those sessions initialled or ticked by parents). This number was compared to the maximum possible number of sessions when the child could have read, taking into account absences, school closures and the like. The number of sessions obtained for each child was expressed as a percentage of the maximum possible obtainable. In this way 'scores' were derived for particular children, or groups of children, to show what frequency of home reading had been obtained over any given period (week, term or year). A frequency of 100 per cent would mean being heard to read the maximum of five times a week; 80 per cent, four times out of five, and so on. This implementation measure is likely to under-estimate the frequency of home reading in so far as unrecorded sessions and lost cards did not count. It might be thought that parents would mark cards falsely, but this is rather unlikely since it would assume extraordinary bad faith on their part. The class teachers, who were well placed to detected erroneous marking from their daily contact with the children, did not report it happening. On the contrary, they believed that quite often a child had read without the card having been marked.

The mean home-reading frequency according to reading cards for all children who completed three years in the project was 74 per cent. Figure 5.2 shows how it varied over time for each cohort. It indicates that for each cohort there was a decrease in the level of parental involvement over the three years children were in the project. Also, at the institutional level, there was a decrease over the five years that the school carried out the project. However, these declines are not very significant set against the overall high level obtained. Only rarely did frequencies for cohorts drop below 70 per cent. This shows that the school succeeded in getting children

Figure 5.2: Mean Frequencies (%) of being Heard to Read at Home during each Term of the Project for each Cohort (from Reading Cards)

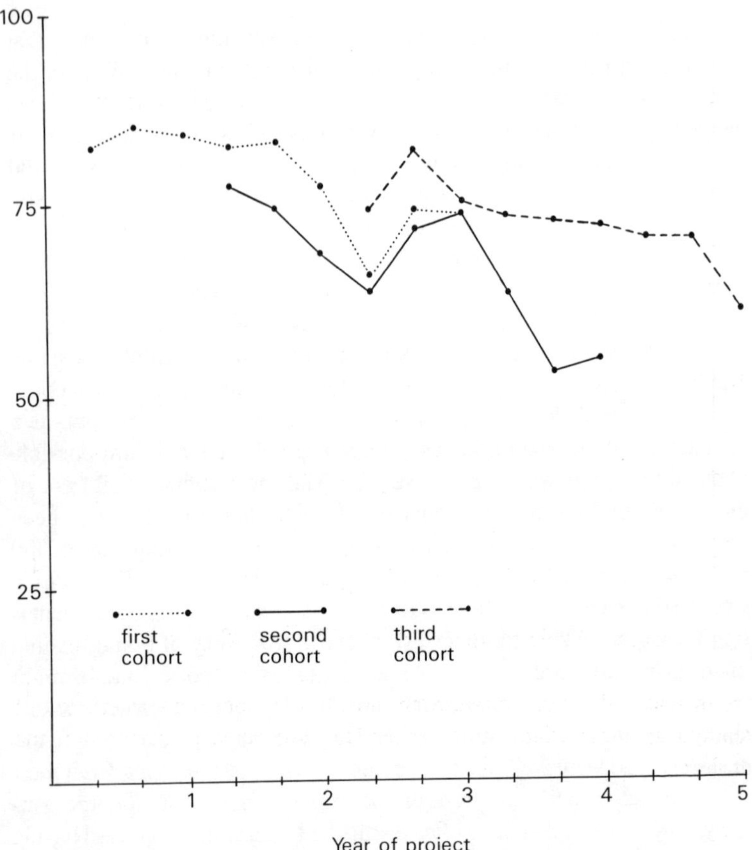

to read to someone at home on average about three or four times a week.

These figures, which are averages for groups, conceal a certain amount of variation between children. Figure 5.3 therefore shows the proportion of children obtaining different sources between zero and 100 per cent. The distribution is strikingly skewed to the right with two-thirds of children compressed in the 70–100 per cent range. It can be compared to the picture revealed in Figure 5.1, which refers to children two years into the project and where the measure of reading frequency was based on parents' reports rather than reading-card records. The two measures

Figure 5.3: Numbers of Children Heard to Read at Home at Different Frequencies during Project (from Reading Cards, N = 78)

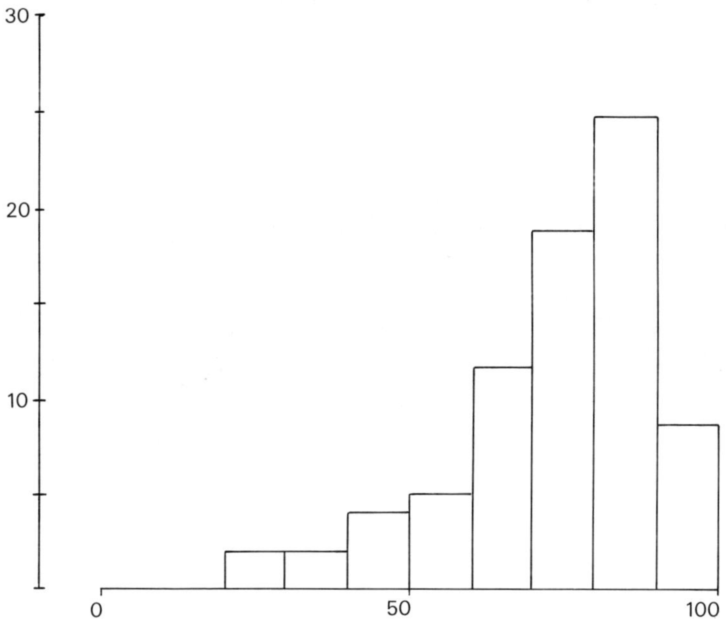

are in reasonable agreement, both indicating a considerable amount of reading at home which was unlikely to have taken place without the project.

Conclusions

This report of a reading project points to a number of questions which deserve further study. The function of educational home visiting and the use made of reading cards for home–school communication are unusual features. There is the question of *how* parents (and teachers) 'heard' children read. And, of course, there is the question of what effects the reading project had on children's reading attainment, or on the parents' experience of involvement. These points are being taken up in other reports.

What we hope to have shown here is how it is possible for a school, in what some might consider an unpromising area, and without extraordinary resources, to secure a very encouraging level of parental involvement over a relatively long period.

References

Hannon, P.W. (1979), *Community Schools for Young Children and Their Families*, Report of the Sixty-sixth Annual Conference of the National Association for Maternal and Child Welfare, NAMCW, London, 36–43

Hannon, P.W. and Cuckle, P. (1984), 'Parental Involvement in the Teaching of Reading: A Study of Current School Practice', *Educational Research*, vol. 26, 7–13

Hewison, J. and Tizard, J. (1980), 'Parental Involvement and Reading Attainment', *British Journal of Educational Psychology*, vol. 50, 209–15

Jackson, A. and Hannon, P.W. (1981), *The Belfield Reading Project*, Belfield Community Council, Rochdale

Newson, J. and Newson, E. (1977), *Perspectives on School at Seven Years Old*, George Allen and Unwin, London

Tizard, J., Schofield, W.N. and Hewison, J. (1982), 'Collaboration between Teachers and Parents in Assisting Children's Reading', *British Journal of Educational Psychology*, 52, 1–15

6 ENCOURAGING PARENTS TO LISTEN TO THEIR CHILDREN READ

Jeremy Swinson

Introduction

The plan to encourage the parents of a group of children to be involved with their reading came about as a result of a series of discussions between two educational psychologists, a peripatetic remedial teacher and the headteacher of a school. We had read of the effectiveness of other schemes, particularly those in Haringey (Tizard, Schofield and Hewison, 1982; and Chapter 4 of this book) and in Belfield School, Rochdale (Jackson and Hannon, 1981; and Chapter 5 of this book), and based much of our planning on their experience. Our project was originally reported in a paper by Dyson and Swinson (1982).

We set ourselves a number of specific aims:

(i) To encourage the parents of children who had difficulty in learning to read to listen to their children read at home every day.
(ii) To evaluate the effect of this daily reading on the reading skills of the children.
(iii) To ascertain whether it was feasible to run such a parental involvement scheme using only the resources of an average primary school.

The School

Our project involved 18 children, from the junior section of a primary school. The school served an area which consisted almost exclusively of a rundown postwar housing estate, and was designated an EPA school.

The Children

The children were selected by the peripatetic remedial teacher who worked in the school. They were already receiving regular remedial help on a withdrawal basis, which continued throughout the project.

The children came from seven different classes, no more than three children coming from any one class. Their ages ranged from 7:6 years to 11:4 years, with a mean of 9:0 years. Their reading delay was in the range 1:1 years to 3:10 years, with a mean delay of 2:2 years.

The Organisation

The project was initiated by the headteacher, who invited the parents of those children who had been selected into school for a discussion about their children's progress. At this meeting the rationale and organisation of the project were outlined. The parents were also asked about their current practice of listening to their children read and were then invited to a group meeting at which the project was to be explained in more detail.

At this meeting the parents were asked to listen to their child read every day after school for between 10 and 15 minutes. Each child would bring home a suitable reading book, together with her or his reading record card.

This card would contain information about the pages the child had read at school that day, comments by the teacher, and a target for the amount to be read that night. There was also room for the parents to make any comments on that night's reading.

The remedial teacher then gave the parents advice on the best way of helping their children when they read. It was suggested that they should make the sessions as relaxed and enjoyable as possible, use a lot of praise, not get angry, and to try to arrange a regular time to listen to their children in a situation with as few distractions as possible. More specific advice was given on what to do when their child met an unknown word, or made mistakes. This advice stressed the use of contextual and syntactic clues as well as basic phonic knowledge.

Whenever the child met an unknown word the parents were advised to:

(i) Ask the child to read to the end of the sentence and then return to the unknown word and guess what it is.
(ii) If that fails, ask the child to work out the initial letter sound, and guess the rest.
(iii) If that fails, tell the child the word and ask for the whole sentence to be reread.
(iv) If the child meets more than one unknown word in each sentence,

then the book is too difficult, in which case read to the end of the sequence yourself and return the book to the class teacher.

Whenever the child made a mistake parents were advised:

(i) If the mistake makes more or less sense, i.e. pony for horse, let your child read to the end of page or paragraph, and then draw attention to the error.
(ii) If the mistake does not make sense, then stop your child, ask if what has just been read made sense, and encourage the child to self-correct and reread the whole sentence.

A booklet containing this advice was given to the parents. A video of a teacher listening to children was then shown. This illustrated the advice the parents had already been given, and provided a valuable stimulus to a discussion.

At the end of the meeting, the parents were invited to sign a contract to reaffirm their commitment to listen to their children. The contract was then signed by the headteacher on behalf of the school.

Originally, it had been envisaged that the project would run only for one term, but such was the enthusiasm generated by the teachers, parents and children, that it continued over the school holidays and throughout the following term.

Results

Prior to the start of the project, each child was assessed on the English Picture Vocabulary Test (Brimer and Dunn, 1962). The mean scale score of those in the project was 92, within a range of 80 to 116. Their reading accuracy was measured on the Neale Analysis of Reading Ability (Neale, 1958). The Neale Analysis was then administered again in its parallel forms at the end of each term. The results of the project in terms of changes in reading ages are given in Table 6.1.

At the commencement of the project the group had reading ages which were on average some two years and two months in arrears. During the course of the first term (ten weeks) their reading ages increased by over six months and in the subsequent term by just over five months. In both terms there was considerable variation in the gains made by individual children, ranging from a measured loss in reading age for one child in the second term, to gains of up to one year and five months in one term

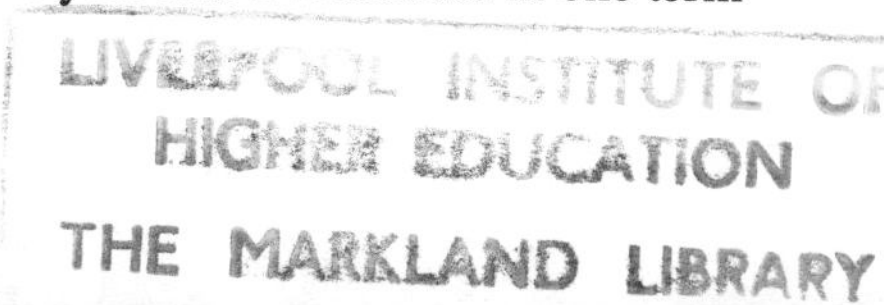

Table 6.1

	Mean years:months	Range years:months
Age	9: 0	7:6–11:4
Reading age at start	6:10	6:0– 8:0
Reading age after one term	7: 4	6:6– 9:2
Reading age after two terms	7: 9	6:6– 9:5
Reading gains	**Mean (months)**	**Range (months)**
First term	6.5	1–17
Second term	5.3	2–13
Total over two terms	11.8	6–20

by others. Overall, there was a tendency for children who had done poorly in the first term to do better in the second, and conversely, children who did exceptionally well in the first term, to do less well in the second.

The fact that the reading ages of the children in the project showed an improvement of almost a year over a seven-month period was a considerable achievement, especially when one considers that prior to the start of the project each previous year had seen the group falling further and further behind. The improvements made by the children were enthusiastically received by parents and teachers alike. It was, therefore, decided to repeat the project in the same school, but in a slightly enlarged form, employing a different experimental design and using a slightly modified record card. This project has been reported by Mannion (1983).

Forty-four children were selected to take part. They came from either the junior or top infants' classes of the school. They all had some degree of reading delay, but this varied from only one month in one case to over two years in others. There was a tendency for the reading delay to be greater for the older children. Mannion (1983) divided her sample into two matched groups. During the first term the parents of one group were actively encouraged to hear them read every night, and record their reading on a record card. During the second term the parents of the second group were likewise encouraged, while the parents who had already joined in the project the previous term were largely left to themselves to decide whether to read to their children or not, and were, therefore, not given a record card to fill in every night. In this way, Mannion hoped to discover the extent to which one term's encouragement of home reading would be continued once active encouragement from the school ceased. The results she achieved can be seen in Table 6.2.

The results showed that while the children were receiving help from their parents within the structured setting of the project they gained on

Table 6.2

	Reading gain	
	Group A	Group B
First term	9.4 months*	2.6 months
Second term	5.2 months	9.0 months*

* Group actively encouraged to read at home each night.

average nine months in reading age over the course of one term. The results of the group who were involved in the project first (Group A) were particularly interesting. In the term in which they no longer took home a reading record card, they showed reading-age gains twice that of their counterparts in Group B who at that time had no experience of parental involvement in reading. It would seem, therefore, that for at least some children, the good practice of having their parents listen to them read appears to have been maintained in the absence of active encouragement from the school.

The reading gains made by the children who were involved in the projects were very satisfying. The fact that the children in the second project made greater gains during the term than those in the first was probably due to the difference in reading delay of the two groups of children. Those in the first project having an average reading delay of two years and two months, while those in the second project had slightly less severe problems and an average delay of only one year and three months.

The positive outcome of these projects was not only in terms of reading-age gains, but could also be seen in the changing behaviour, attitudes and work practices of all those involved.

The Parents

Prior to their involvement in the project, we interviewed all the parents and asked them about their current practice of listening to their children read; 16 per cent said they listened every night, 59 per cent said they did so occasionally, while 25 per cent said they never listened. Throughout both projects the consistency with which the parents listened to their children was extremely high, parents and children rarely missed a night's reading. At the end of the project their responses in a questionnaire reflected their enthusiasm. They said that both they and their children had enjoyed reading together; they felt that their children had also gained a great deal in terms of reading ability and confidence. Many admitted that in the past they had felt helpless when they learned that their children were not doing well in school, but that now they felt relieved that they were able to play a part in helping their children themselves. They all reported that they would continue to listen to their children read regularly, whether the project continued or not. Mannion's (1983) findings seem to suggest that many parents were as good as their word and did continue listening to their children regularly.

The Teachers

The teachers involved in the project reported that they found it relatively easy to organise; the children quickly established a routine of returning their books and record cards from home, and few problems were caused by losing books. Towards the end of the project most teachers felt that there had been improvements in other aspects of school work.

When Mannion analysed her results class by class, she found that the children from two classes appeared to have made substantially greater gains in reading age than their peers in parallel classes, while children from another class made distinctly less gains than their equivalent peers. Mannion attributed these differences in performance to what she called 'teacher enthusiasm', which she had rated prior to her project. However, the results she described could equally well have been affected by other variables, such as teaching style, the priority each teacher gave to reading in her daily classroom activities, or indeed many other factors.

The Children

The response of the children who were involved in the project was on the whole positive, the only exceptions tending to be one or two fourth-year junior children who said they regarded reading as a bit of a chore. It was also this group which tended to make least progress during the course of the project. Mannion found that those top infants' children in her sample made an average reading-age gain of 16.5 months over the two-term period, as compared with 10.1 months for the fourth-year juniors. The attitude and performance of this elder group is possibly a reflection of their general feelings about school and perhaps a product of a low self-concept, brought about by years of being poor readers.

It would seem, therefore, that a project such as this one could be best employed when used in the middle primary school years to prevent this failure, and the development of these attitudes, rather than as a first-aid measure later in the child's school life.

The Psychologist

The advantages to an educational psychologist of being involved in a project like this one are many. Most importantly, she or he can be seen to be involved in influencing the policy and practice of whole schools, and, therefore, have an effect on a larger number of children than would be possible from individual case-work. The psychologist can also become involved in an aspect of education that seems to be aimed at the prevention of failure, rather than its remediation. There is a trend among educational psychologists to move away from an individual case-work model of working (Gillham, 1978), and projects such as this one represent one of the ways in which we are attempting to do this.

Following the project there was, in fact, a marked reduction in the number of children referred by the school to the school psychological services. What is more, because one of the features of the project was a term-by-term record of the children's reading development, it quickly became apparent when one particular child was not making the expected progress and therefore that child almost self-selected for referral to the psychologist.

Discussion

The results of this project were very encouraging. They showed that when parents are invited to help with their children's reading they are very willing to do so, and, given the appropriate materials and advice, can be a very effective support to the class teacher. The children in the project — all of whom had some degree of reading difficulty — were seen to make dramatic progress. What is more, this progress did not appear to be short-lived. The children's gains in reading skills continued to develop — not only when the original project was continued for a further term, but also, as Mannion showed, when the parental involvement was not actively encouraged by the school.

The model we devised had a number of features which, after our discussions with parents and teachers, we felt accounted for a great deal of its successes. These included:

First: the record card. The parents in particular found this useful, because it left no one in any doubt about what was expected from their children on any night, and the children could no longer return home with some excuse for not reading. The value of having the record of one week's reading on a card was also commented upon. Many parents said that this acted as a motivation to the children to collect a mark for each night and hence complete a full card. The teachers also said how easy the card made it to follow up any children who missed a night's reading. The record card, therefore, seems to account for the regularity with which children read to their parents.

Second: the level of reading difficulty of the books. Throughout the project great care was taken to ensure that the reading book given to each child was set at exactly the right level, and that, she or he was not faced with a task that was either too easy or too difficult. Care was also taken to advise the parents to stop the reading session if the child was making more than one mistake each sentence. In this way, we attempted to ensure that each reading session was as unthreatening to the child as possible, but was also reasonably demanding and enjoyable.

Third: the approach we used to the teaching of reading. Throughout the project we used a conventional or traditional approach to listening to children read. The advantage of this approach in contrast to one such as Paired Reading (reported elsewhere in this book) seems to be that both parents and teachers felt comfortable listening in this way, and that a consistent method was adopted both at home and school. There was, therefore, no need to teach a completely new technique, advice was kept to a minimum, and there was no implication that in order to achieve results some specialist technique associated with the psychologist had to be adopted.

This last point is very important, especially when one considers the ease with which a project like this one can be replicated in other schools. The results within at least one LEA have been encouraging. Following the publication of the results of our original project (Dyson and Swinson, 1982), the scheme was taken up by over 20 local schools.

Many schools opted for an exact replication of our original, while others adapted it to their own needs. Many schools did so with only a minimal involvement from the psychological service, and often only a brief consultative discussion was required.

Within the same LEA the value of involving parents in listening to their children read was appreciated by the authority's peripatetic remedial reading service. This resulted in it becoming almost standard practice for the remedial teachers to meet the parents of their pupils, and encourage them to become involved in listening to their children read.

The spread of such projects has not been confined just to one authority. Since the original project, we have been contacted by teachers and psychologists from all over the country, who reported their intention of running schemes. There is also at least one in-service teachers' course run by a college of higher education on How to Run a Successful Parental Involvement Scheme.

The model we used in our project would also seem to be relatively easy to adapt to use in other settings. Swinson (1985) has used the same methods as described in this chapter to encourage mothers to read stories to their nursery-age children. After they had done so on a daily basis for most of the school year, he found that the children had made significant gains in both their vocabulary and comprehension skills. He also found that some of these gains were still apparent after the children had transferred to the infants' school.

Although the parental involvement projects described in this chapter have on the whole been successful, there are a number of points that need to be taken into account by anyone considering running a scheme in their own school.

First, a home-reading project should not be regarded as a substitute for a well-organised reading curriculum. In fact, before any project can begin, it is essential that the school's curriculum is well thought out and that its reading resources are well organised, so that it is easy to ensure that a child is reading a book at the appropriate level.

Second, it is important for a school not simply to copy a successful project from another source, but to consider the needs of its own children and its individual structure, and to devise an approach that can be integrated into the organisation and philosophy of the whole school.

Third, it is important not to over-burden either parents or teachers. In our project the largest number of children from any class was four, it could be counterproductive if large numbers of children from any one class were included, unless the teacher was given help in not only listening to children read, but also in the selection of appropriate books. To over-burden the parents could also have been counterproductive and result in them feeling that listening to their children was a chore, hence in our project we asked the parents to spend no more than ten minutes of their time each day.

If these considerations are taken into account during the planning of any scheme, then the results in terms of improvement of reading skills made by the children can be very satisfying. However, it would be very limiting indeed to look at parental involvement schemes only in these terms. There are implications for psychologists in considering the merits of advisory as opposed to case-orientated work. As far as the schools are concerned, it is clear that it is both possible and necessary to involve parents actively in many aspects of school life — including the actual learning of skills — and that such participation can be very influential in realising the full potential of their children.

References

Brimer, L. and Dunn, L. (1962), English Picture Vocabulary Test, Educational Evaluation Enterprises, Bristol

Dyson, J. and Swinson, J. (1982), 'Involving Parents in the Teaching of Reading', *Journal of the Association of Educational Psychologists*, vol. 5, no. 9, 18–21

Gillham, B. (ed.) (1978), *Reconstructing Educational Psychology*, Croom Helm, London

Jackson, A. and Hannon, P. (1981), *The Belfield Reading Project*, Belfield Community Council, Rochdale

Mannion, M. (1983), unpublished MEd thesis, University of Wales, Bangor

Neale, M. (1958), *The Neale Analysis of Reading Ability*, Macmillan Education, London

Swinson, J. (1985), 'A Parental Involvement Project in a Nursery School', *Educational Psychology in Practice*, 1 (1), April

Tizard, J., Schofield, W. and Hewison, J. (1982) 'Collaboration between Teachers and Parents in Assisting Childrens' Reading', *British Journal of Educational Psychology*, vol. 52, 1–15

7 THE ELMWOOD PROJECT, SOMERSET

David Knapman

Introduction

It is a most illuminating process to ask parents exactly how they help their children with reading at home. Perhaps in the past we have been too quick to accept at face value the assurance from some parents that they listen to their child read regularly, and we have assumed that this, in itself, is a uniform and straightforward matter. For some children this is patently not the case. There exists for future research a mine of information about parent–child interaction in early reading, and many teachers would do well to consider and explore this area further. To ask parents to demonstrate how they work with their child at home can be revealing and instructive. One is often reminded that apart from the formal processes involved in reading, complex feelings and relationship factors are also important; what one observes may be consistent with the teaching at school and the advice given to a child by school staff, or equally it may be quite different.

Some of the more common observations which have been made concerning faulty reading-support work at home include: (a) reading session occurring too late in the evening; (b) individual reading sessions lasting too long or being spaced too far apart; (c) reading work taking place in an inappropriate setting; (d) parents exerting too much pressure on reading; (e) reading work spoilt by anxiety or loss of temper; (f) the use of inappropriate reading material; (g) parents giving too much time to mistakes or difficulties and insufficient attention to praise and encouragement; (h) incorrect or inadequate cues given when a child becomes 'stuck'; and (i) imprudent use of siblings, relations, friends, etc., for reading work.

Especially where there are difficulties, reading practice at home can be a highly emotionally charged process for all concerned. Although research has been conducted on the development of learning processes, on teaching styles, and on various structured materials, relatively little attention — until recently — has been focused on the role of the parent in supporting reading work at home. For some children it may be that this factor is a critical one.

In this particular project, at Elmwood School, Somerset, a group of parents of slow-learning children (traditionally ESN(M)) were invited to a series of evening discussion meetings. Specific advice and tips were given and actual 'modelling' work with the children was carried out. As far as we were aware, few, if any, similar projects had taken slow-learning children as subjects for this type of research. For many parents who may feel confused about modern methods in special education and unsure about how best to help their children, the need for good specific advice on reading work at home is arguably a widespread one. It is this factor which formed the background to the present study.

The Project

The ideas behind the present project sprang jointly from senior school staff at a local authority special school, and members of the support and psychological service. At the time (1982), increasing publicity was being given to studies in various parts of the country, all of which seemed to be demonstrating the value of parent involvement in reading progress. The question naturally arose as to whether this work might profitably be extended to the special-school situation.

First, a letter was sent to the headteacher to parents of one particular class, outlining the idea of the project and asking for volunteers to attend a series of meetings. The letter explained that the project would last for between one and two terms and that it would be essentially experimental. As a result of this, a group of parents of six children was established and at the conjoint meetings that followed the staff group comprised the headteacher, deputy head, special-education support teacher, and the area educational psychologist. All the children (three boys and three girls) had been assessed as functioning in the traditional ESN(M) range of ability and they had in fact (which may be significant) already made a start with their formal reading. With such a small group of quite individual children it was felt difficult and impractical to consider established a matched control group. In its formulation of the overall aims of the project, the staff agreed on the following:

(1) To advise the parent group as specifically as possible how best to manage and support their children's reading work.
(2) To organise a series of evening meetings with the parents to support and maintain the work they would do at home with their children.

(3) To involve staff in practical tutorial sessions with parents and their children.
(4) To provide a good and suitable range of reading material which would be freely available.
(5) To evaluate the results.

Details of the Sessions

It was agreed that the project sessions would take place at school, between 7.00 and 9.00 p.m., and that these would be held on a weekly basis for the first six meetings. This initial phase was, in fact, complemented by a further two 'maintenance' sessions which followed up the work the parents had been doing at home in the intervening period. At all the meetings an informal atmosphere was encouraged, with the provision of coffee and the arrangement of parallel play sessions (from Session 3 onwards) while the adult discussion group was being held. A relaxed and well-knit group did, in fact, quickly develop. A more detailed outline of the content of individual sessions follows.

Session 1 (Parents and Staff Only)

The rationale of the project was explained with an overview of recent research. Various psychological aspects of the reading process were mentioned and members of the group shared their own experiences, both when they themselves were at school, and now with their children's reading. Following this, the plan of the project was discussed in more detail and the parents were given folders which contained basic advice on listening to reading.

Session 2 (Parents and Staff Only)

A further discussion of various factors involved in reading took place, and using a role-play procedure we attempted to illustrate good and bad practices as regards listening to reading. Also in this session the question of rewards was first introduced as a possible incentive for the children, and various possibilities were jointly put forward. The parents were introduced to the initial book supply and some discussion of how to choose appropriate books took place. Parents in fact selected their first books with their children during this session, again with the advice of staff, and it was agreed that the home sessions would begin the following day. The joint agreement was that the reading work would generally last 10–15 minutes, with some stress on the fact that discussion with the child should be part of the aim.

Sessions 3, 4, and 5 (Parents, Staff and Children)

Each of these sessions fell into two parts. During the first part each member of staff took two sets of parents to an adjoining classroom area where individual tutorial sessions took place. In this way it was possible for the parent–child interaction during the reading to be observed and discussed with the parent. During the second part of the sessions a general discussion took place between parents and staff on the question of progress, books, record-keeping, etc. At this time the children engaged in supervised play in the school hall.

Session 6

This session was similar to the preceding ones, except it was agreed that it would be a good idea to involve the children in the general group meeting in order to give them as positive a feedback as possible for the progress which they had been making.

At its inception it was envisaged that the project should be seen as of strictly limited duration — as a special opportunity for parents to gain advice and contact with the school which they would hopefully wish to sustain. It was felt important to make this clear at the first session but by the end of Session 6 the group had consolidated to such an extent that the further two maintenance sessions were finally agreed on. These were spaced at monthly intervals and during this time staff were freely available to parents by telephone, and a number of home visits were also made. Throughout the project parents had ready access to the book supply at the school.

Discussion of the Project

When the idea of the project was first suggested to the parents, there was a ready response from them and the level of interest which was subsequently maintained tended to confirm the feeling that a need might exist for this sort of structured support work. Also, during the 18 weeks' experimental period none of the parents who had volunteered either dropped out or attended irregularly. It was interesting to observe that there was no evidence of the children's motivation weakening as the work progressed. It had been agreed that the parents and their children would aim for an average of five evenings a week to do their reading work. One or two of the parents did admit that they, rather than the children, sometimes found it difficult to make time for their reading sessions in the evening; several parents mentioned that brothers and sisters also wanted to be heard to read in the same way! Certain aspects of the project are worth commenting on individually.

Reading Material

This was felt to be particularly crucial. The initial stock of books quickly proved to be inadequate both in terms of quantity and range of difficulty, but thanks to the good co-operation of the Somerset schools library service, this deficiency was quickly overcome. During the evaluation phase of the project, it was agreed by the staff group and parents that the provision of a good supply of suitable books was of paramount importance and, if lacking, might well jeopardise the success of any similar parent involvement project.

Tutorial Demonstration Work

As well as the more formal discussion and seminar work, it was felt that the actual demonstration of 'listening styles' through role play and individual tutoring was extremely valuable to the parents. Despite their involvement in the discussion periods, certain parents gained greater benefit from 'on-the-job' advice with regard to their particular style. It was also felt by some that the provision of private areas in the school for this aspect of the work was important.

Rewards

When the question of rewards was first discussed, most parents felt that this would be unecessary in order to sustain the motivation or enthusiasm of their children. Subsequently, however, several did agree with their children on suitable reward and found this helpful as the project developed. To some extent the recording charts which were used were found to be self-rewarding, but when a parent suggested that the 'house point' system (currently in use at the school) might be used, this was accepted by the whole group. Criteria for the reward of a 'house point' were agreed upon with the result that each child's weekly chart was returned by the parents to the headteacher for the reward of a 'house point' as appropriate. All the parents commented that, from a reward point of view, the children greatly looked forward to and enjoyed their meetings at school.

Record Charts

These charts (see Figure 7.1) were designed and later modified to record the actual reading work being done at home, to estimate the child's attitude towards this, and also to record any points for future group

Figure 7.1: Record Chart of Weekly Reading at Home

Name:________________________________ Week beginning:__________

	Length of Session (Reading/Talking)	Stars for Attitude				Parents Comments/Title of Book
		V. Good	Good	Fair	Poor	
MONDAY						
TUESDAY						
WEDNESDAY						
THURSDAY						
FRIDAY						

OTHER COMMENTS:

discussion. The charts were completed each evening with the child; for recording purposes, gummed stars or shading-in were suggested. It was observed later from the records that some parents found it hard to limit themselves to the 10–15 minutes agreed upon as the maximum length for reading sessions, but it was felt that a formal recording device such as this was useful to all concerned.

Conclusion

This brief local study examined how a structured and supported effort on the part of parents to hear their children read might affect reading ability. The children taking part were slow learners in the 8–9 age group, who were initially approximately two years 'behind' with their reading. Some caution is required in judging the results: the size of the group was small and the level of motivation on the part of the volunteer parents may have been greater than usual. Different results might hav been obtained from a group of children who had not made a beginning with their reading, and no long-term follow-up of the results was made. Nevertheless, significant gains in reading ability (see Table 7.1) were observed to suggest that this form of intervention might indeed be worth developing, not only in mainstream education but within the field of special education also. The feeling of all concerned was that the project had not only helped the children with their reading, but had significantly affected school–parent relationships and basic attitudes.

Table 7.1: Gains in Reading Ability*

Child	Reading accuracy (Jan. 82)	Reading comprehension (Jan. 82)	Reading accuracy (June 82)	Reading comprehension (June 82)	Accuracy gain (months)	Comprehension gain
Jane	6: 3	6:6	7: 1	7:10	+10	+16
Paul	7: 0	6:6	7: 9	7:10	+ 9	+16
Anne	8: 5	7:6	8: 8	6: 9	+ 3	− 9
Susan	5: 7	6:8	6:10	7: 4	+15	+ 8
Richard	7: 1	7:6	7: 9	8: 5	+ 8	+11
Sarah	5:11	6:9	6: 9	7:10	+10	+13

Mean gain in reading age over 18 weeks

Accuracy (months)**	Comprehension (months)**
9.2	9.2

* Years:months, unless otherwise stated.
** Using Neale Analysis of Reading Ability.

8 PACT: DEVELOPMENT OF HOME-READING SCHEMES IN THE ILEA

Alex Griffiths and Alastair King

The Origins

PACT is an acronym for Parents and Children and Teachers, chosen after some deliberation to signify the underlying ideal of partnership between all three. In the Inner London Education Authority (ILEA) it has not only become an umbrella term for structured home-reading schemes, but also refers to a loosely organised movement which supports all efforts to improve co-operation between parents and teachers.

The roots of PACT are in a programme co-funded by ILEA and Inner City Partnership finance, and called the Pitfield Project. A team comprising an educational psychologist, an advisory teacher, an education welfare officer and a secretary were appointed to work in a small group of Hackney schools, in an attempt to help teachers work more effectively with children with learning difficulties.

The results of a number of research projects into parental involvement in reading enhanced the team's conviction that *all* children would benefit if their parents were involved in their learning. In consequence, the team was instrumental in helping to pilot the first structured home-reading scheme in a Hackney junior school.

It was considered important to test the Haringey results (Hewison and Tizard, 1980; Tizard, Schofield and Hewison, 1982; and Chapter 4 of this book) in a junior school as almost all major projects involving parents — such as the Head-start programmes in the USA (Lazar, 1979) — had all been with preschool or infant-age children. There are a number of small-scale exceptions, of course (Glynn, 1980). The basic premise formulated by the team was that if any parental reading scheme was to be successful, then three criteria had to be met:

(1) Parents and teachers must meet to set up a partnership.
(2) There must be a sharing of teachers' professional knowledge with parents, and of parents' knowledge with the teachers.
(3) Reliable structures must be instigated to sustain a dialogue between parents and teachers.

Pilot School

In many senses these criteria are obvious, but fulfilling them is not so easy (Griffiths and Hamilton, 1984).

The junior school which piloted the first scheme took each of the criteria in turn, and critically examined its policies in relation to them. It quickly became apparent that if the school was going to involve parents genuinely in their children's learning then a combined, committed staff effort was needed — later individuals and groups of teachers in other schools successfully operated similar schemes, though this put some considerable burden on those involved.

Perhaps the most difficult decisions that the school had to make concerned which elements of 'good teaching technique' should be shared with parents. After all, most teachers have years of training and several years of practice before they regard themselves as experienced exponents of their art. How could it be encapsulated into a few essential elements and still retain its quality? After much discussion it was decided that parents would be encouraged to keep any reading sessions short (approximately ten minutes), give lots of praise to their child, ensure that the session was enjoyable both to themselves and to their child, and spend much time talking with their child. Parents were also to be given specific guidance as to what to do when their child made a mistake, e.g. 'count to five slowly to yourself and then give them the word'. Of course, this advice will sound familiar to many but it was important at the time for it to be articulated and clearly formulated within the school.

Another important decision for the school was how to maintain good contact with parents over a long period of time. Having regular contact with individual parents can be extremely time-consuming, especially with a class of 30 children! Although the pilot school had a fairly flexible open-house approach to parents, it was decided to introduce a record card for home reading. This card went home with the child's reading book and parents were asked to comment on the session they had had with their child. The teacher also made comments on the card and was *expected* to encourage parents to make comments. The record-card system has proved crucial in maintaining parent–teacher links. Also many schools have supplementary 'back-up systems', such as teachers being available for a short while after school on a particular day of the week.

Much thought was also given by the school as to how to launch a scheme which would appeal to parents. 'Help us to help your child' proved a useful slogan for persuading parents to participate, but the staff carefully examined the detail of working with parents. They looked at their own attitudes and expectations, as well as the practicalities for parents of absorbing large amounts of information. The pilot school actually launched its scheme at a large meeting, with great care given to how the new material was presented and ensuring that parents had every opportunity to attend. (For instance, the school ran a crèche so that parents, especially single parents, were able to come.)

Within only a few months 98.5 per cent of the children in this school, which was in a very deprived area of London, were heard reading regularly by adults in the evenings. A figure this size can only be attributed to the massive amount of interest that parents have in their children's learning. The benefits were clear. Over a period of 18 months reading ages improved dramatically (Griffiths and Hamilton, 1984). Teachers felt that they had grown in their knowledge and awareness of parents, and felt they had gained a much higher regard for parents — both as parents and as effective teachers. Parents stated their belief that the school had made an effort to meet their needs, that they felt closer to the school and its aims and frequently took the trouble to express this both in attitude and in words.

This brief description fails to convey the tremendous amount of effort and time that teachers gave to make the original scheme work, let alone the efforts of headteachers and teachers elsewhere in ILEA. But the idea clearly struck a chord and the effort was thought to be worth while, because the idea spread rapidly, other schools quickly implemented similar schemes and the Pitfield Project team was soon inundated with requests for information, advice, support materials and in-service training, far beyond the original group of project schools. Interested people in the community came together and the PACT committee was formed to support parental involvement initiatives. It consisted of the Pitfield Project team, an inspector, headteachers, a local children's librarian, community relations workers, representatives of adult education, and, of course, parents. The committee has undoubtedly been an important influence in the development of parental involvement in Hackney. Recently, this organisation has been able to look critically at PACT schemes in a number of schools.

The Spread of PACT in ILEA

The experience of the Pitfield Project suggested that schools were taking up PACT schemes, or very similar schemes, in large numbers. But what was *actually* happening in Hackney schools, and what were teachers' views about it? Some evidence has been gathered recently to try and answer these questions.

In the spring of 1984, the project team carried out a telephone survey of all the headteachers of primary schools in Hackney, asking about their use of PACT-style home-reading schemes. Of the total 73 schools canvassed, 43 claimed that their schools were using, specifically, a PACT scheme. A further 13 planned to introduce one in the near future, and 12 said that they encouraged children to take books home to read with their parents but had no formal scheme. Therefore, on the surface at least, it seemed that a high proportion of Hackney schools were showing interest in this kind of approach. No similar data is available for the rest of ILEA, but again, take-up undoubtedly appears to have been extensive. Four over-subscribed, centrally based INSET courses on introducing PACT were run during the spring and summer terms of 1984, each catering for 30–40 headteachers and teachers. A follow-up questionnaire of one course group after a six-week gap found that 22 schools, out of 23 replying, had plans for introducing a PACT scheme within the next term or two.

However, it is difficult to be sure whether all of this apparent interest and activity is an accurate reflection of what is actually going on between individual parents and teachers and children, and whether any really significant change in practice is taking place.

It is important, therefore, to go below the surface activity and ask some questions about what is happening at classroom level.

Survey Results

An attempt was made recently to investigate some important questions by interviewing class teachers in 15 randomly chosen schools whose heads had claimed in the earlier telephone survey to be operating PACT schemes. Of the 132 class teachers in these schools, 117 were questioned. The results have not been fully analysed yet, but a preliminary examination of the findings yields the following picture.

(1) There are considerable differences in practice and apparent effectiveness, both between schools and between teachers within schools. The 'school factor' and the 'teacher factor' seem important, presumably reflecting qualities of commitment and organisation. Some schools had a whole school policy towards PACT with most teachers operating a scheme, while in others one or two teachers were working a scheme in isolation from colleagues and with little sense of support.

(2) Schools, and individual class groups, were at quite different stages of development as far as PACT schemes were concerned. Some had recently established schemes which still carried the enthusiasm of novelty. Others had been established for longer and were felt by staff to be in need of a shot in the arm. This suggests a continuing need for INSET and support, and for the development of other, complementary strategies for involving parents in education.

(3) There is a tail-off effect with older year groups. Reading aloud, whether at home or at school, is in any case probably not an appropriate regular activity for older and more fluent readers. Undoubtedly, some such children still enjoy doing this, but many others, and their parents, feel that it is unnecessary. That does not mean that the parents of older and more fluent readers cannot be directly involved in their children's education, only that other ways of involving them have to be found. Some teachers in the survey had developed interesting ideas about this, such as setting homework involving 'higher order' literacy skills, with clearly structured tasks to be shared with parents (e.g. dictionary work, criticism, etc.). It is worth noting, incidentally, that a number of ILEA secondary schools have introduced formal schemes along these lines, which are reported by the teachers concerned to be very successful.

(4) Perhaps the main difficulty reported by tachers was that of finding time to monitor the scheme, to follow up individual children and to talk to parents. It was usually found necessary to reorganise the timetable in some way. Other difficulties mentioned included the need for extra resources (more books, the production of folders and record cards, etc.); providing for families whose first language is not English; involving more reluctant parents; maintaining the enthusiasm — of both teachers and parents — for the scheme.

(5) Despite the difficulties, the vast majority of teachers questioned found PACT a useful framework. About 80 per cent of those interviewed used a PACT scheme, and most of the 20 per cent not using one were third- and fourth-year junior teachers (see point 3 above). Only five teachers questioned thought PACT was not useful, and *all* of the teachers who actually used a scheme found it beneficial — over half of them found it *very* beneficial.

(6) On the teachers' estimates, 57 per cent of the children in their classes read regularly (twice weekly or more) to their parents at home. This is certainly a lower figure than in some research projects, but higher than seems to occur spontaneously in inner-city areas. A further 22 per cent read at home to parents occasionally, and 21 per cent did so rarely or never. This last figures needs to be treated cautiously, since it includes

a high proportion of fluent readers for whom, as already suggested, reading aloud at home is not necessarily appropriate anyway; it also includes a number of families whose first language is not English.

(7) Teachers varied considerably in the extent to which they had contact with individual parents. As would be expected, there is, on the whole, more personal contact in infants' departments. Most teacher–parent contacts were either informal (e.g. parents coming to school to collect children) or occurred when parents were summoned to school to discuss problems. However, several teachers had set up regular 'surgeries' to which parents could come if they wished.

(8) About 40 per cent of the teachers questioned had had parents working with children — not necessarily their own — in their classrooms during the year. A total of 122 parents in the 15 schools had been involved in this way.

(9) A number of teachers said that they thought home visiting would be useful, and eight had actually made home visits during the year.

(10) The benefits mentioned by teachers included improved reading levels, increased pleasure in books, improved attitudes to school, and better home–school relationships.

These findings suggest that there has been a genuine move to involve parents in education in Hackney primary schools, and that large numbers of parents have been successfully engaged in home-reading schemes. They also suggest that many teachers are taking active steps to extend the notion of a home–school partnership (e.g. by bringing parents into the classroom). It may be, of course, that Hackney schools were already moving towards this before PACT came along, but it does seem that PACT has helped to promote a much more rapid growth in this area than would have occurred otherwise, possibly stimulated by the PACT organisation directly contacting groups and individuals in the community.

It has proved difficult to gather hard evidence about the effects of PACT schemes on actual reading ages. Very few schools evaluate their schemes in any systematic way, and control groups are seldom used. When the overall reading levels of schools using PACT schemes are examined, the picture is confusing, with some showing little change and others showing large gains, but with confounding factors (e.g. changes in key members of staff; change from ITA to traditional orthography). It may prove difficult in general practice to repeat the very rapid and marked gains in reading levels which are found in research projects; but this does not diminish the value of PACT-type schemes, for other benefits may be equally important in the short term, and it may take longer for gains to be established in general practice. Indeed, even research projects have taken up to two years to obtain overall school effects. Teachers need to be aware of this because unrealistic expectations may be set up which lead quickly to disillusionment.

Good Practice

There is no doubt that there are many schools and individual teachers in Hackney who have gone a long way towards establishing the conditions for a genuine partnership with parents. A visitor could not help but be impressed by the ethos in such schools and classrooms and by the arrangements which have been made to foster good home–school relationships, of which the home-reading scheme is just one aspect.

We have tried to pick out some of the characteristics of such schools which appear to be of importance in helping to sustain effective parental involvement schemes, and some of the factors which contribute to good practice. Effective PACT schemes occur:

(1) In schools where the home-reading scheme has been developed as part of an overall policy towards language. That is, where a school view on the essential elements of the reading process has been carefully thought out, and consideration has been given to the relative contributions of psycholinguistics, phonics, etc. The school's reading scheme has often been reviewed in the light of this and usually placed a major emphasis on the notion of books for fun and enjoyment — essentially *shared* fun and enjoyment — rather than on reading as a task to be mastered (see point 6).

(2) Where the headteacher is enthusiastic and supportive towards the scheme.

(3) Where teachers have taken into account the need to organise the classroom and timetable to accommodate PACT. After all, individual children have to be followed up, as do their parents' responses.

(4) Where clear strategies have been developed to deal with difficult areas (e.g. families with limited resources; situations in which English is not the family's first language; 'reluctant' parents, etc.). It seems important to have a realistic appreciation of the difficulties involved and a commitment to continue exploring new ways of overcoming them.

(5) In schools which are effective in other areas, too, and where parental involvement is one part of the overall philosophy, organisation and ethos of the school. A school may be a very effective educational

institution and have good home–school relationships without necessarily using a formally structured PACT scheme. And introducing a PACT scheme will not in itself make a poor school good!

(6) In schools where the implications of parental involvement for resources have been explored. Most schools with successful schemes have a named member of staff with responsibility for co-ordinating parental involvement efforts within the school. Sometimes this is a scale-post, and in some schools a home–school liaison teacher has been appointed, with home visiting as part of their job description. The subject of home visiting by teachers is a contentious one which needs careful thought, but the fact is that most of the seminal research projects in the area of home–school-reading schemes have used it and regarded it as an essential element. One must ask what qualities and skills a home-visiting teacher would need and what support and resources (e.g. INSET) would be required to help promote and foster these skills. There is clearly a very real question here about the extent to which education authorities are prepared and able to make resources available for this kind of work, and individual schools may also have to look carefully at the way in which their existing resources are organised. The fundamental issue underlying these questions, of course, is that of the priority to be given to parental involvement initiatives.

The PACT experience in ILEA suggests that resources and support mechanisms operating from outside the schools can be very potent influences. The Pitfield Project and the PACT committee have provided an important central point for the collection and dissemination of information, advice and materials, as well as helping to provide a focus and an identity for parental involvement schemes. Advisers, inspectors, educational psychologists, teachers, and education welfare officers have all played a part, as have such 'non-educationalists' as parents, librarians, and community workers, reflecting the fact that forging links between schools and the communities of which they are a part is a multidisciplinary task which transcends professional boundaries. Moreover, educational professionals are quite likely to find their existing roles affected by these developments. In the authors' personal experience, this has certainly been so with the traditional aspects of their roles as educational psychologists, involving work with individual children. In the first place, when a child with learning difficulties is referred, an attempt is often made to try to work out with the parents and the school a home-based programme as part of a treatment plan. Second, there appear to be increased possibilities of work in partnership with teachers and parents in situations where behaviour is a problem (e.g. by having the parents in the classroom). These strategies would not be possible if teachers and parents were not receptive to the idea of working together and accustomed to this approach. PACT schemes, we would argue, have helped to foster these conditions.

The PACT committee, working through the Pitfield Project team, has tried to meet the demands of schools by providing regular in-service training both school-based and centre-based. Until recently there has been a tendency to concentrate on the practicalities of running a home-reading scheme, how to set it up, how to keep it going, how to encourage parents, how to advise parents, how to find the time to do all this! Although many schools in Hackney now have PACT-type schemes, there is a continuing demand for such practical courses, but there is additional need for courses of a more experimental, reflective nature which focus on more personal aspects of working with parents.

PACT schemes are now operating in many infants' and junior schools, but the ideas underlining PACT have also been incorporated into a number of initiatives for preschool children, as well as for secondary-age children. At the present time many nursery schools and classes are encouraging parents to read to their children. Indeed, nursery teachers are reporting exciting and fruitful discussions between themselves and parents about books, literacy and child development. A growing number of secondary schools have also developed schemes mainly with English and special-needs departments to encourage reading with first- and second-hand children. Although many of these secondary schemes are in their early stages, early reports suggest a high degree of parent and child interest as well as an excitement about literacy and literature. But secondary schools will probably need to think even more deeply about certain aspects of parental involvement. For instance, parents of secondary age children often ask how they can be more helpful to their children at homework time and many are confused by the organisation and curriculum of secondary schools. The foundations for parental involvement should have been laid at the primary stage, but advice about learning skills or study skills may need to be explored further with parents at the secondary stage and it is essential that the rationale and objectives of the curriculum be made accessible to parents, particularly in the way it relates to their individual children.

Much investigation still needs to be done, teachers' ideas need to be evaluated. However, there is sufficient evidence to suggest that schools can run successful schemes without a lot of outside help. But backing from some kind of support organisation or a Local Education Authority does appear to be necessary to share out the available expertise and encourage schools in their efforts towards parent–teacher co-operation.

References

Glynn, T. (1980), 'Parent–Child Interaction in Remedial Teaching at Home', in Clark, M.M. and Glynn, T. (eds), *Reading and Writing for the Child with Difficulties*, University of Birmingham

Griffiths, A. and Hamilton, D. (1984), *Parent, Teacher, Child: Working Together in Children's Learning*, Methuen, London

Hewison, J. and Tizard, J. (1980), 'Parental Involvement in Reading Attainment', *British Journal of Educational Psychology*, vol. 50, no. 3, 209–15

Lazar, I. (ed.), *Lasting Effects after the School*, US Government Printing Office, Washington

Tizard, J., Schofield, W.N. and Hewison, J. (1982), 'Collaboration between Teachers and Parents in Assisting Children's Reading', *British Journal of Educational Psychology*, vol. 52, no. 1, 1–15

9 PARENTAL INVOLVEMENT PROGRAMMES AND THE LITERACY PERFORMANCE OF CHILDREN

Paul Widlake and Flora MacLeod

Coventry, unlike some other Local Education Authorities which take part in community projects, has sustained innovation and given it a permanent place within its education service (despite changes in political control within the city's council).

In its infancy the Community Education Project (CEP) consisted of a small team placed in an infants' school in the heart of the city's multi-ethnic and disadvantaged area. Its work ranged over twelve primary schools and a nursery centre and involved the Sidney Stringer community school. The team provided additional support and innovative services to teachers, pupils and parents in the area by:

(i) Developing a programme in schools designed to encourage home–school and community–school links.

(ii) Developing in-service training and support programmes for teachers in: the use of the latest teaching techniques; development of communication skills; understanding of the culture of people in the inner-city area.

(iii) Supporting teachers in their first year from college.

(iv) Developing an adult programme seeking to respond to community needs rather than present the community with additional education possibilities offered from an institution.

(v) Establishing a home-tutoring scheme for immigrant mothers.

(vi) Assisting with the extension of preschool provision. In 1975 the idea of a 'decentralised' team was replicated in four other areas of the city. These areas were selected on the basis of degree of disadvantage suffered by the pupils in the schools, thus retaining the original 'positive discrimination' policy in the new areas. Community education strategies have developed in each area, and differ in detail, but all regard home–school relationships as a priority.

Home–School. Strategies and supporting materials have been developed which have widened, deepened and informalised parental involvement in many of the schools concerned. Parents are being accepted as genuine partners in the educational process. The following list gives some idea of the kind of possibilities and activities which are being offered right across the city: parents' rooms; family clubs; dressmaking; English lessons; school youth clubs; subject evenings (e.g. modern maths); do-it-yourself evenings; film nights; discos; social evenings; lunchtime concerts; craft club evenings; keep-fit classes.

Preschool. Work in this area has included development of mother and toddler groups in many schools, ready-for-school groups, and a wide range of home-visiting strategies. The training element in these strategies has laid the foundation for adult education work.

In 1973, the Van Leer Foundation provided a grant for an experimental scheme using local mothers, trained and supervised by qualified teachers, to run annexes to the Hillfields Nursery Centre. Three years later the Foundation offered to provide sufficient additional funds to enable the scheme to be extended to a second area for a three-year period.

Adult Education. From informal beginnings, dealing with a content mainly concerned with the development and education of young children, a more formal provision has developed. Courses on local history, simple graphics, Indian dancing, and GCE 'O' Level English are examples of provision made at several primary schools. Many adults attend regular classes in day schools to study for 'O' and 'A' Level examinations.

Leadership courses are also being run to train some parents to take over the leadership of a wide variety of groups in schools. This generation of self-help skills is further exemplified by the training of a multiracial group of parents who carry out home-visiting duties in their school catchment area. These visitors work under the direction of the school headteacher and in close liaison with health visitors and social workers.

Some schools are now beginning to evolve a parents' syllabus from their home–school programmes. Each school's syllabus is structured to ensure that during their time with the school, parents will be given a share in most aspects of the curriculum side by side with their child's progress through the school.

Regular radio broadcasts by CEP staff on educational matters are backed up with specially prepared materials across the city.

Curriculum. Materials have been devised to encourage situations in which parents, children and teachers work together on the development of observation, analysis, diagnosis and social action skills in terms of the local environment.

Four of the five areas have seen the influence of the community on the curriculum as a priority which is exhibited in several patterns — using the local community as a resource for learning, taking the local community as a starting-point for wider urban studies, or taking a particular aspect of the community as the basis for developing a specific curriculum strategy. The publication of various teaching kits has evolved out of these initiatives. Particular interest has been centred on the teaching of reading skills and has resulted in the production of a highly structured and monitored scheme to measure and describe the effects of parental involvement in a school-directed reading programme, preschool reading material, a booklet specifically designed to stimulate parental involvement in a school reading programme, and reading books containing children's imaginative stories.

Home-tutoring services for Asian adults have been operating throughout the period under review, 1971–7, and families in many parts of the city are in receipt of regular help. In addition, there are a variety of afternoon and evening classes, which are regularly attended by 120 women but with many more attending occasionally as and when other commitments permit.

Other activities of the CEP include the provision of in-service training for teachers, the publication of regular communication links with schools — bulletins, news-sheets, staffroom folders, etc. — and holiday playtime schemes engaging the practical support of students attending Lanchester Polytechnic and Warwick University.

It is apparent that 'reading', in an extended form which includes many aspects of language development, has always featured prominently in the Coventry CEP programme. In the early 1970s, school work was displayed on buses and some famous people were associated with the programme, which was focused on school activities of all kinds, especially reading and mathematics. The children whose work was used then are now in their twenties, and many have preschool children themselves. From 1972 onwards, a local news bulletin was sent out which included articles about reading, morning assemblies, home-tutoring schemes, and so on.

A booklet, *Reading: Involving Parents*, contains details of 15 methods of involving parents in reading, ranging from parents observing in the classroom and listening to children reading in school, to helping at home by making sure that the children have books and use them. During the last two years, a somewhat different approach has been taken. Following initial meetings organised by the schools, parents have been asked to hear their children read at home and to keep a systematic record on a card prepared by the school.

Many schools are attempting to create an atmosphere which is conducive to the development of reading: book displays are arranged throughout schools; community assemblies are arranged based on stories, new library books, etc.; community libraries based in schools are run by parents and other community members; slides, filmstrips and films of stories are shown to parents and pupils. Children are allowed to take home any books in the school except those borrowed from the city library.

Books taken home are treated as something rather special and so are transported to and from school in a specially prepared plastic folder. In addition to the child's reading book, many schools also make available a selection of very attractive books for children to choose from. Although these books are generally arranged roughly according to readability level, the children are always free to make their own choices.

Pre- and early reading and language workshops for parents have been run by some schools. There have been many local radio broadcasts, listening groups and phone-ins, followed up by discussion groups in local schools.

An invitation was received to evaluate the effects of a current CEP reading drive. It was intended to collect base-line data and to retest in all schools, but it soon became apparent that the programmes were at very different stages of development. Some schools had been following open-door policies for a decade, others were more recently involved. It became apparent that we were looking at both the long-term and short-term effects of programmes initiated by the Coventry CEP teacher advisers. They identified eight schools (plus an infants' department) which were particularly welcoming and effective in integrating parental contributions in many ways. We decided that the classical research design we had hoped to achieve would not be feasible, and instead studied schools selected from this sample who were known to involve parents effectively.

The Hunter-Grundin Literacy Profiles used for the study consist of five tests: four group tests assessing attitudes to reading, reading for meaning, spelling and free-writing; and one individual test assessing spoken language. None of the tests takes longer than ten minutes to complete. Reading for meaning is a multiple-choice cloze procedure test, i.e. instead of the deletions in a conventional cloze test there are four alternative words from which the child has to choose one. This eliminates the influence of writing ability on the reading test result. In a conventional cloze test a child might know the right word that goes in a deletion, but may be unable to write it in an intelligible form; or may be able to write the words, but the writing may be very time-consuming and tiring. The 'Reading for Meaning' test can thus be said to be a more 'pure' test of reading ability than a conventional cloze test.

Despite the importance attributed to reading, it is desirable that progress should be assessed in a wide spectrum of language skills. The Hunter-Grundin battery uses a picture as a stimulus to conversation and distinguishes five elements in oral language at infants' level: confidence, enunciation, vocabulary, accuracy and imagination. These are assessed using a five-point scale. Older children can be assessed on their 'free-writing' performance, using measures of legibility, fluency, accuracy and originality. These are also assessed on a five-point scale. Finally, and very importantly, the profiles provide a measure of attitudes towards reading. Level One is intended for use at the end of the children's infant schooling, i.e. around the age of seven years; Level Two is intended for use after one year in the junior school, i.e. around the age of eight; Level Three contains scales for the nine- to ten-year-olds and Levels Four and Five are also available.

The sample was structured so as to enable comparisons to be made with norms provided in the manual of the chosen tests, which give a breakdown of schools by socio-economic status; 765 children of junior school age (seven to eleven years) were tested and 116 of infant school age (five to seven years), constituting a survey of the language attainments of children at different age levels. Additionally, 137 children in three junior schools were retested after one year on Reading for Meaning.

Spoken Language in the Infant School

A large, representative sample of white and non-white children were individually tested, using picture stimuli provided in the test manual. The response was quite remarkable:

81 per cent scored high on confidence;
more than 90 per cent were categorised as having 'intelligible speech' and more than half as possessing 'precise and carefully enunciated speech';
nearly 80 per cent scored well on vocabulary.

Attitudes to Reading

Unusually for schools designated as social priority schools, a very high proportion of infant (72 per cent) and junior (86 per cent) children revealed positive attitudes towards reading.

Free-writing

Samples were collected from cohorts of seven, eight and nine year olds.

These were graded according to a system provided in the test manuals, which identifies the following elements: legibility, fluency, accuracy, originality. The proportions of children scoring high on each element increased at each year group: by nine years, over 90 per cent could write legibly and nearly as many fluently and accurately. The only negative aspect was that on the measures of accuracy and originality, the results suggested there were few 'high fliers'.

Reading for Meaning

The Survey. The mean scores of the Coventry sample were compared by socio-economic groupings with those provided in the test manuals. At Level One the Coventry means were consistently below those of the Hunter-Grundin. At Levels Two and Three they were much better. The overall Coventry means were, in fact, equal or superior to those of the 'middle-class' schools as provided in the test manuals.

The Retest in Schools A, B and C. School A, in an inner city, with a multicultural population, had outstanding test scores in both 1982 and 1983, equal to and superior to the middle-class norms. School C, with a similar population, had much lower results. In all schools, there was a linear relationship between reading scores and amount of parental support.

As a consequence of deliberate policy-making over a period of twelve years, community schools have grown up in many parts of the city and a tradition of parental involvement has been established in Coventry such that most primary schools take the presence of parents for granted, and they are included in many activities. In some parts of the city, two generations of parents have now worked in partnership with teachers. Through support from schools, parents have been encouraged to take direct action in relation to their own lives as well as making a positive contribution towards the psychological and educational development of their children. In short, children have been socialised into a school system where there are few barriers between the home and the school. There can be no doubt about the effects of involving parents in their children's reading, but the significant difference between the schools which were retested also point to the school's crucial role in this process.

Note

Further details of the study summarised here will be found in the book *Raising Standards*, by Paul Widlake and Flora MacLeod, available from the Community Education Development Centre, Coventry.

10 TEACHERS WORKING TOGETHER: A WORKSHOP APPROACH

Mary Robertson*

Purpose of the Course

Home involvement in children's school work since the 1960s has largely been in response to a regional policy, like the Coventry Community Education Project (see Chapter 9) for example, or as a result of the commitment of teachers and heads in individual schools. More recently, Jenny Hewison's research project in Haringey (see Chapter 4) articulated the interest of those who had long considered the idea of fostering home–school links.

Parents and Community in Education (PACE) in Newham was designed to explored these approaches by making available a series of workshops, general enough to be applicable to a range of schools but sufficiently specific to accommodate individual needs. It was, therefore, an 'off-site-school-focused' model in which the in-service group was seen as a starting-point for subsequent involvement of course tutors assigned to each school.

In the June before the first autumn term meeting was planned, schools in the London Borough of Newham were contacted and invited to state their interest in the six-week after-school course, held at the Language Reading Centre. They were advised of the proposed content of the two-hour sessions and asked to specify at what stage in the forthcoming year they considered starting a programme of parental involvement.

The three infant, two junior and three secondary schools which attended were each represented by two or three teachers so that continuity could be effectively maintained and within-school dissemination facilitated.

Responsibility for post-course contact and continuity with each of the schools was divided between the two teachers from the Language Reading Centre — Evelyn Gregory and Yvonne Elden; Sheila Wolfendale — course tutor of the MSc educational psychology course at the North East London Polytechnic; and Mary Robertson — a trainee educational

* With acknowledgement to Evelyn Gregory, Yvonne Elden, Sheila Wolfendale.

psychologist. The opportunity to plan an individualised programme in close collaboration with one of the course tutors was therefore established at the outset.

Such flexibility made the presentation of a wide range of alternative approaches feasible and, as a result, a handbook was prepared by Evelyn Gregory, Yvonne Elden and Sheila Wolfendale to accompany the course (*Parents and Community in Education*, details on page 322 of this book). It described established schemes, provided information on the organisation of home–school links and contained a comprehensive reference section citing many publications which included those available in the Newham Language Reading Centre.

Outline of the Course

The course itself was divided into six broad sessions intended to provide a choice route through a selection of schemes and materials, parental training approaches and monitoring and assessment procedures.

In session one, the rationale behind parental involvement was examined, a range of schemes was presented and guidelines intended for initial approaches to parents suggested. It was hoped that such an introduction, together with the information contained in the handbook, would be sufficient to generate tentative proposals by the participating schools by the next session in which a more definitive examination of materials and methods was undertaken.

The usefulness of subsequent meetings was therefore largely dependent on clarity of general intent by session three, in which teachers were required to have decided upon method, content and materials specific to their chosen scheme. Only by establishing plans at this stage could the most effective use be made of testing, assessment and monitoring procedures which constituted the fourth and fifth sessions.

Before the final meeting, a period of four weeks was set aside for tutor-supported scheme organisation within each school so that by the sixth session, teachers had the opportunity to discuss parental responses to school meetings and finalise administrative details.

Outcomes

It would have been encouraging to report that every school interpreted the sessions in the way most appropriate, and mounted a scheme in the spring or summer of 1984. The fact that this was not so served a two-fold purpose.

First, it was possible to isolate the components which — in combination — produced positive consequences in some schools. Second, by examining the problems which frustrated the soundest intentions in others, it became feasible to direct a course between the practical and theoretical for future use.

Let us look, therefore, at the schools in which aim and outcome were effectively matched.

School A: Secondary School for Boys

From the outset, the aims of the two remedial teachers were modest: a two-month scheme involving first-year boys from mixed-ability classes reading to their parents.

Although they had the support of the headteacher, they envisaged no more than departmental commitment and therefore perceived course attendance, preparation of materials and home visits as a two-handed affair. Some books within the department were reserved for home use and new materials, including computer programmes, devised for use at school. The teachers selected pupils on the basis of experiential knowledge of the families concerned and offered an in-school alternative to those for whom a home programme would have been inappropriate.

Of the 15 families selected, seven attended a school-based meeting and another eight received a home visit from one of the two teachers.

The scheme was not formally evaluated but the home–school relationship was so favourably affected that staff became very much aware of the need for a school liaison officer within the school. The workshop sessions had thus been interpreted as developing understanding between parent and teacher. As a result, staff were able to form more ambitious expectations for written work at home and formulate a realistic approach to the boys' learning difficulties.

School B: Infant School

For this school, the scheme articulated enduring attempts to develop closer liaison between family and school. It gave informal teacher–parent discussion definition and elevated maternal interest to the level of a specific educative contribution. Incidental information from home now assumed importance, and progress which had formerly been casually mentioned now constituted part of a structured scheme.

Two teachers and the headmistress attended the workshop sessions and with the active support of the staff mounted a continuous scheme in Parental Participation in Education throughout the whole school.

Alternative strategies of literacy development were suggested. These included the child reading to his or her parent, a reading-related activity designed to develop phonic and sequencing skills, for example, and the parent reading a story book to his or her child. The existing colour-coded system of the school was therefore extended to include a range of graded games and activities together with new materials generated by the teachers themselves or adapted from resources in the Language Reading Centre and Portage programme.

An informal handwritten letter was sent to the parents advising them of a school-based meeting to launch the scheme. Sixty per cent of the parents attended the training session in which the drama team demonstrated the dos and don'ts of the home-learning situation in a light-hearted way. It was explained that if a parent was not able to visit the school regularly in order to collect materials, then a home visit could be made by the child's teacher. For those able to visit, staff arranged to be available for half an hour one day a week and the headmistress each morning.

Response from parents and children was such that no fundamental changes were implicated after the scheme had been in operation for three months. Staff reported 'positive gains in literacy and motivation' and were encouraged by the indirect but significant effects of local interest which added to the status of the school.

School C: Secondary School

Cautious that the parental co-operation reported in schemes for infants and juniors might not be reflected in the secondary sector, the three teachers who attended the workshop sessions initiated a continuous school-based scheme, using not the children's own parents but adult 'partners'. In this way, the eleven first- and second-year pupils selected on the basis of their reading difficulty were able to share an hour a week with a partner engaged in their own joint activities or those provided by the school.

It was felt that children who might benefit from parental involvement should have the opportunity to do so by taking advantage of a team of parent partners randomly assigned to any one child. A 'community room' was made available for this interchange and parents encouraged by phone or letter to take part in weekly meetings.

For these teachers, the course had served to develop a community centre within the school in which parents and children, bound not by family ties but common interest, could define their own roles.

Repercussions within the Newham School Community

Although some schools did not attend the workshop sessions, the interest of teachers was such that members of the course team were invited to develop a community approach to reading and language within certain schools. Evelyn Gregory was involved in two of these collaborative operations in which policy change came about as a result of regular meetings and informal discussion.

School D: Junior School

Fourth-year children experiencing reading difficulties were selected on the basis of interview, taped miscue analysis on a chosen book, an attitude questionnaire (APU) and the Primary Reading Test.

Their parents — all mothers — were invited to meet the course tutor once a week in a purpose-built 'parents' room' in the school. These sessions were devoted to discussions on reading and all aspects of school life, the preparation of appropriate books and materials and work programmes undertaken by mothers and their children as a group. In such a context, the educative purpose of the meetings for the children was equally as important as the supportive role performed by the course tutor.

School E: Secondary School

Using similar screening procedures for first-year remedial pupils, teachers invited parents into the school to discuss a home-reading programme. By maintaining regular availability of staff at a specific time each week, it was possible to modify initial parental scepticism and sustain enthusiasm within a setting which sought to provide encouragement rather than expectations, and support rather than specific direction.

A development from this initiative in 1984 and 1985, involves a trainee educational psychologist from the MSc course at North East London Polytechnic, collaborating with the Remedial Department, to effect parental involvement in a spelling programme, both school and home-based, which has demonstrated positive results.

Conclusion

These examples are not intended to imply that only the schools mentioned possessed realistic expectations, marshalled existing parental support to a definitive end or responded positively to regular intervention from a member of the course team. Indeed, considerable planning was undertaken by schools from which there appeared to be no apparent outcome.

Yet even discounting those ambitious schemes which escalated from a single-class, short-term experiment to a change of policy taken across a whole year-band and requiring considerable preparation, there were schools in which aim and outcome were poorly matched. A range of contributory factors could have accounted for this.

First, the workshops were available for all age-level teachers — infants to secondary. In order to offer a balanced programme applicable to all groups, it was necessary to present much verbal and written information which, while ensuring a non-directive approach, also introduced a broad spread of alternatives. For some, this substantiated ideas which had been formulated earlier; for others, such choice merely increased indecision and — in some cases — fragmented hitherto united teams of teachers from a particular school. Some of the issues are posed below as a series of questions.

Should there be a system of pre- and post-testing in order to present tangible findings? Should a philosophy of parental intervention be adopted as a matter of policy without monitoring procedures? Should a whole junior year group be involved? Should one class remain as a control? Should the scheme run for a limited period? Should it be continuous?

Aware of issues which, for some, were irreconcilable, course tutors did not advocate any one approach but attempted — by visits to the schools and discussion with the staff — to help teachers select the most appropriate course of action.

Second, the understandable presupposition that parental involvement was 'a good thing' led both course tutors and teachers alike to underestimate the commitment required by staff members concerned.

Some teachers envisaged prohibitive programmes of home visiting, made plans for extensive material preparation and considered much after-school availability in enthusiastic response to discussions on the benefits of what could accrue from such commitment.

This in turn led to the personal responsibility perceived by course members. For example, if a single teacher was allowed to assume major responsibility for this extra workload, the scheme would not only be wasteful of greater staff involvement, but also be vulnerable to the effects of illness and disenchantment as goodwill diminished. Conversely, if democratic decisions were sought at each substage of the intended target, then the probability of disagreement would be increased and the long-term aims lose purpose and clarity. As both these approaches were evidenced to some extent, it could be concluded that a certain state of 'readiness' is implied prior to course attendance.

In fact, the most successful programmes of parental involvement emanated from schools in which classification of books, composition of home-teaching guidelines, presentation of parents' meeting and planning of training sessions were undertaken in an almost pioneering spirit of professional unity. Better the whole school than some of the parts within it.

What, then, are the advantages of this model of in-service training concerned with parental involvement in children's learning? Certainly the outcomes cannot be predicted as neatly as those following courses in specific subject areas, and so what is sacrificed for this apparent lack of academic control? It is, after all, easy enough to present the pattern of PRINT and PACT and suggest a copy, or to insist that formal evaluation is the only scientific way to approach a new system of learning: but such directiveness lends itself more to convenience than creativity.

We have mentioned that teachers within schools did not necessarily agree. Their co-operation was derived, however, from an examination of impartially presented alternatives which could only be made meaningful within their specific context and with the collaboration of head and secondary department or head and infant/junior school.

Although the ethic of in-service training has usually been dissemination of information, it has always been possible for teachers to pursue professional interests either isolated from or rejected by their colleagues. This familiar pattern cannot be reconciled with the PACE model which depends upon the cohesion of staff, just as much as on their co-operation of parents.

PART 2:

PARENTAL INVOLVEMENT IN READING IN ACTION

B. PAIRED READING

11 AN INTRODUCTION TO PAIRED READING

Keith Topping

> A man ought to read just as inclination leads him, for what he reads as a task will do him little good.
>
> Dr Samuel Johnson (1709–84)

Paired Reading is a straightforward and enjoyable way for non-professionals to help children develop better reading skills. The method is adaptable to any reading material, and children select books which are of intrinsic interest to them. Encouragement to read 'little and often' is usual.

The technique has two phases. During the first, 'simultaneous reading', tutor and child read together out loud in close synchrony, adjustment to the child's pace being made as necessary by the tutor. The child is required to read all the words out loud correctly, and errors are corrected merely by the tutor again giving a perfect example of how to read the error word, and ensuring that the child repeats it correctly — then the pair continue.

The second phase is known as 'independent reading'. When the child feels confident enough to read a section of text unsupported, the child signals by a knock, nudge or other gesture for the tutor to be silent. The tutor praises the child for taking this initiative, and subsequently praises the child *very* regularly, especially for mastering very difficult words or spontaneously self-correcting. When the child makes an error, the tutor corrects this as before, by modelling and ensuring perfect repetition, *and* then joins back in reading simultaneously. Any word not read correctly within four seconds is treated as an error — the child is not left to struggle.

Initially, much reading is usually done simultaneously, but as the child improves and makes more appropriate choices of reading materials, more and more independent reading occurs. Any tendency to rush on the part of the pupil is usually resolved by consistent use of the correction procedure and visually 'pacing' the reading by pointing to each word as it is to be pronounced.

Does it Work?

This simple and non-technical procedure has been demonstrated to have a profound and extraordinary impact on children's reading ability. The procedure has been used with children aged between five and 14 years, in projects catering for from three to 76 children. The children have ranged from average readers, through children retarded by five and a half years, to total non-readers. The assumed cognitive abilities of the children have been very various; bright 'dyslexics' and children in special schools for those with moderate learning difficulties have benefited equally. Paired Reading 'projects' have shown positive results with populations of all levels of socio-economic status over periods as short as four weeks and as long as twelve months, with the most usual initial period being eight weeks. 'Tutors' have included natural parents, adult volunteers and other children of similar or greater age.

If an increase of one year in 'reading age' on a standardised test during one actual year is considered 'normal', children in Paired Reading projects have shown gains ranging from one and a half to seven *times* 'normal' in reading accuracy, and from one to twelve times 'normal' in reading comprehension. Gains of three times 'normal' in reading accuracy and five times 'normal' in comprehension seem typical.

In addition to the chapters which follow this introduction, and some chapters in the section on 'Variations' which incorporate some aspect of Paired Reading, reference may be made to: Jungnitz, Olive and Topping, 1983; Morris, 1984; Pitchford and Taylor, 1983; Evans, 1984; Topping and McKnight, 1984; Bruce, 1984; Winter and Low, 1984; Winter, 1984; Grigg, 1984; Gollop, 1984; and Gillham, 1984.

The amount of follow-up support in different projects has varied enormously. Some projects offer weekly home visits, others none at all; some projects stage follow-up feedback meetings, others do not; many projects utilise some form of home–school recording and reporting, but certainly not all; and some incorporate individual consultations with teachers in schools. Although it is too early to detect obvious trends, it seems likely that the more vulnerable and unskilled the target group is, the more extensive the support and follow-up will need to be. However, many schools in supposedly 'disadvantaged' areas have had an excellent response from their parents.

Why Does it Work?

There is a degree of theoretical conflict and a paucity of empirical evidence concerning this question. What empirical evidence there is tends to be enigmatic. Toepritz (1982) noted that while an increased percentage of independent reading appeared over time, neither this nor the degree of synchrony proved a good predictor of post-project gains on reading tests. Scott (1983) noted that although Paired Reading improved children's reading ability, it did not improve their scores on 'underlying subskills' as measured by the Aston Index, although miscue analysis indicated improved usage of contextual clues. Andy Miller and his colleagues describe further relevant evidence in Chapter 14.

The original theoretical conception of Paired Reading was totally behavioural, based on the concepts of 'participant modelling' and reinforcement, and Roger Morgan describes this in the following chapter. Later workers have found that the technique has strong psycholinguistic overtones, and it is clear from evaluation results repeatedly showing massive increases in comprehension skills that Paired Reading is certainly not just improving mechanical skills.

Bushell *et al.* (1982) note that the effects of the technique are explicable within a conceptualisation of the reading process in which the child's self-esteem is crucial and capable of stimulating various psycholinguistic aspects of the reading process. Failure is eliminated, and tutor and pupil usually learn the technique together from scratch. Fragmentation of the reading process by over-focusing on difficult words is much reduced, and this creates the opportunity to use contextual clues to aid semantic and syntactic prediction. However, it cannot be denied that the factors of modelling, prompting and reinforcement described by Morgan are also in play, and Heath's work (see Chapter 13) shows that the positive effects of the technique are not solely due to the reinforcement aspect.

Other advantages are evident: children pursue their own interests and read for their own purposes — just like adults. They become more in control of the proceedings. The emphasis on fluency and continuity facilitates meaning-getting. The technique is highly flexible, able to accommodate not only to difficulty of text but also to current levels of interest, mood, tiredness, confidence, and so on. Children are able to copy expressiveness, pacing and rhythm from the tutor, as well as merely accuracy of word recognition. Not only do the children get more attention, which may itself be beneficial, they also get more sheer practice at reading. Not least, tutors and pupils have a clear, simple structure to follow — so neither (hopefully) will get confused, worried or bad-tempered about reading.

Where Does It Fit?

Although Paired Reading as such came into being in the mid-1970s, it had certainly been foreshadowed. While it might seem novel to the parents of current schoolchildren, their grandparents would ahve been entirely familiar with group reading of favourite Bible passages in synchrony. Likewise, speech therapists have for some time used the technique of 'shadowing' with stammerers — providing a continuous model and prompt of fluent speech.

The positive effect of adult modelling pure and simple on children's reading had begun to be noticed elsewhere (e.g. Smith, 1979). In this study, the adult read the first section of text fluently and the child carried on unaided from where the adult left off. The child's reading ability was even further raised with the introduction of a correction procedure for errors involving adult modelling of the correct response. Still greater improvements were found when the child commenced reading back at the start of the text, having had a 'preview' with adult modelling.

As early as 1968 Neville had noted that listening to a reading or recording of a text while following it visually helped increase fluency. In 1975 a further study of 180 children of normal reading ability showed that the slowest of three speeds of simultaneous listening with silent reading resulted in the highest level of comprehension. This 'pacing effect' seemed even more marked in a small sample of 'remedial' readers, and seemed to be more prominent among boys. The very poor recall performance of boys as compared to girls on a silent reading task, in contrast with their equal recall performance after listening to and after orally reading a message (Johnson, 1982), is a related finding indicating a sex differential. Wilkinson (1980) also reported that simultaneous listening and reading facilitated comprehension, even with highly skilled readers.

It seems that simultaneous reading and listening, as in 'reading together', frees the struggling reader from a preoccupation with laborious decoding and enables other reading strategies to come into play. If the 'limited processing capacity' (Curtis, 1980) of the remedial reader is totally devoted to accurate word recognition or phonic analysis–synthesis, no processing capacity is left to deploy other strategies, such as using contextual clues. Hutson, Cowger and Wallbrown (1980) and Potter (1982) both provide evidence that weak readers are usually less able, and consequently less willing, to use psycholinguistic strategies, and tend to depend heavily on a phonic approach.

Paradoxically, teachers tend to reinforce this over-dependence, not only by assuming that given sufficient phonic nuts and bolts the child will spontaneously prove able to assemble a machine, but also by interrupting weak readers to give phonic cues far more often, in proportion to mistakes made, than they do with competent readers. This constant interruption further reduces the contextual clues available to the reader (Allington, 1980). It is perhaps unsurprising that weak readers tend to display characteristics of learned helplessness (Butkowsky and Willows, 1980). These features of reading failure are precisely those which Paired Reading seems so effective in remedying.

Another major advantage of Paired Reading is that its practice has no confusing or otherwise harmful effects on the school reading curriculum. Paired Reading at home lies down perfectly happily with a school reading curriculum based on look-and-say, phonics, language experience, pictograms, precision teaching, direct instruction or any other kind of approach. Indeed, there is considerable advantage in home and school pursuing different approaches, since Paired Reading is complementary to all and is a labour-intensive method which is often impossible to carry through consistently in school.

References

Allington, R.L. (1980), 'Teacher Interruption Behaviors During Primary-grade Oral Reading', *Journal of Educational Psychology*, vol. 72, no. 3, 371–7

Bruce, P. (1984), 'The Stile Common Middle Infant Paired Reading Project', unpublished paper, Stile Common Infant School, Huddersfield

Bushell, R., Miller, A. and Robson, D. (1982), 'Parents as Remedial Teachers', *Journal of the Association of Educational Psychologists*, vol. 5, no. 9, 7–13

Butkowsky, I.S. and Willows, D.M. (1980), 'Cognitive-Motivational Characteristics of Children Varying in Reading Ability: Evidence for Learned Helplessness in Poor Readers', *Journal of Educational Psychology*, vol. 72, no. 3, 408–22

Curtis, M.E. (1980), 'Development of Components of Reading Skill', *Journal of Educational Psychology*, vol. 72, no. 5, 656–69

Evans, A. (1984), 'Paired Reading: A Report on Two Projects', unpublished paper, Division and Institute of Education, University of Sheffield

Gillham, W.E.C.G. (1984), 'Paired Reading in Practice', unpublished paper, Department of Psychology, University of Strathclyde

Gollop, S. (1984), 'A Paired Reading Project in a Junior School', *Focus on Language*, vol. 6, 10–11, Essex Reading and Language Centre

Grigg, S. (1984), 'Parental Involvement with Reading: An Experimental Comparison of Paired Reading and Listening to Children Read', unpublished MSc (Educational Psychology) dissertation, University of Newcastle-on-Tyne

Hutson, B.A., Cowger, D.E. and Wallbrown, F.H. (1980), 'Assessing Psycholinguistic Orientation and Decoding Strategies for Remedial and Nonremedial Readers', *Journal of School Psychology*, vol. 18, no. 3, 263–70

Johnson, S. (1982), 'Listening and Reading: The Recall of 7 to 9 Year Olds', *British Journal of Educational Psychology*, vol. 52, 24–32

Jungnitz, G., Olive, S. and Topping, K.J. (1983), 'The Development and Evaluation of a

Paired Reading Project', *Journal of Community Education*, vol. 2, no. 4, 14–22

Morris, A. (1984), 'A Paired Reading Approach — Parental Involvement at a Comprehensive School', unpublished paper, Division and Institute of Education, University of Sheffield

Neville, M.H. (1968), 'Effects of Oral and Echoic Responses in Beginning Reading', *Journal of Educational Psychology*, vol. 59, 362–9

Neville, M.H. (1975), 'Effectiveness of Rate of Aural Message on Reading and Listening', *Educational Research*, vol. 18, no. 1, 37–43

Pitchford, M. and Taylor, P. (1983), 'Paired Reading, Previewing and Independent Reading', unpublished paper, Leeds Psychological Service

Potter, F. (1982), 'The Use of Linguistic Context: Do Good and Poor Readers Use Different Strategies?', *British Journal of Educational Psychology*, vol. 52, 16–23

Scott, J. (1983), 'Process Evaluation of Paired Reading', *Occasional Papers of the Division of Educational and Child Psychology, British Psychological Society*, vol. 7, no. 1, 82

Smith, D.D. (1979), 'The Improvement of Children's Oral Reading through the Use of Teacher Modelling', *Journal of Learning Disabilities*, vol. 12, no. 3, 39–42

Toepritz, P.I. (1982), 'A Study of Parent–Child Interaction in a Paired Reading Project', unpublished MSc (Educational Psychology) thesis, University of Sheffield

Topping, K.J. and McKnight, G. (1984), 'Paired Reading — and Parent Power', *Special Education: Forward Trends*, vol. 11, no. 3, 12–15

Wilkinson, A.C. (1980), 'Children's Understanding in Reading and Listening', *Journal of Educational Psychology*, vol. 72, no. 4, 561–74

Winter, S. (1984), 'A Short-term Paired Reading Workshop for Parents: A Controlled Study', unpublished paper

Winter, S. and Low, A. (1984), 'The Rossmere Peer Tutor Project', *Behavioural Approaches with Children*, vol. 8, no. 2, 62–5

12 PAIRED READING: ORIGINS AND FUTURE

Roger Morgan

My intention in this brief chapter is to identify the origins of Paired Reading and to suggest some areas for its future development and evaluation.

I designed Paired Reading a decade ago with the twin aims of introducing a technique suitable for a wide variety of children with reading problems, and capable of being used with minimum specialised instruction by a wide range of people working with children, not solely by psychologists and teachers. The technique was designed to meet the first requirement by being inherently flexible, so that it might adjust to children's differing reading levels and different reading strategies. The intention was to maximise reading performance regardless of the child's existing method of attack upon words, through the use of generally applicable and flexible learning principles. By making the technique 'standard' and simple to communicate in a short space of time, it was intended that Paired Reading should be a 'package' that could readily be passed on to parents, volunteers and others perhaps not normally undertaking reading work with children, hopefully without too much variation in the procedures being introduced in the process. The initial hope, which appears to have been substantiated by much of the subsequent research, was that Paired Reading would be sufficiently 'robust' to tolerate use over periods of weeks by adult tutors having received very limited instruction and supervision, and, eventually, to withstand use by parents at home in competition with the hurly-burly and distractions of family activity.

These initial requirements of Paired Reading led to some encouraging early observations. Having allowed children free choice of reading material, the technique showed useful adaptability to differing levels of difficulty in the material some children chose, through changes in the relative proportions of simultaneous and independent reading. It proved easier than expected to train volunteer tutors in Paired Reading, so that by 1977 we were training parents to use it at home, rather than relying on our own 'clinic-based' tuition. In relation to ease of transmission, it is notable that in a few cases, having trained a mother in Paired Reading, the father turned up to subsequent monitoring sessions — having been unofficially trained to a wholly acceptable standard by mother and child at home. It is also interesting to me that Paired Reading has proved simple enough to be used, evaluated and published upon by numerous professionals after no more detailed original transmission than its description in the two original papers on the subject (Morgan, 1976; Morgan and Lyon, 1979).

Paired Reading was originally derived from behavioural principles. Simultaneous reading was designed as participant modelling, in which the child receives a model and a continuous prompt for correct reading, during his or her own attempt to read the words. Independent reading aimed to provide positive reinforcement, by praise, of correct reading responses. Praise for signalling the wish to read independently was introduced to reinforce the selection of independent reading, which then gave opportunity to practise (and be praised for) responses acquired during simultaneous reading, and thus opportunity for their learning to be 'sealed in' by successful and praised use. Free choice of reading material was intended to escape the aversive and learning-inhibiting effects of simplified or special texts, and to increase motivation to read in the relatively unmotivated, through the intrinsic reward of reading something one wanted to read. Avoiding being made to try any word for more than four seconds before being given the answer was a means of limiting anxiety, a known inhibitor of learning when excessive. In designing paired reading, I was much influenced by earlier work demonstrating operant influences upon children's reading (e.g. Rachman, 1962; Staats, 1973; and see Chapter 19 of this book).

The relevance of behavioural principles to Paired Reading is questioned by some contributors to this book. This does not matter; one's theoretical bases are working hypotheses for generating approaches to be tested in practice, and are unlikely to represent the whole theoretical picture. Given the complexity of the reading process, and the multiplicity of theoretical approaches to it, it would indeed be surprising if Paired Reading were to exclude a contribution from learning principles other than the behavioural ones upon which its initial design drew. What does matter is whether or not outcome evaluation supports continued use of Paired Reading, and whether there are theoretical considerations yielding ideas for its further development in practice.

While the findings to date do support some behavioural explanations, they also suggest other processes at work in Paired Reading, including those described in the psycholinguistic literature. Paired Reading appears to improve the child's attitudes towards reading, and it creates a different and more 'partnering' role for the parent working with the child. It provides constant cueing of correct responses, and capitalises on existing word-decoding strategies without introducing competing strategies. It may well work as much as lifting previous inhibitions upon learning reading (aversive pressure, failure, boredom, anxiety, uninteresting material), as by introducing anything new. Paired Reading perhaps reintroduces reading to the failing reader, through a major shift in both parent's and child's attitudes towards reading, followed by a period of minimised adverse influences on progress and maximised opportunity for, and reinforcement of, success. Its relative neutrality to the child's mode of word attack, with a concentration on successful performance, effectively selects and strengthens any successful decoding strategies an individual child may be using, and culls out ineffective strategies.

The early Paired Reading studies are summarised in Table 12.1. In the initial pilot study, Paired Reading was used by the author with three children at a small charitable reading tuition centre in Birmingham (Morgan, 1976). The second report (Morgan and Lyon, 1979) involved parental use of Paired Reading at home, with initial training and regular supervision at an LEA remedial reading unit, a model widely adopted by later researchers. The third study (Morgan and Gavin, 1985) was a small controlled trial of parental use of Paired Reading in three primary schools in East Anglia.

Table 12.1: Paired Reading Studies: Results

Study	n	Results
Morgan (1976)	3	(i) Average Neale accuracy gain for 2 children of 5.5 months over 19 weeks (ii) Percentage of words correctly read increasing (to statistically significant level) over 13 sessions for 2 children (ANOVA) (iii) Average Neale comprehension gain for 2 children of 16.0 months over 19 weeks
Morgan and Lyon (1979)	4	(i) Average Neale accuracy gain of 11.75 months over 6.25 months (ii) Average Neale comprehension gain of 11.5 months over 6.25 months
Morgan and Gavin (1985)	7 Paired Reading, 8 control	(i) Average Neale accuracy gain of 6.29 months over 3 months of tuition, compared with 2.0 months gain in the same period for controls (ii) Average Neale comprehension gain of 9.29 months after 3 months of tuition, compared with a change of *minus* 0.4 months for controls in the same period.

Paired Reading has shown itself an acceptable and useful technique for parental involvement in reading. It has also demonstrated the unanticipated but very welcome and useful bonus of being fun. Future directions for development and evaluation should, I would suggest, include the following: (i) identification of the proportion of failing readers for whom Paired Reading is useful; (ii) identification of any prognostic indicators for the selection of children who may benefit; (iii) further appraisal of Paired Reading with different groups having reading problems; (iv) exploration of which elements of Paired Reading produce which effects, for refinement of the technique; (v) evaluation with a range of dependent variables, including attitudinal measures (and reducing reliance on the Neale Analysis of Reading Ability); (vi) exploration of the use of Paired Reading as a 'primer' or 'remotivator' with subsequent use of other approaches; (vii) follow-up of reading practice and performance after both continued and concluded Paired Reading; (viii) the effects of Paired Reading as an element in early teaching of non-reading-retarded children; (ix) further comparison of Paired Reading with other forms of parental involvement in reading; and (x) investigation of the stage(s) during tuition at which most improvement occurs.

Overall, Paired Reading has matured from the initial studies to the healthy stage where large-scale evaluation has shown its further exploration to be worthwhile, but where also its efficacy and theoretical content are subject to research-based critique. I am gratified by the practice and research interest in Paired Reading so far, and look forward to the outcomes of the projects now running and being initiated on Paired Reading and its derivatives.

References

Morgan, R.T.T. (1976), ' "Paired Reading" Tuition: A Preliminary Report on a Technique for Cases of Reading Deficit', *Child Care, Health and Development*, vol. 2, 13–28

Morgan, R.T.T. and Gavin, P. (1985). 'A Trial of Paired Reading Tuition' (in preparation)

Morgan, R.T.T. and Lyon, E. (1979), ' "Paired Reading" — A Preliminary Report on a Technique for Parental Tuition of Reading-retarded Children', *Journal of Child Psychology and Psychiatry*, vol. 20, 151–60

Rachman, S. (1962), 'Learning Theory and Child Psychology — Therapeutic Possibilities', *Journal of Child Psychology and Psychiatry*, vol. 3, 149–63

Staats, A.W. (1973), 'Behaviour Analysis and Token Reinforcement in Educational Behaviour Modification and Curriculum Research', in C.E. Thorensen (ed.), *Behaviour Modification in Education*, NSSE, Chicago

13 A STUDY OF THE EFFECTIVENESS OF PAIRED READING

Alan Heath

Pilot

The pilot project, involving a total of twelve children, was designed to test the effectiveness of the Paired Reading technique against a more simple method, also involving parents, which emphasised praise for only the words successfully read by the children. This we called the 'reinforcement' technique. A third group of children, where no direct intervention was made over and above what was already being done (control) completed our groups.

Selection of Children

In one inner-urban primary school, where the number of children with reading difficulties was high, we asked the staff to select a group of children from the age range 7–9 years who were having difficulty with reading (this was defined as children whose measured reading age was one year or more below their actual age). From the resulting list, the children were randomly allocated to one of the three groups, i.e. Paired Reading, Reinforcement and Control. An assessment of ability and reading age was then conducted for each child, following negotiations for consent and co-operation from their parents.

Methods of Training

Initially, each parent was invited to school to discuss the project and to be trained in the appropriate procedure. Parents were first asked to listen to their child reading in as normal a way as possible with one of the research team observing. This was to establish a base-line of what normally happened or (more realistically in the context) what the parent and child thought was ideal practice. The observations made at this stage were startling in themselves, and should not pass without comment.

Base-line

We were surprised, in observing mothers listening to children read, by the dearth of encouragement or praise. Even when encouragement was forthcoming, it tended to be mothers' suggesting children spell out or sound out words. The mothers, well intentioned and supportive, seemed unaware that their children rarely had skills to do either of these things.

In view of these findings, it cannot be emphasised enough how important it is to undertake this observation — of ourselves, perhaps, as well as of parents. It provides an invaluable insight into the home reading context to which the children are exposed. It also gives an indication of the degree to which reading may often be made a puzzle to be unravelled with minimum cues — and answers never given.

Training — Paired Reading

Following base-line observations, mother and child were tutored in the Paired Reading technique. It was found helpful to demonstrate the 'togetherness' of the technique by counting to five aloud with the children, to model the sound of speaking simultaneously. The initial training took two half-hour sessions, during which both stages of the technique of Paired Reading were shown and practised. All mother and child pairs accomplished the technique in these sessions. Each pair was subsequently invited to fortnightly monitoring sessions (15 minutes), which were used to discuss issues and problems of practice (e.g. children's reluctance to practise; choice of books; parental concerns) and to ensure that the technique did not fade away inappropriately. Though not often emphasised, it is our view that these monitoring sessions may be critical in making successful gains in reading ability and confidence.

Training Reinforcement

The mothers and children in the Reinforcement Group were given the same experiences as the Paired Reading Group (i.e. tuition, discussion and monitoring sessions). The technique, however, was restricted to reward (by saying 'good', 'well done', etc., or in one instance by passing a Smartie to the child) every three words read correctly, and quickly to supply any word the child was unable to read or had misread.

Control

The reading ages of the control group were measured and, so far as possible, no further educational interventions were made.

Results

For economy of words and space, the results outlined in Table 13.1 are discussed in conjunction with the main project results. It will be clear, however, that they were very encouraging and suggested that the Paired

Table 13.1: Reading Age Gains (in Months) over Three-month Period of Study (Neale Analysis A and B)

	Paired Reading (n = 4)	Reinforcement (n = 4)	Control (n = 4)
Average 'accuracy' gain	8	5	0.25
Average 'comprehension' gain	15	4	0.25

Reading technique was successful and more powerful than simply involving parents in their children's reading and encouraging praise with quick answers. Our results also suggested that the intelligence of the child was not of critical importance to the success of the technique.

The Main Study

The main study was concluded in two further schools. The procedures used were as described for the pilot study, except that

(i) children were assigned only to two groups, Paired Reading and Control;
(ii) not all children had an intelligence assessment;
(iii) a teacher-tutor from the school staff was involved in training and monitoring a group of mothers and children in the Paired Reading technique.

The children were selected on the same basis as the original study. Their average age was 7:11 years, and the study spanned three months. The random selection of children into the two groups produced a bias against the Paired Reading Group, and the results need to be interpreted in this context.

Results

Table 13.2: Reading Age Gains (in Months) over Three-month Period of Study (Neale Analysis A and B)

	Paired Reading (n = 19)	Control (n = 16)
Average accuracy gain	6.8 (initial ARA 6:5 years)	3.3 (initial ARA 7:3 years)
Average comprehension gain	10.7 (initial CRA 6:8 years)	6.4 (initial CRA 6:8 years)

Table 13.3: Reading Age Gains (in Months) Boys and Girls (Neale Analysis A and B)

	Paired Reading	Control
Boys' accuracy	7 (n= 9)	2.6 (n=8)
Girls' accuracy	6.7 (n=10)	4.1 (n=8)
Boys' comprehension	9 (n= 9)	7.1 (n=8)
Girls' comprehension	12 (n=10)	5.7 (n=8)

Discussion

It is clear from the information presented (Tables 13.1 and 13.2) that the children in the Paired Reading Groups made considerably more progress with their reading during the study than children in other groups. What is not revealed in the figures is the very positive change in attitude towards reading conveyed to us by both parents and children. The children frequently commented that our books — i.e. those in the rooms used for the training and monitoring sessions — were 'better' than those available in school. We took this not to be literary criticism in its infancy, but as a reflection of the access to all books given to the children by the Paired Reading procedure.

Work by Hewison (1981, and see Chapter 4) has demonstrated that parental collaboration in hearing children read has resulted in significant improvements in children's reading attainment. What this study shows is that additional gains are made when mothers and children are offered a technique which reduces uncertainty and difficulties for both parent and child. In a sense, the Paired Reading technique offers a transitional step between reading to a child and listening to him or her read. The transitional step is reading *with* the child. As a transitional step the Paired Reading technique seems to tap into the language processes indicated — for example by Rutter and Yule (1977) — to be so important in the acquisition of reading skills. More speculation about the way in which the process of Paired Reading works is offered elsewhere in this volume, and in Heath (1981).

It is worth noting that evidence from the study suggested that level of intelligence is not a significant contributor to the success of the Paired Reading technique. None of the correlation between the extent of gain in reading age and intelligence levels achieved statistical significance. A further frequently mentioned associate of reading failure or success is sex differences. Table 13.3 shows an interesting sex difference. It will be seen that the boys in the Paired Reading Group made a significant gain over the control group boys in reading accuracy, but did not make a similarly significant gain in comparison to the Control Group in reading comprehension. The girls, on the other hand, produced an almost opposite result, the Paired Reading Group making significant comprehension gains over the Control Group, but a much smaller gain in reading accuracy. Thus, the usual sex advantage of girls in learning to read was maintained, but its effects seem slightly reduced by the Paired Reading technique.

Several issues arise from the study which seem worthy of further comment here. First, the choice of children and parents. Clearly, parental illiteracy is an insurmountable bar to involvement — yet indexes a major 'at risk' group of children for reading failure. Here may be a role for voluntary help inside or outside school. It also highlights, however, another possible way to deal with the problem: involving fathers in the procedure. It has been suggested to me that one reason for boys' vulnerability to reading failure is a cultural link between reading activities and femininity. It is impossible to comment on the validity of this analysis, but there seems to be no reason not to involve fathers in the Paired Reading procedure, and thus avoid possible cultural impediments to reading success.

The major study was conducted in schools already operating some kind of home reading scheme. But it became apparent during the study that despite this, many parents in the study — in both Paired Reading and Control Groups — were unaware of the extent of their child's failure in reading. The effect of simply informing parents of this failure was a major uncontrolled variable in the present study, and may account for some of the progress in both Paired Reading and Control Groups. The comparatively greater improvement in the Paired Reading Group, however, suggests that the technique is still more powerful than simply alerting parents to their children's failure. More positively, it seemed that the Paired Reading technique could readily be offered by teacher-tutors as a natural adjunct to the now very common 'school bookshops' — making these into a more constructive educational enterprise.

Finally, with regard to organisational issues, one must express continuing surprise at the overt and covert resistance of many schools to adopting the Paired Reading technique as a simple and effective addition to their repertoires of skills and activities to both involve parents closely in their children's learning and to facilitate children's learning to read. The technique is very time- and cost-effective, and has already been demonstrated to be more effective with children with reading difficulties than many other 'remedial' techniques which are more costly in terms of teacher time and resources. Paired Reading provides a very successful background against which reading may be taught and learned — not only for children failing to learn, but for all children learning to read.

References

Heath, A. (1981), 'A Paired-reading Programme', *Edition 2* (ILEA Schools' Psychological Service), vol. 2, 22–32

Hewison, J. (1981), 'Home Is Where the Help Is (The Haringey Project)', *Times Educational Supplement*, 16 January, 20–1

Rutter, M. and Yule, W. (1977), 'Reading Difficulties', in M. Rutter and L. Hersov (eds), *Child Psychiatry: Modern Approaches*, Blackwell Scientific, Oxford

14 THE DEVELOPMENT OF PAIRED READING IN DERBYSHIRE

Andy Miller, David Robson and Roger Bushell

Paired Reading was initially used in Derbyshire by a few educational psychologists with individual children who showed persistent reading difficulties. Early successes led to an attempt to deliver the approach to larger groups of children and their parents, from which followed a more detailed research study. This has culminated in an increasing number of schools in the area being encouraged to run their own individually tailored Paired Reading schemes.

Phase One: the Pilot Study

This was planned and seen as a means of developing a project focus within our team, as well as an investigation of the possibilities of working more cost-effectively with groups of parents and children rather than individuals. This pilot phase lasted eight weeks in the spring term (1981) with parents encouraged to read with their child for 20 minutes each night, using the Paired Reading techniques described and demonstrated in two meetings for parents, held in the schools prior to the commencement of the project. The psychologists visited each pair at home at fortnightly intervals, using a skills checklist to provide a structure for observation and advice during these sessions, which were of approximately 20 minutes' duration each. The results of testing of reading ages before the pilot study and at its conclusion were analysed and then discussed with each pair. The results (presented elsewhere — see Bushell, Miller and Robson, 1982), led us to conclude that most children made good gains in reading accuracy and/or reading comprehension. In addition, the positive evaluation by the parents and children of the enjoyability and usefulness of the technique, together with some of the more theoretical issues in need of further clarification, led to the design of a main study.

Phase Two: the Main Study

This was an attempt to mount a controlled study, involving more children (54 in total) from a wider selection of schools. The methods for introducing the parents to the Paired Reading techniques remained as in the pilot study. The Paired Reading techniques remained as in the pilot study. The Paired Reading, however, was to last only six weeks. All testing was carried out by remedial advisory teachers, who were unaware of assignation to groups — one doing Paired Reading (X) and the other not (Y). The children were all tested in January 1982, before Group X parents received tuition, and then again eight weeks later, immediately after Group X's Paired Reading activities. In March 1982, Group Y commenced a Paired Reading phase, whilst the Group X children, no longer doing Paired Reading, engaged in home reading along lines similar to those described in the account of the Belfield scheme (Jackson and Hannon, 1981; see Chapter 5 of this book).

Phase Three: Encouraging School Initiatives

This describes the period from May 1982 onwards, when schools (including those which had not been involved with the pilot or main study) were encouraged to offer Paired Reading schemes to parents. The educational psychologist offered to be available to assume any role which the school thought most useful in implementing Paired Reading for parents. The role requested most often was that of consultant to schools wishing to set up their own Paired Reading schemes. In addition, we were asked to attend initial meetings with the parents, to describe the methods to be used, and to contribute to a general discussion about reading.

Phase Three: Follow-up

We wished to see whether the experience of participating in the Paired Reading main study had produced any effects, which had informed the schools' perception and use of parents as helpers with their children's reading. This was examined one year later, in May 1983, by means of a structured interview with the headteachers of the schools involved in the main study, and was conducted by two post-graduate students. Results are presented in detail elsewhere (Crowther and Wilson, 1983), but in summary it appeared that schools had welcomed the Paired Reading approach with parents.

Characteristics of Target Children

Age

The average age of the 23 subjects in the pilot study was 9:11, and that of the children in the main study was 9:10.

Reading Age

For the children in the pilot study, the average reading-age delays were 1:11 (accuracy) and 2:0 (comprehension). For the children in the main study, the average reading-age delays were 2:0 (accuracy) and 2:1 (comprehension).

English Picture Vocabulary Test

The average EPVT score for pilot study children was 87, and for main study children 83. The scores ranged between 140 and 60.

Social Characteristics

A high proportion of the children in the main study were in receipt of free school meals (38 per cent, against a general average for the 13 schools involved of only 16 per cent).

Sex

Four times as many boys as girls participated in the studies.

Types of Schools Attended

These were all primary or junior schools, ranging from very small rural schools to large neighbourhood schools. Some schools donated only a few children, with more coming from the larger schools. Three of the schools which supplied the greatest proportion of children to the main study had catchment areas including large council housing estates.

Main Study Results

The main study showed Paired Reading to have a statistically significant effect upon reading accuracy, but not comprehension, when carried out for a mean time of 7.6 hours over a six-week period. The gains in reading ages were similar to those found in other Paired Reading studies, that is, at least two and a half to three times the 'normal' rate of progress for children with similar reading difficulties (see Table 14.1).

We have been frequently asked whether it is possible to identify any

Table 14.1: Changes in Mean Reading Ages (in Months) over an Eight-week Period during the Main Paired Reading Study

	Group X (Paired Reading)	Group Y (control)	Group Y (Paired Reading)
Accuracy	2.43	0.81	4.85
Comprehension	4.36	1.69	6.31

characteristics of the children who are likely to do well with Paired Reading, or whether we can say which aspects of the technique are most and least essential for success. For instance, does Paired Reading work better for those children with the most serious reading difficulties or for those with less extreme problems? Will older or younger children benefit more? And can we expect children with lower intelligence test scores to experience only lower rates of progress, or even none at all? In terms of the technique, does it matter whether children and parents operate more in the simultaneous, or in the independent mode? Does the technique need to be performed precisely in all its aspects or will various rough approximations do just as well?

From the statistical analysis it was possible to differentiate between factors which had no responsibility for the improvements in reading performance and those that might be implicated (see Table 14.2). None of the factors examined exerted a very high influence on either accuracy or comprehension gains. Consequently, this study is able to identify those factors which had very little bearing on reading progress more easily than it can highlight the components which might be crucial to success.

So, for reading accuracy, the findings suggest that the measured characteristics of the children themselves — age, EPVT scores, sex, accuracy and comprehension reading ages and delays — had a minimal effect. In other words, within the range of ages and abilities studied, these are no grounds for attempts to select or exclude children by means of such criteria.

In terms of the technique itself, the experiment has shown that one need not be overly fastidious in pursuing each and every element of the technique, provided that certain features related to the independent mode are included. The implication is that the reading materials and the child's confidence should be such that the child will progress to a stage of reading a high proportion of words independently. One of the main aspects of a high quality of independent reading is the parent's ability to make an easy transition back to the simultaneous mode if the child makes an error while reading alone. The experiment suggests that this ability is also an

Table 14.2: Factors Contributing and Not Contributing to the Gains in Reading Accuracy and Comprehension during the Main Paired Reading Study

Contributory factors*		Non-contributory factors**	
Accuracy gains	*Comprehension gains*	*Accuracy gains*	*Comprehension gains*
Quality of independent reading (0.27) Percentage words read independently (0.25)	Chronological age (0.32) Percentage words read independently (0.31) Starting accuracy (0.30) Comprehension delay (0.28) Quality of independent reading (0.22)	Comprehension delay Accuracy delay EPVT score Chronological age Sex Quality of simultaneous reading Time spent Starting comprehension Starting accuracy	EPVT score Sex Quality of simultaneous reading Accuracy delay Total words read Accuracy delay Total words read Starting comprehension

* Correlation 0.2 or greater.
** Correlation less than 0.10.
Qualitative factors were derived from ratings structured according to the Paired Reading Elements Checklist (see Appendix to this chapter) based on observation during home visits.

important influence on reading progress, and many parents have described to us the 'crises' which used to surround errors when their children were previously reading to them.

The fact that the quality of simultaneous reading did not have a direct effect upon gains was initially surprising. However, Paired Reading is not just simultaneous reading. It is a means by which children are enabled to progress from an initially hesitant and dependent style towards greater fluency and independence. This process begins with the simultaneous mode. Similarly, successful independent reading is not merely reading alone; even here simultaneous reading has an important role. Independent reading is a technique which, when used efficiently, provides an immediate and consistent strategy for dealing with reading errors.

Thus, the recommended format for a successful period of Paired Reading appears to be:

(a) The establishment of a form of simultaneous reading with which parent and child feel comfortable. (This allows the child to be able to exercise control over the selection of books, at least at this stage.)

(b) A move towards a greater proportion of words being read independently.
(c) The encouragement of a smooth transition back to simultaneous reading when the child makes an error.

Practical Problems of Implementation

In the rural area in which we work, travelling time has been a problem. We tried to introduce some efficiency by holding the introductory meetings for parents in the main study at the main donating school. This meant that parents of children at the other school had to travel to the host school, as did the liaison teachers. In practice, this discouraged some parents from participating. In our experience, a project for pupils from a single school is more likely to yield a high level of interest and commitment among parents.

Often, the introductory sessions in schools were the focus of much parental anxiety, and sometimes anger and resentment. Partly, this was about why their child was being singled out for this sort of approach. There are very clear implications for the preparation by the headteacher and/or the project teacher of all potential participating parents. We also found parents who were often angry and confused about the school's perception of their child's reading ability. The meetings raised many issues about reading, the role of parents in helping, and either the lack of advice or the conflicting advice parents may have received in the past. In a small number of cases, it emerged that poor parental reading, or even illiteracy, was a factor to be contended with. These cases need sensitive identification and preparation, with perhaps a joint parental effort, or the involvement of the child's older sibling.

A problem which we encountered was the selection by children of inappropriate books. Often, these were too easy, or very familiar books chosen by the child as a guarantee of early success. We did not discourage this, but hoped that parents might encourage more challenging selections. On the other hand, there were some children whose reading choices seemed to us to be too difficult — either on the grounds of the level of readability, or of inherent 'technicality' and irrelevance, or both. In such cases, unless a very strong motivation by the child to read that chosen book was apparent, we did not discourage changing the reading material. However, one's perception of what is inappropriate reading material can be wrong! One girl in the pilot study ploughed her way determinedly through an ancient *Book of Railway Stories*, where tattered and missing pages frequently disrupted the plots. Another, displaying endurance beyond the call of duty, read an old copy of *Derbyshire Life* from cover to cover. On one home visit, a child emerged carrying a huge, leather-bound Webster's Dictionary! Thankfully, it was not his chosen reading material, but a conveniently sized and nicely resonant device on which to knock! In general, however, we found that most children adjusted fairly quickly to choosing books whose readability was within, or almost within, their capabilities.

Our own visits to parents and children at home have usually been between 4.00 p.m. and 7.00 p.m., which is not very convenient for parents, especially those with a demanding spouse or younger children to look after. We have tried to urge parents, where possible, to take on Paired Reading as a joint venture. In our experience, parents and children often found a mutually convenient time of the day when distractions were at a minimum.

The experience we had in the schools, especially during the introductory sessions for parents, pointed out to us the need for schools to be 'welcoming' — not only in a socially desirable way (cups of tea, biscuits, pleasant room, etc.), but also in ways which demonstrate a genuine desire to take advantage of and value the resource which the parents are offering to provide. Most notably, this involves being willing to take time in listening to parents' views and opinions and not to be too hasty in offering 'expert' advice. Certainly, the role of project teacher as a facilitator is vital, as is a willingness to visit parents and children at home, to discuss associated problems, and to give constructive feedback about the pair's performance. Provision of extra, attractive reading materials, and extended 'browsing' opportunities for children and parents on any Paired Reading project is also desirable.

Future Developments

We see two areas as deserving further active experimentation. One is concerned with the means of evaluating the effects of short-term interventions, such as Paired Reading, on children's reading abilities. Standardised reading tests are not typically constructed to measure changes over a short period of time for small numbers of children. Indeed, although with fairly large groups our main study was able to demonstrate statistically significant gains as a result of Paired Reading, within both the control and experimental groups there were a few individuals whose reading ages changed by dramatic amounts in both directions. In action research, these few rogue scores create practical problems of interpretation, as teachers and parents are naturally anxious to consider the gains and losses made during experiments very much on an individual basis. We also feel it to be important that projects employ evaluators who are not otherwise in contact with the children, as familiarity with testers, leading to greater confidence in a test situation, may well exert a considerable influence on performance and subsequent reading test scores.

An alternative to standardised tests is a criterion-referenced evaluation, which might be based, for example, on changes in children's sight vocabulary. Such evaluations present their own problems, however. In order to use sight vocabulary change as a yardstick, it may be necessary to limit and control the child's selection of books (Forrester and Bushell, 1984) thus changing the form of the intervention.

There appears to be a need to look critically at such factors as changes in children's reading purpose and strategy, attitudes towards reading, general self-esteem and practical aspects such as take-up rates (Robson, Miller and Bushell, 1984).

The second area we feel to be worthy of examination is the way in which schools and Local Education Authorities employ the Paired Reading technique in schemes aimed at greater collaboration between home and school. At the school level, our Phase Three follow-up revealed that although most schools reported favourably on their experiences with Paired Reading, the factor most instrumental in inhibiting their further involvement was the commitment of time and energy necessary for future schemes to be a success. Various local schools, however, have devised methods for overcoming these difficulties. Brockwell County Primary in Derbyshire has invited parents to come into school for the monitoring session, while Thornsett Primary School involved the whole of a first-year junior class — not just those with reading difficulties — thus giving the project a high priority within the school's curriculum. At Wildbank County Primary School in Tameside, the problem of time was overcome by involving for home visits as many individuals as possible, drawn from the teaching and non-teaching staff of the school as well as members of the educational psychology and language support services.

Our professional interest lies in the way in which Local Education Authorities can encourage and support schools in the development of parent collaboration schemes. Our view is that the Paired Reading technique, because of its novelty and dissimilarity from what is normally done in schools, is particularly useful where there is a reluctance to begin — reluctance on the part of the child, parent, teacher or headteacher. Where there is a greater confidence we see Paired Reading as a useful stimulus to devising schemes similar to those carried out at Belfield.

We feel that it is unrealistic to expect initiatives of this type to flourish and, more importantly, be maintained without some form of supportive management structure. We feel there is a need for the type of pyramidal support system initially developed for the Portage Home Teaching System for Preschool Handicapped Children (Bluma *et al.*, 1976) and later amended in Derbyshire to facilitate the delivery of programmes to slow learners (Miller *et al.*, 1984). This would mean that each parent-and-child pair would be monitored by the child's teacher. Information on the progress of each child would be collected from the teachers by a supervisor who would collate this and pass it to a senior administrative officer of the LEA, who would be able to designate resources where required and provide written feedback and encouragement to all participants. Such a system would keep all informed of the variations in different schools' initiatives as new means of extending the collaboration between teachers and parents are devised.

Appendix: Derbyshire Psychological Service Checklist of Elements of Paired Reading

Elements (Child's name ....)

Simultaneous reading	*Dates checked*						*Notes*
(a) Are parent and child in close synchrony?							
(b) Does the parent adjust the pace when necessary?							
(c) Does the child attempt each word?							
(d) Does the parent allow time for a second attempt when necessary?							
(e) Does the parent remodel a word when the child cannot make second attempt?							
Independent reading							
(a) Does the child remember to knock?							
(b) Does the parent heed the knock?							

	Dates checked						*Notes*
(c) Is the child praised for knocking?							
(d) Does the parent indicate *minor* errors?							
(e) Does simultaneous reading reoccur after about four seconds if child is unable to read a word?							
(f) Is the child praised after each period of about five seconds of independent reading?							
General							
(a) Is the reading material of the child's choice?							
(b) Does the parent avoid negative and anxiety-provoking reactions?							

Acknowledgements

The Derbyshire Paired Reading studies would not have been possible without the efforts of a large number of teachers, parents and children. In particular, the demanding testing schedule was carried out by Mrs Mildred Beard, Mrs Meg Nelson and Mrs Margaret Longstaff, advisory teachers (special needs), to whom we are extremely grateful. Our thanks are also due to the helpful advice on statistical matters provided by Mr Ben Jones, Sheffield University.

References

Bluma, S.M. *et al.* (1976), *Portage Guide to Early Education*, Portage, Wisconsin (Portage Project)

Bushell, R., Miller, A. and Robson, D. (1982), 'Parents as Remedial Teachers: An Account of a Paired Reading Project with Junior School Failing Readers and their Parents', *Journal of the Association of Educational Psychologists*, vol. 5, no. 9, 7–13

Crowther, C. and Wilson, D. (1983) 'The Derbyshire Paired Reading Project: Phase III:

A Summary of Results', unpublished paper, Derbyshire County Educational Psychology Service

Forrester, A. and Bushell, R. (1985) 'Paired Reading: Done to Death or More to Learn?' (in preparation)

Jackson, A. and Hannon, P. (1981), *The Belfield Reading Project*, Belfield Community School, Rochdale

Miller, A., Robson, D. and Bushell, R. (1984), 'Parental Participation in Paired Reading: A Controlled Study and an Examination of the Role of the Technique in Home–School Collaboration' (unpublished paper)

Miller, A., Jewell, T., Booth, S. and Robson, D. (1985), 'A System for Delivering Educational Programmes to Slow Learners', *Educational Psychology in Practice* (in press)

Robson, D., Miller, A. and Bushell, R. (1985), 'The Development of Paired Reading in High Peak and West Derbyshire', unpublished paper

15 PAIRED READING AT DEIGHTON JUNIOR SCHOOL

Avril Bush

Deighton Junior School is situated in an area of high unemployment and poor housing conditions in Huddersfield, West Yorkshire. The pupils are from several racial groups, currently 15 per cent Asian, 13 per cent Caribbean, 9 per cent half-caste and 62 per cent white. In recent years, the Asian proportion has increased and the white proportion decreased, as the school roll has fallen from 360 in 1979 to 201 in 1984.

In 1979, a Special Needs Department (to be called the Red Room) was set up to diagnose and remedy serious lack of achievement in literacy skills. Initial testing revealed a large number of children (86–23 per cent of the roll) with reading ages two years or more below their chronological ages. Because of these large numbers, a withdrawal system was adopted in place of the single vertically grouped 'remedial' class already in operation.

At the time of writing, five years later, only exceptionally weak children reaching the fourth year still need remedial help after three years' Red Room work. This means that, although a serious lack of achievement remains one of the criteria for entry into the department, a programme of prevention can be operated for larger numbers of children lower down the school to reduce the likelihood of remedial help being required later.

The advent of Paired Reading to this school in November 1981 has played a significant part in the development of this preventive role.

Parental Involvement

Parental involvement prior to January 1982 was limited to formal open evenings or an occasional summons to discuss a child's bad behaviour or poor progress. Community evening classes organised by a teacher failed through lack of support, as did social events such as West Indian evenings. A very small core of parents belonged to the Parent–Teacher Association, and staff had become disillusioned with their attempts to involve the community.

Knowing the value of parental contact from previous work in a special school, the writer viewed this situation with considerable regret. A request by local psychologists for Deighton to try to replicate work done with Paired Reading in Derbyshire was taken as an opportunity to try a different approach to involve the community. In the event, it was found that participation in the education of their children did in fact appeal to many previously uninterested parents.

The Deighton Project

The Deighton project is called PRINT (Paired Reading Involving Non-Teachers). Phase One was set up in January 1982. A group of 30 children whose reading ages were two or more years below their chronological ages was chosen. The parents were invited by letter to a meeting on introducing a new way to help children to read. The method would only take a few minutes of their time each evening. Only seven parents were interested at this stage, but the success of their children with PRINT (see Table 15.1) was so spectacular that the news spread rapidly. In two and a half years, 138 children have been involved in nine phases of PRINT. Of these, 73 per cent have been Red Room children.

Table 15.1: Results of Phase One: Neale Analysis of Reading Ability

November 1981			March 1982		
Actual age	Reading age Accuracy	Reading age Comprehension	Actual age	Reading age Accuracy	Reading age Comprehension
10:7	8:5	10:1	11:0	10:1	12:6
10:5	8:4	8:10	10:9	9:1	9:5
10:6	8:1	9:3	10:10	9:5	12:0
10:6	8:2	6:11	10:11	9:2	9:1
10:6	7:3	6:6	10:10	8:0	8:2
9:8	6:8	6:8	10:0	8:0	7:10
10:0	8:0	8:8	10:4	8:8	8:10

Of the 1983–84 roll of 201 children, 84 have taken part and twelve others who took part have since left. This is seen as quite a remarkable percentage of the school's population, considering the type of area involved.

Setting up PRINT

Parents are initially made aware of the project when their child visits school in the July prior to entry in September. It is stressed that all children, regardless of ability, can benefit from PRINT, since reading improvement is not the only positive outcome. In September, the parents of first years are invited by letter to an evening meeting. The evening begins with refreshments to relax the atmosphere. Early phases begin with a short introductory chat about PRINT's previous successes, followed by a light-hearted use of role play contrasting the old and new method of helping children with their reading. Many parents recognise themselves in our exaggerated version of the 'old' method, which is full of tension and aggravation between mother, father and daughter. The new way, in contrast, is relaxed and happy, generating a mutual excitement in the chosen book. The role play is now available on video, along with examples of a number of our parents and children engaged in Paired Reading. The staff role play is a source of much amusement and usually dispels any remaining tension.

Each parent-and-child pair then chooses a teacher to visit them at home five times during the eight weeks.

The Importance of Home Visiting

The involvement of school staff in the home visiting — instead of psychologists, as in the earlier Derbyshire projects — is now seen as a vital element in the success of PRINT. Only a minority of parents whose children attend the Red Room visit the school on open evenings. Therefore PRINT provided the first contact with many of these parents.

Since PRINT began, staff have been invited into the homes of over 50 per cent of all the children in school. It has been possible to observe the complex relationships within each home and appreciate the effects on the child. One sees the efforts of those who, despite the surrounding decay and vandalism, have made their homes into attractive, caring places.

Each visited child-and-parent pair develops a relationship with the staff visitor, who is often asked to provide advice or practical help with personal problems. One comes to understand more clearly the problems of the half-caste child in an all-white home; the West Indian child in a matriarchal home (contrasting with a more liberal discipline at school); the child of a non-English-speaking Asian family providing the only link with the English-speaking world outside; the Asian child with parents ambitious but quite unable to provide practical help; the child of a one-parent family; the child of unemployed parents; the child presented with yet another change of father; the child of a father in prison. In spite of these problems, the majority have achieved a measure of success. Many have improved to a phenomenal degree.

Implications for Teachers of Ethnic Minority Children

The percentage of ethnic minority groups taking part in PRINT is shown in Table 15.2. This shows an encouraging percentage of West Indian parents taking part. Achieving an equal partnership with some of our Caribbean community is more difficult than with the more assertive white population. Education has been, and still is, the preserve of the trained teacher in the Caribbean. However, once persuaded that they can play a vitally important role in their child's education, the parents are conscientious and reliable.

Table 15.2: Ethnic Groups Participating in PRINT

	Asian		West Indian		Half-caste		White	
	School	PRINT	School	PRINT	School	PRINT	School	PRINT
1981–2	24	2	40	4	22	3	181	9
1982–3	31	9	35	14	23	7	179	57
1983–4	31	4	26	6	19	2	125	10
Totals	86	15	101	24	64	12	475	76
Percentage		17		24		19		16

The Asian question is more difficult to overcome. Unless an older sibling or younger relative is available, PRINT at home is often impossible. The older child is therefore the most vulnerable, and these children need to do PRINT at school. Parents working in the Red Room (a partnership which evolved directly from the improved relationship developed by PRINT) willingly give these children an opportunity to do Paired Reading with an adult. If this is not possible, a sympathetic older child can serve as a 'helper', after training. Gains in these situations have not been as impressive, but nevertheless sufficient to justify continuance of the practice. All staff have adopted the method, but without any expectation of achieving gains similar to those the parents produce.

The half-caste group presents probably the most difficult ethnic problem encountered at Deighton. Not being able to identify entirely with either the white or West Indian communities causes worries and fears which intrude on the learning situation. Many try to 'prove' themselves to both communities. They have not, on the whole, been found to be as successful as other groups. Unlike the participating West Indian family units, the West Indian fathers of half-caste children have often been aggressive towards the scheme, and some have prevented white mothers from taking part.

Results

The Neale Analysis of Reading Ability was used to evaluate the first five phases of PRINT (see Table 15.3).

Table 15.3: Summary of Results on Neale Analysis of Reading Ability

	Phase One (Jan–Mar 82)	Phase Three (Sept–Nov 82)	Phase Four (Jan–Mar 83)	Phase Five (Apr–June 83)
Number in group	7	23	35	21
Average improvement (months) accuracy	12.6	12.4	10.3	12.6
Average improvement (months) comprehension	18.7	16.6	16.5	14.7

The approach to Phase Two was different and it has not been included here. After Phase Five, the Neale test was abandoned when it became too time-consuming owing to the increasing numbers involved. The reliability of the test seemed a little suspect in some cases. The Spar Test (a group test covering a wide age range) was tried for PRINT Phase Six, but proved not useful. Test results were disappointing in relation to the changes seen by teachers and parents. Phase Nine (September 1984) has introduced evaluation via the Edinburgh Reading Tests.

Case Studies

One case study out of 138 is rather selective. These cameos will provide a wider range of PRINT experiences.

Child M

A timid child in a 'tough' area is unwilling to draw attention to himself. M was such a child. He had lost his father in a road accident and was well behind with his reading. He attended the Red Room on entry to the school at seven. He took part in PRINT 3 at the start of his third year and PRINT 4 just prior to going to the high school. He became much less withdrawn, and more able to speak up for himself and assert his own point of view.

Having been over one and a half years behind, he left the school over a year ahead on the Neale Analysis (see Table 15.4).

Table 15.4: Results of Neale Analysis

	Actual age	Before Reading age Accuracy	Before Reading age Comprehension	After Reading age Accuracy	After Reading age Comprehension
PRINT 3	10:4	8:9	9:1	11:0	12:3
PRINT 5	11:0	11:0	12:3	12:3	12:6

Twins V and S

In cases where success has not been so extreme, as in the case of M, it is usually possible to identify the reason. This can be illustrated by looking at twins who took part in PRINT 3. Their parents both attend Red Room lessons, dividing their time equally between the two girls. V is eager and conscientious in both academic work and leisure activities. S is very easy-going and less well motivated. After the eight weeks, S had improved much more than V, which was unexpected. However, sustaining the effort of eight weeks over the subsequent one and a half years' work proved to be a different matter. Table 15.5 shows current reading ability in class tests compared with Neale results at the time of PRINT involvement.

Table 15.5: Twins S and V, Neale Analysis and Later Class Reading Ages

		Neale Analysis			
		Pre-PRINT		Post-PRINT	
	Actual age	Accuracy	Comprehension	Accuracy	Comprehension
S	7:9	7:11	8:2	8:7	9:5
V	7:9	8:1	8:5	8:7	8:11
		Class tests (after 18 months)			
S	9:3	Burt	Daniels and Diack		
V	9:3	8:0	8:1		
		8:6	9:8		

These results have implications for other children in the project. Is the improvement apparently showed by Neale results maintained in later years?

Maintenance of Results

Other Paired Reading researchers have expressed concern about the inflated individual scores sometimes obtained using the Neale test, and work is being done to find a more reliable method of quantifying the benefits of Paired Reading. At Deighton some evaluation is in progress by comparing class tests on entry to the school at seven with the same tests (Burt Word Recognition Test and the Daniels and Diack Test 12) taken by 54 fourth year children at the end of the school year. Comparisons for 1983–84 will also be made with Neale and Edinburgh Reading Test 3 results. It is hoped to be able to determine whether these tests have any value in quantifying maintenance of gains apparently achieved after PRINT. Studies of this nature are hampered by the mobility of the school population. Only 40 of the 54 children who entered the school in 1980 completed their four junior years at Deighton, and 73 children have been in this year group altogether.

Improvements beyond Reading Gains

There have been a number of positive results arising from the scheme which cannot be quantified. Both parents and children were in a downwards spiral of failure. Both were predisposed to believe that improvement in reading was beyond their personal control. Through PRINT they have established this control.

Comments collected from parents, children and staff have highlighted fewer behaviour problems, the establishment of a closer and more understanding personal relationship, greater confidence in themselves and each other, a real knowledge of the child's abilities and the generalisation of skills into other curriculum areas.

Perhaps the most important aspect of PRINT can be seen in the PRINT library at lunchtime, which even on warm summer days will be full of eager readers and those seeking new books. Parents 'complain' that they are buying books now, an unheard-of expense before PRINT. For many children, only their very own copy is now good enough.

16 A RESEARCH PROJECT IN PAIRED READING

Leslie Carrick-Smith

A project was undertaken to replicate and extend the Derbyshire study (see Chapter 4), and to examine the various possibilities of establishing the technique with greater economy of service delivery, and hence on a much wider basis. Led by a senior educational psychologist, the project was carried out by him, three remedial support teachers and the author, who was responsible for the research design and statistical analysis. The aim of the study was to show that those children who take part in a Paired Reading programme do better on a variety of parameters than a group of children who do not, and to this end hypotheses were posed to examine the effect of Paired Reading on three facets of reading age: accuracy, comprehension and rate; and also on self-concept as an indicator of attitudes and relationships. It is reading accuracy and comprehension that are of first interest in this present account; details of other aspects may be found in the original documentation of the project (Carrick-Smith, 1982).

Previous work in the field had generally assumed teachers or perhaps parents as partners in the technique. In the interests of a wider-ranging study, and also in the interests of more economical service delivery (since teachers are a relatively scarce resource, and some parents may be not suitable), the effect of using different types of partner (in this case, older school children) as well as teachers and parents was examined. It was not the prime intention to examine the effects between three rather different comprehensive schools, but the necessity to establish the project across those schools facilitated this to some extent.

The Sample

Three rather different comprehensive schools were chosen. Within these, identification was made of pupils with a common reading problem as defined by a score on the Neale Analysis of Reading for accuracy of below nine and a half years (i.e. a delay of some three years), but with some existing skills. Twenty-eight pairs of pupils (for experimental and control purposes) were matched for reading accuracy and age, ten pairs in each of two schools and eight in the third. It transpired also that overall pre-test means for reading comprehension and rate between the experimental and control groups were very similar. Furthermore, the majority of scores on a measure of 'general intelligence' were below the fiftieth percentile, and socio-economic status was similar. There were no ethnic considerations. Statistical manipulation subsequently enabled results to be analysed as if there were ten pairs in each school.

The Project Staff

While the senior educational psychologist and the author held overall responsibility for the design and co-ordination of the project, there was a vital need for specialised teachers to carry the project into the field, and for whom — assuming the project to be successful — it would become a useful working tool. Such teachers would be able to undertake the future dissemination of Paired Reading in schools. The remedial support teachers fulfilled this role. In many ways the project was theirs. The mediatory role of such staff is very important, they have the contacts with both staff and pupils in many schools, and already are familiar with the workings of individual schools. Without this role, a project of this size would probably be too large for psychologists to handle alone — particularly in the training stages. These teachers, acting as 'agents' in the schools, with their local knowledge, also had the necessary flexibility of working required to accommodate to the varied constraints encountered.

Training

About one month before the actual Paired Reading was scheduled to commence, training was undertaken with the projected partners. In the case of parents, a meeting was held with them so that they could share their past anxieties concerning their children's reading. In the case of volunteer teachers, it was pointed out that reading problems were shared across all subjects and thus affected all staff. In the case of the sixth-form volunteers, the social aspect of a reading weakness compared with their own mastery was stressed. These early meetings promoted the importance of intervention. The technique was initially introduced.

To keep progress simple and uniform, it was decided to introduce the technique in two parts: first, the aspect of simultaneous reading only, to be practised for about a week; subsequently, the 'tapping' (signalling) and independent reading to be introduced for the remainder of the programme.

Partner training was done by means of a printed information sheet, discussion and demonstration by role play between the workers, and with one-to-one provision for individual help. Record folders were produced with provision for partners to record progress and comments. The schools made a suitable selection of books available for pupils to choose their own (this independent choice is important). The first phase (i.e. of simultaneous reading only) was commenced, about 15 minutes a day at an agreed time and place convenient to each pair.

A 'worker' training session was held about this time, where agreed uniform practices were emphasised in terms of promoting a steady rhythm, appreciation of the storyline and continuity between sessions, and very frequent praise. This was reinforced by a videotape which had been prepared by the senior and trainee educational psychologists in one of the schools.

Following this, each partner and pupil was visited in the home or school during the first week to provide an individual check and advice upon the technique, demonstrations being given where necessary. Initially (although this was a major draw on resources), particularly in the case of parents at home, two workers were present to promote uniformity of practice.

After the first week or so, further meetings were held in school to discuss progress, share problems, and to introduce the second phase of 'tapping' and independent reading, again by demonstration and role play, as a natural progression.

For the remainder of the six-week experimental period, each pair was to be visited for observation and monitoring by a worker on two occasions. A checklist was prepared for this purpose, both to 'tick off' the various features of the scheme, and also as a means of gathering further, subjective information.

The final experimental component was to conduct the Neale Analysis retests. Each pupil (both experimental and control) was retested by the same worker on an alternative form of the test to avoid an obvious source of error, and also the choice of form was distributed as evenly as possible.

A final meeting was held in each school to 'round off' the interactive component, and to stress the ongoing nature of the technique although the experiment as such was over.

In several subsequent 'worker' meetings, analysed data were considered, and although there was some concern in the case of several individual scores, the pattern of success emerged.

An important follow-up session was held at which all three schools and the LEA were represented at senior level. The results were presented, together with an outline of the technique and a videotape. A discussion forum was held, and major implications for the technique were considered, not least at curricular level.

Practical Difficulties

The practical difficulties of such a project are only those, by and large, which might be anticipated. However, if this account is to be used as a model, it is as well to be prepared for problems which will inevitably develop.

To obtain enough partners who will be prepared to give a reliable daily commitment is not easy. Parents are the obvious choice, but what if they cannot read very well, or home circumstances are not conducive? More able peers or teachers are possibilities; even auxiliaries, dinner ladies and caretakers may participate if care and discretion are used. To slot another activity into the school day, or to withdraw two people by mutual consent, is notoriously difficult. Getting to school earlier or using part of lunchtime or assembly seem to be ways of overcoming this, but the time and place must be regular, and faithfully kept. Even more difficult is the arrangement of training sessions at a time and place convenient to the majority; this is no different from problems encountered in arranging any other meeting, but it can mean that some volunteers may be lost, or receive secondhand, inadequate or incomplete training.

A vital feature of Paired Reading is the fact that aversive reaction to failure and anxiety-provoking feedback is avoided. Particularly insidious are those few partners who cannot relinquish the role of teacher, or who 'know better' in some way. They are few, but for them it seems that the technique might not work. If phonics, for example, have failed in the past, then they will fail again if incorporated into this technique. The method is very simple; keep it so!

A number of parents reported difficulty in the natural progression to 'tapping' and independent reading from simultaneous reading. Perhaps this was not helped by the way this particular study was set up, but partners should be prepared to encourage this development if necessary.

In setting up a project of this type, the warning should be heeded that to check the technique properly with individual pairs on several occasions will stress resources. With the numbers discussed in this account, and five committed workers, this was a strain — particularly where home visiting was involved.

The Results

The results are summarised in Tables 16.1 and 16.2, and illustrated in Figures 16.1 and 16.2.

The figures given below are group means in months for scores from the Neale Analysis of Reading for accuracy and comprehension respectively, both for the experimental period and for follow-up after one year.

Table 16.1: Reading Accuracy

	Experimental	Control	School
Pre	102	102	1
Post	106	103	
Change	+4	+1	
Follow-up	105	107	
Long-term	+3	+5	
Pre	105	105	2
Post	109	106	
Change	+4	+1	
Follow-up	113	113	
Long-term	+8	+8	
Pre	104	103	3
Post	111	103	
Change	+7	0	
Follow-up	116	109	
Long-term	+12	+6	
Pre	104	103	Overall
Post	109	105	
Change	+5	+2	
Follow-up	112	110	
Long-term	+8	+7	

Table 16.2: Reading Comprehension

	Experimental	Control	School
Pre	103	109	1
Post	111	112	
Change	+8	+3	
Follow-up	110	115	
Long-term	+7	+6	
Pre	107	101	2
Post	113	107	
Change	+6	+6	
Follow-up	115	110	
Long-term	+8	+9	
Pre	103	101	3
Post	116	104	
Change	+13	+3	
Follow-up	119	106	
Long-term	+16	+5	
Pre	104	104	Overall
Post	113	108	
Change	+9	+4	
Follow-up	115	111	
Long-term	+11	+7	

Figure 16.1: Reading Accuracy Changes

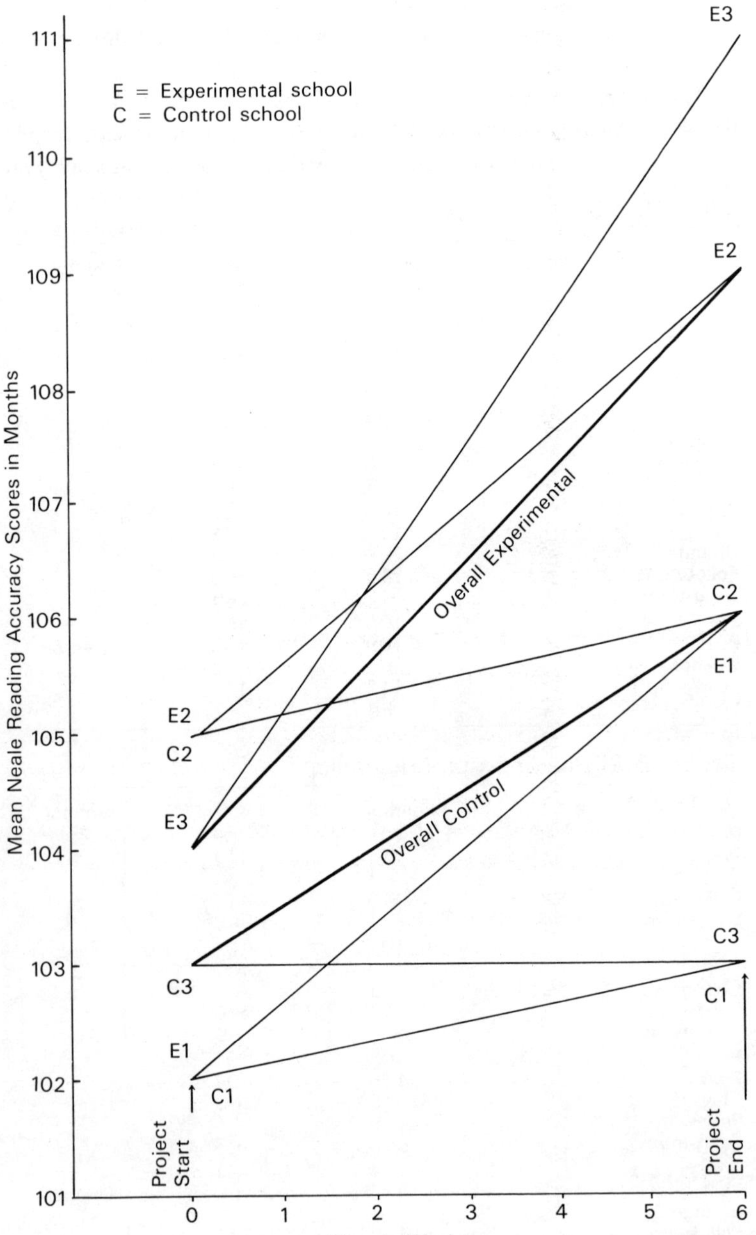

Figure 16.2: Reading Comprehension Changes

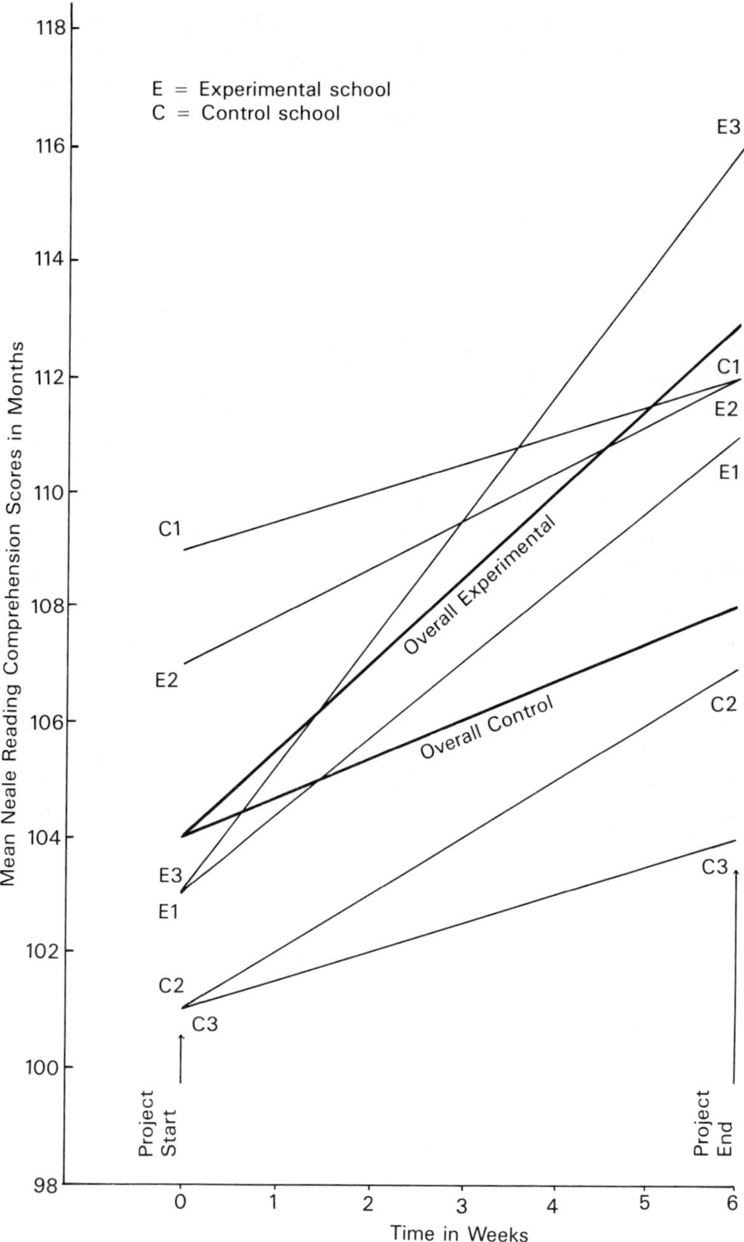

In short, it was found that over the two-month experimental period, gains for the pupils who had taken part in Paired Reading were in excess of twice those of the control group for both reading accuracy and reading comprehension. Statistical analysis suggests little possibility that these results could have occurred by chance. While there were differences in results obtained by different schools and types of partner, these were not statistically significant and do not reasonably require comment.

Validity of Findings

While several individual results seemed to be either exaggerated or pessimistic, the overall results show a very definite and dramatic improvement to have been made. Thus, while in a few cases we might question the reliability of individual results, and therefore have certain misgivings with regard to the Neale Analysis, overall it is felt that if there is any question as to the validity of the findings, it must be to suggest that the results are very conservative in comparison to subjective impressions. Partners reported all manner of benefits, not only in reading skills, but in behaviour and interpersonal relationships, even in the few cases where radical improvements in scores did not occur. Thus we had a high level of 'user approval'.

Follow-up

In the interests of sound research, a follow-up study was carried out after one year. The remedial support teachers carried out Neale Analyses of Reading on the original experimental and control groups using the remaining alternative form of the test.

Graphical representation (Figure 16.3) of the results shown in Tables 16.1 and 16.2 illustrates that Paired Reading gave a most marked boost to reading accuracy and comprehension, which was maintained after the experimental period, albeit at a much reduced level. The control groups made steady progress in both reading accuracy and comprehension over the year following the experiment. However, despite the restored freedom to apply specialised intervention — and presumably the lessons learned from the experiment — the controls had *not* caught up. Thus, it would seem that particularly in reading comprehension, and to a lesser extent in reading accuracy, the experimental groups maintained the gains given by the 'boost' of the Paired Reading course, beyond the control groups.

Figure 16.3: Paired Reading: Long-term Follow-up

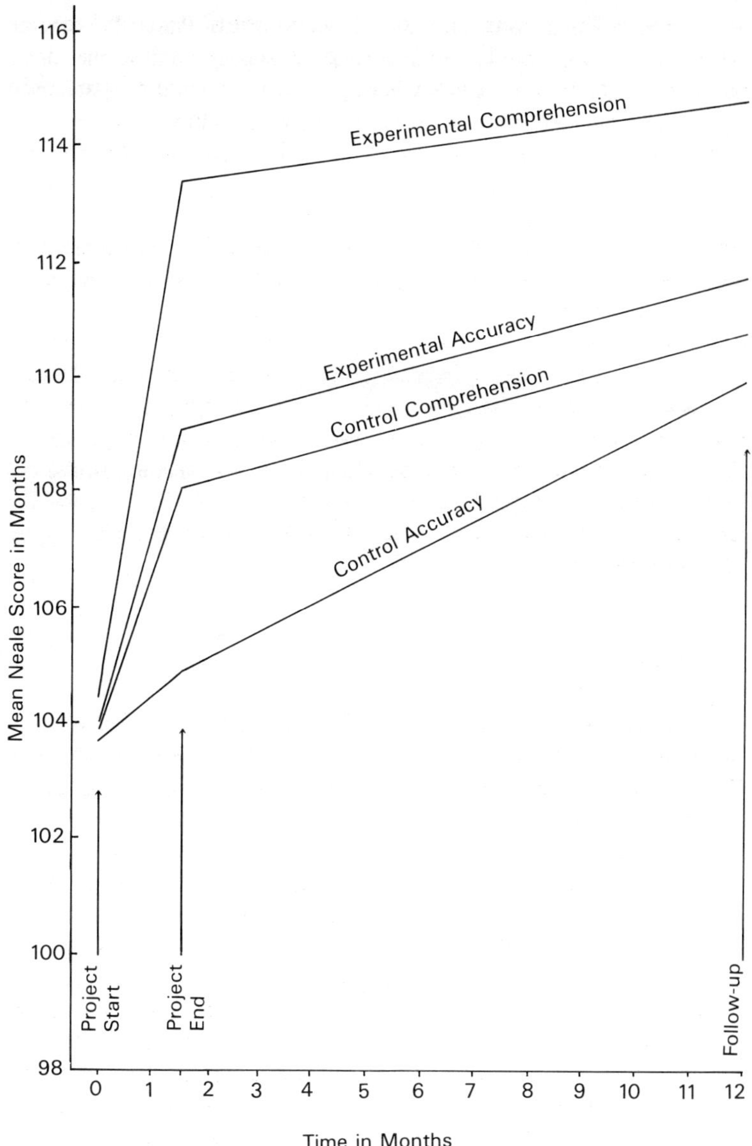

Implications

There would appear to be ample evidence to justify Paired Reading as a form of intervention. The long-term study suggests that it may be of particular value in those cases where pupils are referred to specialised centres for 'booster' courses of about a term's duration.

However, the initial heavy investment of time in training partners for this particular project illustrates the need for in-service training to ensure that the procedure is self-maintaining as a technique in schools. This has been an ongoing task for the remedial support teachers in Sheffield, and one which has been approached in various other ways by other authorities.

Reference

Carrick-Smith, L. (1982), 'An Investigation into the Effectiveness of Paired Reading', unpublished MSc thesis, University of Sheffield

17 A PAIRED READING PROJECT WITH ASIAN FAMILIES

Greta Jungnitz

The research reported here is part of a wider study (Jungnitz, 1984) designed to explore the introduction of Paired Reading to a group of Asian parents and their 'remedial' children. The main aim of the study was to identify and report on issues which may bear upon successful implementation of this and other such programmes with ethnic minorities. This chapter describes only that part of the research which was directly concerned with the introduction, implementation process and parents' and children's perceptions of Paired Reading. Additionally, reading test results for three groups are compared.

Development of the Project

The project school is a large multi-racial social priority junior school of about 470 pupils, approximately 75 per cent of whom are of Asian origin. The school serves a wide catchment area in an industrial northern town. All of the children involved in the project attended the mixed first- and second-year classes in the Remedial Department of the school. The parents involved were mainly employed as shiftworkers in local factories, although one or two were self-employed owning small shops, which were usually open in the evenings or at weekends. Immediately prior to the research commencing the school had managed — mainly through persuasive verbal messages sent home via the children — to involve ten families in a home–school reading programme based on the Belfield model (see Chapter 5). The second group (the Paired Reading group), consisting of ten Asian families, was established by the researcher. Partners in this group were taught and supported in the use of the Paired Reading technique. The third group consisted of those children whose parents were neither contacted by the researcher, nor responded to overtures made by the school.

In order to establish contact with the parents in the project group, letters in appropriate languages introducing the researcher, describing the purpose of the project, and arranging a time for an initial visit, were sent out.

Apart from misunderstandings with one family, who initially thought the researcher to be 'a private teacher touting for business', contact was easily established, and all of the families expressed willingness to join in the project.

Lack of proficiency in written and spoken English prevented all except one parent acting as partners. This is in contrast to the Belfield model group, where all except three children were supported by one (and in a few cases, both) parents. The age range and educational level of the partners differed widely. Two pupils were supported by an intellectually able, self-educated father, one by an 18-year-old sibling studying for four 'A' levels, while others had to rely on teenage brothers and sisters from the middle or lower bands of comprehensive schools.

Non-specific support by the parents was encouraged, and in most cases undertaken. Some fathers were particularly eager to offer encouragement. This was evidenced by praise, small gifts for having completed a long session or a difficult book, and later on in the project by escorting their children to the library to choose additional books. In one family, however, extra sessions of Paired Reading were used as a reward for carrying out small chores or errands.

In only one case was implementation of Paired Reading hindered by language barriers. Pressure from these parents, and a very strongly felt natural desire to help their child, resulted in the researcher introducing a small innovation. In short, the child was trained to read in unison with tape-recorded stories, while mother 'sat in' and gave non-specific support. This child made above-normal progress on all three tests, six months, eight months, and 15 months respectively, but these results are not included in the main evaluation.

Implementation of the Paired Reading Process

Implementation of the first stage, reading together, where training sessions were carried out individually in the homes, was quickly and remarkably easily achieved. Follow-up checks showed all of the families to be responding well. The second stage, reading independently, was introduced at a group session at the school. All of the families except one attended, and for many this was their first ever visit to the school. Many were acutely shy and nervous. These factors and others prevented full advantage of the session being taken, and the educationalists involved felt that the training would be more effectively carried out by the researcher in the homes.

All of the families found the second stage more difficult, and it was only in the final stages of the project that satisfactory implementation of this stage began to occur over the whole group.

Evaluation

Data were available on 28 first- and second-year junior remedial pupils, all of whom, except one, had a reading age significantly below their chronological age at pre-testing. Eleven pupils had experienced Paired Reading at home regularly, ten pupils had received non-specific reading practice, and seven children had no known home tuition. The last group is a comparison rather than a control group, since the factors determining the pupils' inclusion were varied and non-random. The mean ages of the groups were not significantly different from each other.

A number of similarities emerged between the Paired Reading and Home–School Reading groups. All of the children in the Paired Reading group were of Asian origin, as were all except one child in the Home–School Reading group. Numbers of boys and girls were fairly evenly matched (six to five and six to four, respectively), as were the numbers of first- and second-year pupils. The third group consisted originally of ten children. A loss in sample of three children occurred in this group. Factors affecting inclusion to all the groups were varied and non-random. These especially affected the non-involved group, where there was a greater racial mix.

All of the children were tested, pre-treatment, in the week ending 3 February on the Schonell Word Accuracy Test, and in the week ending 10 February on the Neale Reading Accuracy Test and Neale Reading Comprehension Test. Post-treatment testing was carried out between 16 and 26 May.

In order to identify significant differences between mean test results, a one-way analysis of variance followed by a Student Newman Keuls Test was used with the pre-treatment and post-treatment data separately for the three groups. In addition, a paired t-test was carried out to compare the pre-test and post-test means for each of the three groups separately, for each of the tests. All the means which were significantly different are shown arrowed in Tables 17.1, 17.2 and 17.3.

Results of the Schonell Word Accuracy Test

Significant progress was shown between pre- and post-tests for all groups, indicating effective teaching by the Remedial Department of the reading

Table 17.1: Schonell Word Recognition Test

Group*	Pre-treatment score (months)	Significance of inter-group difference	Post-treatment score (months)	Significance of inter-group difference
Group A	80.7	↔	88.4	↑
Group B	82.7	↔	87.0	↑ │
Group C	79.3	↔	82.1	↓ ↓

* Group A = Paired Reading group; Group B = Belfield Model group; Group C = non-involved group.

Table 17.2: Neale Reading Analysis: Accuracy Test

	Significance of inter-group differences	Pre-treatment score (months)	Significance of inter-group differences	Post-treatment score (months)	Significance of inter-group differences
Group A	↑	80.0	↔	93.1	↑
Group B	↓	84.9		92.0	↑ │
Group C		81.4		85.3	↓ ↓

Table 17.3: Neale Reading Analysis: Comprehension Test

	Pre-treatment score (months)	Significance of inter-group differences	Post-treatment score (months)	Significance of inter-group differences
Group A	78.9	↔	94.5	↑ ⇑
Group B	82.0	↔	88.8	↑ ↓ ‖
Group C	81.0		82.0	↓ ⇓

↔ $p < .05$
⟺ $p < .01$

skills measured. Significant differences between the post-treatment mean scores of the Paired Reading group (Group A) and the Belfield Model group (Group B), in relation to the non-involved group (Group C), suggest that help with reading at home has assisted in raising attainment levels.

The Neale Reading Accuracy Test

At pre-treatment testing the mean attainment score of Group B was significantly better ($p < .05$) than that of Group A. Post-treatment testing showed that this difference had been eradicated by the large and significant gains in reading accuracy by Group A. Mean gains in progress by Group A and Group B (13.1 months and 7.1 months, respectively) were both significantly better than that of Group C (3.9 months), although the gain of Group C exceeded 'normal' progress in relation to time passed (12 weeks).

The Neale Reading Comprehension Test

The mean gains of Group A on this test were substantially and significantly higher than those of Group B ($p < .05$). The results suggest that reading at home, and especially use of Paired Reading, significantly raises achievement levels in reading comprehension.

The rather worrying results of Group C may be due to a number of extraneous factors. A loss of three pupils from this group resulted in a smaller sample, and additionally the regression of one pupil — for which no explanation can be given — may have distorted the result.

Recently, results of Paired Reading experiments have often been expressed in terms of rate of progress. The comparative results in rates of progress for the different groups are shown in Table 17.4.

Table 17.4: Rate of Progress of Different Groups Compared to 'Normal' Rates (% increase)

Group	Schonell Word Accuracy	Neale Reading Accuracy	Neale Reading Comprehension
Group A	250	400	500
Group B	150	250	200
Group C	100	133	33

The results of the Paired Reading group (A) in this experiment fit neatly into an emerging pattern where the largest gains are shown in comprehension tests (for example, Bushell *et al.*, 1982; and see Chapter 14; Bush, 1983; and see Chapter 15; Topping and McKnight, 1984).

A number of features of the Paired Reading model appear specifically to foster comprehension skills. The whole exercise depends on the child wanting to understand and enjoy what he or she is reading. The embracing atmosphere of interest by supporters and families, not only in the reading *process* but also in the *content* of the books, seems likely to lead to conversations which are based on comprehension of the text.

Conclusions

Before any conclusion can be drawn a number of important points imposed by the limitations of the research design must be raised.

(1) Samples, especially Group C, were very small.
(2) Selection of the groups was not entirely satisfactory.
(3) Since the Schonell Test is frequently administered in the school, the results of this test may reflect practice effects.
(4) Reliability of the Neale Comprehension Test is not completely satisfactory.
(5) Exact comparison between non-specific reading help at home and the Paired Reading model cannot be made, since the implementation of the second phase of the latter (independent reading) was not entirely satisfactory.
(6) Enthusiasm of both children and parents in Group A may have been due, at least to some extent, to a 'Hawthorne effect', since many of them understood that they were taking part in an experiment.

However, the findings reported here suggest the following. First, a causal relationship exists between families supporting their own children in reading practice at home and gains in reading attainment. These gains are enhanced by the use of Paired Reading.

Second, implementation of the Paired Reading model, rather than non-specific help at home, significantly enhances gains in reading comprehension. No other comparative research on the effectiveness of the two models is known to the researcher, but a number of studies which employed the Paired Reading model give evidence of large gains in reading comprehension.

Third, the age, educational level, and level of spoken English of the supporters does not appear to have affected outcomes.

Parents' and Children's Perceptions

All of the supporters and children said that they had enjoyed Paired Reading. The children were especially enthusiastic and frequently said they 'loved it' and 'were not bored at home now'. Books brought into the homes were found to be intrinsically interesting, and a beneficial spin-off was evidenced in increased use of the public library by the families. Many supporters felt that their own English and that of the children had improved as a result of the project.

References

Bush, A.M. (1983), 'Can Pupils' Reading be Improved by Involving their Parents?', *Remedial Education*, vol. 18, no. 4, 167–70

Bushell, R., Miller, A. and Robson, D. (1982), 'Parents as Remedial Teachers', *Journal of the Association of Educational Psychologists*, vol. 5, o. 9, 7–13

Jungnitz, G. (1984), 'An Investigation of Paired Reading with Asian Families', unpublished MA thesis, University of York

Topping, K.J. and McKnight, G. (1984), 'Paired Reading — and Parent Power', *Special Education: Forward Trends*, vol. 11, no. 3, 12–15

PART 2:

PARENTAL INVOLVEMENT IN READING IN ACTION

C. BEHAVIOURAL METHODS

18 AN INTRODUCTION TO BEHAVIOURAL METHODS

Keith Topping

Four basic methods of parental involvement in reading are dealt with in this part of the book. All four embody a preoccupation with the surface behaviour of the participants, rather than supposing or implying mysterious and intangible cognitive processes. The methods act directly to change the reading behaviour of participants. At first glance, some of them may seem crude, simplistic or rigid. But all of them are very effective.

The methods are: (a) Reinforcement; (b) Pause, Prompt and Praise; (c) Precision Teaching; and (d) Direct Instructions.

Reinforcement

For many failing readers, the act of reading is far from intrinsically rewarding. On the contrary, it is often associated with struggle, pain and despair. Unsurprisingly, many such children come to devote more energy to avoiding the source of this anguish than to attempting to overcome the problem.

In the absence of any natural incentive to read, teachers often find themselves obliged to resort to authoritarian tactics, and try to 'make' the child read. While punishing non-reading may have some brief effect within the confines of the classroom, it does not establish a behaviour which generalises out of school, and at best establishes a few mechanical tricks.

The principles of learning established by B.F. Skinner and his forerunners, now so widely known that citation of specific references is unnecessary, stipulate that behaviour is increased in frequency, and subsequently maintained, by the rewards or reinforcement accruing as a result thereof. This implies that where failing readers lack intrinsic motivation to read, stronger or more frequent reinforcement is required. This may perforce be of an 'artificial' nature — by definition, reinforcement is not occurring frequently enough in the natural environment, or there would not be a problem.

The most readily available form of reward is 'social' reinforcement — smiles, hugs, pats on the back, praise, and so forth. The rate of teacher usage of such reinforcement is much lower than teachers commonly suppose, and international research consistently documents that teachers utter three negative and critical comments for every single positive one they emit. As we noted in Chapter 2, teachers give excessive emphasis to errors with failing readers. While social reinforcement will not be effective if offered by an adult of no significance to, or negative valence with, the child — and may be counterproductive if offered before an audience of the recipient's peer group who may have contrary expectations — it does seem to be an under-used technique.

Some workers carry reinforcement principles further, arguing that massive incentives are necessary to redress the effects of a long history of failure. In such cases, it is proposed, tangible rewards may need to be offered in addition, such as sweets, periods of favoured play activity and other 'treats' for increases in quality and/or quantity of reading behaviour. The intention is not that children subsequently read *only* if offered rewards — care is taken to link social and tangible reinforcement, eventually fading out the latter as increased competence results in greater success and the development of intrinsic motivation.

As such, reinforcement procedures can be allied to any form of educational programme or curriculum content. The role of parents is particularly significant, since the range of tangible reinforcers available in the privacy of the home enviroment far exceeds anything a busy teacher can offer at school. Social reinforcement by the parents, who in most cases are more significant in children's lives than the current class teacher, also tends to be more potent.

Many of the methods documented in the various sections of this book place some emphasis on social reinforcement, at the least in making some vague statement about the importance of praise and 'encouragement'. Some of the methods outline the reinforcement aspects much more specifically. Relatively few, however, incorporate direct tangible reward. It is worth considering the latter in greater detail.

Of note are papers by Staats *et al.* (1970) and Ryback and Staats (1970). Children with severe reading problems were rewarded with tokens exchangeable for cash for successful reading of flashcards of individual words drawn from their reading scheme. In the first study, the involved adults were non-related unqualified volunteers; and in the second, they were the natural parents of the children. The two groups of children made substantial gains in reading ability, in the first study markedly so in comparison to a control group. Staats first began work in this area in 1959 and many other studies involving him are reported in the literature. Camp and Van Doornick (1972) obtained similar results.

By 1973 Koven and LeBow had extended the procedure to cover spelling as well as reading, and had introduced greater reinforcement for faster child responses. Results were favourable, and follow-up two months post-project showed good maintenance of gains in most cases. Concurrently, Lahey *et al.* (1973) were applying a similar reinforcement procedure to reading activities which placed much greater emphasis on comprehension. Chapter 19 summarises a more recent and sophisticated project.

Despite the evidence from these subsequent studies that such procedures need not be mechanical or raise doubts about relevance to more complex reading skills and generalisation over time and space, tangible reinforcement procedures have never achieved the widespread popularity of other methods. Certainly careful planning, supporting and monitoring of phasing out tangible reinforcement in favour of social reinforcement alone would be necessary to ensure enduring gains. A common view is that such procedures are better held in reserve for use with particularly intractable cases, rather than being suitable for application across whole target groups.

Pause, Prompt and Praise (PPP)

In many ways this technique, developed by Ted Glynn and Stuart McNaughton, owes as much to miscue analysis and a psycholinguistic analysis of the reading process as it does to straightforward 'behaviourism'. It is included here because it does also have strong behavioural features, not least in that its developers have taken great pains to examine changes in parental tutoring behaviour following training in great detail. No other studies have scrutinised the links between training, changed parent behaviour and subsequent changed child behaviour so scrupulously.

McNaughton and Glynn (1981) cite evidence that excessive and immediate adult attention to reading errors *reduces* reading accuracy by limiting processing of contextual clues and inhibiting the facility for self-correction which Clay (1969, 1979) regards as so important. Hence, the first step in the PPP technique for parents — pause to allow the child to self-correct.

The procedure typically involves controlled and graded reading material, such as books from a reading scheme. A simple method of checking error-rate on the first 50 words is explained to parents, to enable them to determine if a book is of a 'suitable' level, and to use as a measure

Figure 18.1: Pause, Prompt and Praise Procedure

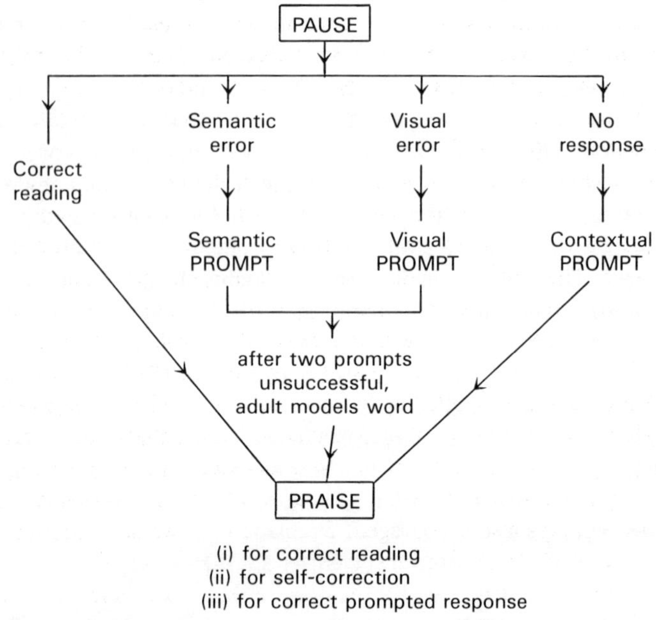

of increased child competence.

Parents are asked to pause to allow self-correction, and if this does not occur to make a tripartite discrimination as to the nature of the error made. If the mistake makes no sense, the parent prompts the child with clues about the meaning of the story. If the mistake does make sense, the parent prompts with clues about the way the word looks. If the child stops and says nothing, the parent prompts by asking the child to read on to the end of the sentence, or re-read from the beginning of the sentence (to search for contextual clues). If the error word is not read correctly after two prompts, the parent tells the child what the word is.

Praise is given liberally, for correct reading, for self-correction, and for successful reading after prompting. This three-step procedure is rendered diagramatically in Figure 18.1.

The PPP protagonists describe the results of the use of the technique with eight children in New Zealand in McNaughton *et al.* (1981), and with four children in Birmingham, England, in Glynn (1980). These are summarised in Chapter 20. Further work is reported in Scott and Ballard (1983) and Glynn (1985). In the first study, detailed data on parental tutoring behaviour *before* training are given. Training was by verbal and written instruction, modelling, verbal recall, practice and post-practice feedback on a weekly basis. After training, the number of books read greatly increased, as did the proportion of self-corrections, but the proportion of words read correctly overall did not increase greatly as the children were tackling progressively harder books. Results of five children were less impressive at school than they were at home and additional tutoring at school was introduced.

In the Birmingham study (Glynn, 1980), the children were allowed to choose their own books, but nevertheless the results at home were equally positive and the generalisation to school more substantial and clear-cut. The children made twice 'normal' gains on Neale Accuracy during the project. The Scott and Ballard (1983) study involved tutoring at home and school, and recorded gains of three times 'normal'.

Related work was reported in the UK by Traxson (1980), but this eight-week project was supported by twice-weekly home visits. The technique in which parents were trained included pausing and praising, but prompting procedure was different and included prompting specifically by giving initial sounds of words. Re-reading of sentences containing many error words was also encouraged. Dramatic improvements are reported in nine out of ten children involved.

The PPP technique clearly has promise, but more widespread usage and evaluation is obviously necessary. A step in this direction is reported in Chapter 22.

Precision Teaching

Precision teaching (PT) is not a teaching method, but rather a system of procedures for evaluating the effectiveness of teaching. By daily direct measurement, PT finds out which teaching methods result in rapid learning in particular cases. PT programmes are usually individually tailored to meet the specific educational needs of single pupils.

A number of American texts describe the procedures in detail (Haring and Schiefelbusch, 1976; White and Haring, 1977; Formentin and Csapo, 1980). Only a brief outline can be given here.

The first step is to specify an area of curriculum content. What the child has to *do* to demonstrate mastery of the content is then specified. This involves framing the learning tasks as operational targets or behavioural objectives. (For example, 'Given a sheet of 20 single-digit addition sums in horizontal form with total not exceeding 9, the child will write correct answers'.)

Large behavioural objectives representing big steps in learning are then broken into smaller component steps (a procedure known as 'task analysis'). The steps are made as small as is necessary to ensure success. These smaller steps are then sequenced into the most sensible order for the child to learn them, with more complex tasks following simpler subtasks in the 'learning hierarchy'. Each target includes a specification of pupil behaviour, the way in which the task is presented, and a criterion for how 'good' the behaviour should be to be acceptable.

The next step is to check out which of the sequence of learning tasks the child can already perform satisfactorily. A brief test or 'probe' on each task serves to determine where in the learning hierarchy the child already is. This is known as 'probing for placement', and establishes the point at which teaching should begin. The child's speed as well as accuracy of performance is noted. A response rate of ten correct items per minute, with correct items outnumbering errors, is usually considered to indicate a reasonable point to start teaching.

Having determined the starting-point of the teaching programme, it is necessary to determine the child's competence on this target *without* support or teaching to errors, to give a clear idea of initial or 'base-line' functioning. 'Probing for base-line', as with other probes, yields results expressed in 'rate per minute' — number of correct responses per minute elapsed. The teacher now needs to determine what is to constitute an acceptable level of performance on the target — the criterion for 'pass'. Complex formulae exist for this, but many teachers set criteria by reference to the expectations they might have of other children in the class.

Careful daily record-keeping of 'probe' results is essential. Many teachers find it helpful to graph numbers of correct responses and errors made each day on a 'ratio chart' (semi-logarithmic graph paper). The ups and downs on the graph clearly indicate changes in the pupil's response as new teaching strategies are introduced or existing ones modified, and the effectiveness of teaching strategies is thus readily evaluated. The criterion for 'pass' can also be marked on the graph, at an appropriately distant point, and by joining 'base-line' and 'criterion' correct response scores a 'minimum acceleration line' is drawn, below which the pupil's daily probe scores should not fall if he or she is to reach criterion in a reasonable time. A 'minimum deceleration line' for errors is drawn in the same way. If the child falls below the acceleration line or above the deceleration line for three consecutive days, it is time to modify the teaching strategies.

All of this may seem fiendishly complicated, and likely to result in far more time spent drawing graphs than in actually teaching. In fact, the time involved in probing, recording and charting is typically less than five minutes per day, leaving the rest of a ten-minute one-to-one session available for teaching to errors. One-to-one teaching is not implicit, however, as PT can equally be used to evaluate the effectiveness of group teaching methods on individual children.

Some curriculum areas obviously lend themselves far more to this approach than others, mathematics being an example of the former. In reading, PT lends itself readily to sight recognition of words on flashcards. However, a moment's thought will show that it can also be applied to reading phonically regular words by phonic analysis–synthesis in isolation or in context, and indeed to any form of oral reading. It can also be applied to comprehension of material read silently, as tested by responses to comprehension questions. In fact, any educational activity wherein what constitutes a correct response and what constitutes an error can be unambiguously defined, and where correct responses and errors can be counted over time, can be precision taught.

Nor are the procedures too complex to be effectively taught to parents. Quite apart from the work reported later in this book (in Chapters 21 and 23), Pennington (1980) reports a successful project with six families over an eight-week trial period. School Psychological Services in Coventry and Leeds, among others, report successful use of PT techniques with increasing numbers of parents. While PT may not be the easiest technique to 'give away' to parents, there is no doubt that it is possible.

Direct Instruction

Not that dreadful DISTAR stuff?! Well, yes, more or less. Direct instruction (DI) is famous for its capacity to incite teachers to cling fiercely to their prejudices against it in the face of overwhelming empirical evidence about its effectiveness.

The most striking evidence is perhaps that stemming from the evaluation in the US of the Follow-through programme, comparing different approaches to the education of disadvantaged children of primary school age range, subsequent to the compensatory Head-start programmes. Becker (1978) concludes that of the nine very different programmes evaluated, 'the data analyses show rather overwhelmingly that the Direct Instruction model was more effective in terms of basic academic goals *and* affective outcomes' (my italics).

In the UK context, substantive evaluations are provided by Gregory *et al.* (1982) and Branwhite (1983), while Gregory (1983) provides a useful review of research. Current literature mainly concerns itself with commercially produced DI packages of materials, predominantly marketed by Science Research Associates. However, other companies are beginning to introduce competing formats, such as METRA. Even though the principles of DI may eventually be widely understood in the teaching profession, it is doubtful whether many teachers will ever have the time required for the independent development of adequately structured DI materials and procedures. There is thus always likely to be considerable reliance on the commercial packages, where cost is no small consideration.

All the commercial DI packages have a number of common features. They are all highly organised, with materials provided and arranged in sequence and teaching sessions pre-specified. They are designed to be delivered to small groups of pupils, with a great deal of emphasis on quick verbal responding in turn or in unison. The amount of 'engaged' or 'on-task' time is thus very high. All DI programmes specify sequences of behavioural objectives, propose problem-solving strategies, articulate well-developed teaching procedures, give massed practice in discrimination of appropriate strategies with a widening variety of problem examples to promote generalisation, ensure over-learning to mastery, and provide a very carefully arranged sequence of tasks in a learning hierarchy.

The materials are often fully scripted for the teacher, and the format includes words to say, which words to emphasise, what questions to ask, how to signal the pupils to respond, and how to correct errors.

In action, DI is characterised by the breathtakingly fast pace of the teaching. Small groups of roughly similar attainment levels are usual and levels of pupil attention are maximised by close teacher monitoring of pupil behaviour. Having ready-scripted dialogue and prepared materials actually frees the teacher to scrutinise pupil behaviour much more closely and respond to it much more effectively and immediately.

Correction procedures in the event of error usually follow the model — lead–test–recheck cycle. The teacher demonstrates the correct response, cues or prompts the child as necessary to emit the correct response, tests that the child can give the correct response unaided, returning at a later stage to that item to ensure the child can still emit the correct response unaided.

To a naive onlooker, DI in action might seem rigid and over-structured, mechanical and meaningless, oppressive and boring, and unpleasantly transatlantic in flavour. To the less naive, it rapidly becomes clear that a great deal of intensive teaching and learning is occurring, and that the children, far from being bored, are really enjoying themselves. In practice, generalisation of skills learned in the DI format does occur spontaneously to other curriculum areas and other environments.

DI can be carried out by parents, although as yet there is limited UK work in this area. Levey and Emsley (1982) report an early initiative in the area, and give interesting descriptive evaluative data, but little hard evidence on attainment outcomes. Further work is reported later in this book (see Chapter 23).

Summary

Many teachers will be familiar with the principles of reinforcement, but rather fewer manage to put these principles into action systematically and consistently. Pause, prompt and praise will be unfamiliar to most UK teachers. Precision teaching and direct instruction are still only just coming into significant usage among UK teachers.

It thus takes an unusual degree of initiative to develop projects designed to transmit the skills outlined in this part of the book to parents. But it is here where there is most room for development, and perhaps where the greatest potential lies as yet largely untapped.

References

Becker, W.G. (1978), 'The National Evaluation of Follow-Through: Behaviour-theory-based Programs Come Out on Top', *Education and Urban Society*, vol. 10, no. 4, 431–58

Branwhite, A.B. (1983), 'Boosting Reading Skills by Direct Instruction', *British Journal of Educational Psychology*, vol. 53, 291–8

Camp, B. and Van Doornick, A. (1972), 'Assessment of "Motivated" Reading Therapy with Elementary School Children', *Behaviour Therapy*, vol. 2, 214–18

Clay, M.M. (1969), 'Reading Errors and Self-correction Behaviour', *British Journal of Educational Psychology*, vol. 39, 47–56

Clay, M.M. (1979), *Reading: The Patterning of Complex Behaviour*, 2nd ed, Heinemann, Auckland

Formentin, T. and Csapo, M. (1980), *Precision Teaching*, Centre for Human Development and Research, Vancouver

Glynn, T. (1980), 'Parent–Child Interaction in Remedial Reading at Home', in M.M. Clarke and T. Glynn (eds), *Reading and Writing for Children with Difficulties*, Educational Review: Occasional Paper no. 8, University of Birmingham

Glynn, T. (1985), 'The Mangere Home and School Remedial Reading Procedures: Continuing Research on their Effectiveness', unpublished paper submitted to *New Zealand Journal of Psychology*

Gregory, R.P., Hackney, C. and Gregory, N.M. (1982), 'Corrective Reading Programme: An Evaluation', *British Journal of Educational Psychology*, vol. 52, 35–50

Gregory, R.P. (1983), 'Direct Instruction, Disadvantaged and Handicapped Children: A Review of the Literature and Some Practical Implications (Parts I and II)', *Remedial*

Education, vol. 18, no. 3, 108–14 and 130–6

Haring, N.G. and Shiefelbusch, R. (eds) (1976), *Teaching Special Children*, McGraw-Hill, New York

Koven, J.T. and LeBow, M.D. (1973), 'Teaching Parents to Remediate the Academic Problems of their Children', *The Journal of Experimental Education*, vol. 41, no. 4, 64–73

Lahey, B.B., McNees, M.P. and Brown, C.C. (1973), 'Modification of Deficits in Reading for Comprehension', *Journal of Applied Behaviour Analysis*, vol. 6, 475–80

Levey, B. and Emsley, D. (1982), 'Involvement of Parents in the Teaching of Distar Reading to Slow-learning Children', *Occasional Paper of the Division of Education and Child Psychology, British Psychological Society*, vol. 6, no. 1, 43–6

McNaughton, S. and Glynn, T. (1981), 'Delayed versus Immediate Attention to Oral Reading Errors: Effects on Accuracy and Self-correction', *Educational Psychology*, vol. 1, no. 1, 57–65

McNaughton, S., Glynn, T. and Robinson, V.M. (1981), *Parents as Remedial Reading Tutors: Issues for Home and School*, New Zealand Council for Educational Research, Wellington

Pennington, A. (1982), 'Parental Involvement in Precision Teaching', *Occasional Papers of the Division of Educational and Child Psychology, British Psychological Society*, vol. 6, no. 1, 39–42

Ryback, D. and Staats, A.W. (1970), 'Parents as Behaviour Therapy — Technicians in Treating Reading Deficits (Dyslexia)', *Journal of Behaviour Therapy and Experimental Psychiatry*, vol. 1, 109–19

Scott, J.M. and Ballard, K.D. (1983), 'Training Parents and Teachers in Remedial Reading Procedures for Children with Learning Difficulties', *Educational Psychology*, vol. 3, no. 1, 15–30

Staats, A.W., Minke, K.A. and Butts, P. (1970), 'A Token-Reinforcement Remedial Reading Program Administered by Black Therapy-Technicians to Problem Black Children', *Behaviour Therapy*, vol. 1, 331–53

Traxson, D. (1980), 'Working with the Parents of Seven-year-old Children Who are Slow in Developing Reading Skills: An Individualised Approach', unpublished MA thesis, University of Nottingham

White, O. and Haring, N.G. (1977), *Exceptional Teaching*, Charles E. Merrill, Columbus, Ohio

19 REMEDIAL READING USING A HOME-BASED TOKEN ECONOMY

Lyn Fry

Introduction

This study was an attempt to involve parents in a project which would make a significant difference to children's low reading achievement with a limited input of professional time.

The impetus came from an earlier study in a junior school (Fry, 1973). In that study, testing identified 30 remedial readers. Ten children, randomly selected, were the experimental group, and were taught words from the Dolch list. The others formed two control groups. The first received the same type of tuition but for learning mathematical tables rather than reading. The second had no further attention of any kind.

The ten children in the experimental group continued with the regular school programme, but also met the headteacher for five minutes daily, as a group, with a partner chosen from the high-progress readers in their class. They were given two reading cards, with a word on the front and a sentence containing the same word (underlined) on the back. At each subsequent meeting the child gave his or her cards (increased beyond two as progress warranted it) to the high-progress partner, who showed each card and asked what the word was. If all the words were read correctly, the child was given a coloured sticker by the headmaster and was praised. These stickers were placed on the child's personal card, and could be exchanged immediately or at the end of the day for a sweet, privilege or small toy (maximum value 20p). For the larger privileges or toys the child had to save tokens.

In the eight-week period of the programme the group gained an average of seven months in reading age as measured on the Burt Test. The average gain in comprehension, measured on the Neale Analysis of Reading Ability, was five months.

The present experiment evaluated the effectiveness of parents' systematic use of token reinforcement in teaching word-recognition skills to children who were significantly retarded in reading. The study was of reversal design, in which reading ability was assessed at the beginning and end of a two-month base-line. The experimental phase lasted two months, and was followed by a further two months' return to base-line, with assessments at the end of each of these phases.

Method

Subjects

Thirty 7–10 year old children were selected from the junior part of a primary school. The school was in a rapidly developing lower-middle-class area, with an unusually large immigrant population. The annual turnover of the school population was 35 per cent. It was common for both parents to work. The sample was composed of 20 boys and ten girls.

At the beginning of the study chronological ages ranged from 7 years 1 month to 10 years 11 months. Reading ages on the Burt Test ranged from 4 years 5 months to 7 years. Retardation in reading ranged from 1 year 10 months to 4 years 1 month. The selection criteria were reading age less than 7 years and retardation more than 18 months.

Seventy-five children were identified as possibly retarded in reading, and these children were then assessed on the Burt Word Recognition Test by the experimenter. (The Neale Analysis was discarded on this occasion because of the non-continuous results it gave. Children would make sudden jumps in reading age on it without demonstrating a substantial increase in other reading skills.) Thirty-six children satisfied the selection criteria. Six of these children were not part of the final sample; two children left the area, two had very recent major family disturbances, one child suffered from muscular dystrophy and one family were recent immigrants who spoke no English.

Setting

All the reading was carried out by the parents in their homes. It was recommended that work be done in a quiet period after dinner, and most parents reported working in this time. It was stressed that reading sessions should not exceed 15 minutes daily. When parents indicated that they were working longer than this, they were cautioned not to, on the grounds that satiation would rapidly occur if the child were allowed to continue each night until he or she lost interest. Three group meetings were held at night in the school to introduce the parents to the programme and discuss any common problems. Two individual sessions were conducted with each set of parents in their own homes.

Design: Base-line One

Two months after the start of the school year the children were tested and selected. Teachers were told the nature of the project when they were asked to identify suitable children, but were not involved further. No action was taken for two months. At the end of this time all children were reassessed to establish the rate of reading progress over the period. At the same time they were all checked by the experimenter on the Dolch List of words occurring with high frequency in English prose. It contains 400 words, graded in difficulty. The child read through the list and any unknown words were noted. These error words then became the child's personal set of stimulus cards, which had the stimulus word on the front and a sentence containing this word (underlined) on the back. The cards were made by the children's parents from materials supplied by the school.

Treatment. All children continued with their regular school reading programme, but their parents were informed by letter that their child had a severe reading problem and were urged to take advantage of extra assistance offered by the school. They were told that the programme used had previously proven extremely effective and parents had had no problems in running it on previous occasions. The parents were invited to attend three meetings at weekly intervals. During these the programme would be explained and any questions and issues discussed.

In the first of the three meetings general points were covered. It was suggested that retarded readers usually meet with considerable difficulties in most aspects of school life. They frequently come to dislike school in general and reading in particular. It was stressed that the programme was designed to give the child new confidence in reading, by making the sessions at home relaxed and happy and by rewarding with both praise and something tangible for effort. The importance of adult praise was stressed, and it was suggest that retarded readers receive negligible praise at school. The parents were given a handout with the programme clearly specified, and it was then discussed point by point.

The specifics of the programme were as follows.

Helping Your Child Learn

(1) Prepare cards with the unknown word on them. Ask your child to give you a sentence containing the word. On the back of the card print

the sentence containing the word. The word should be underlined in the sentence.

(front) (back)

(2) Choose a quiet time to work with your child. Usually this is best just after dinner when the family has settled down for the evening, or just before bed at night. The absolute maximum time spent with the child should be 15 minutes. You may find that your child becomes irritable. In this case stop and try again the following night. You may also find that your child wants to go on longer than 15 minutes. I would not recommend this as with long periods of the same activity, motivation is easily lost.

(3) Work out a 'reward menu' with your child. You may like to include privileges around the house — e.g. breakfast in bed, TV time, stay up later, play cards with dad (or football, or any other game), do some cooking, etc. You may also want special family activities — an outing, picnic, trip to the cinema or restaurant, visit to special friend, ride on ferry, fishing trip, football game, museum, zoo, special game for whole family (Monopoly, Cluedo, cards). Material rewards are also very successful — sweets, ice-creams, chocolate, pencils, paints, small toys, newsprint scribbling pads, jigsaws, puzzles, etc. Pocket money is often a very effective motivator. You and your child should work out together those things he or she finds most rewarding. Write these down on a chart. They should be in order, from the most difficult to the least difficult to earn.

Your child will be earning points for learning the words, so assign a point value to each item and write this beside it. For example:

Lunch with Mum at coffee bar	250 points
Zoo	200 points
Museum	180 points
Money for cinema	100 points
Game of Monopoly	80 points
Breakfast in bed	70 points
Stay up 30 minutes	50 points
5p	30 points
One ice-cream (10p)	20 points
One Smartie	6 points

You should have 15 to 20 items. They should be changed (in consultation with your child) about once every two to four weeks. The items at the top of the menu should take about two weeks to earn, but the child should be able to earn something every night.

(4) For the first session select three cards. Two of these should be words already known to the child. Now you are ready to teach the unknown words.

Show the first card.

Say: 'What is this word?'

Praise if the child gets it right. Give one point. These may be marks on a card, or counters into a box.

If the child gets it wrong, say: 'No, that word is . . .' Pause, then present the card again, and say: 'What is this word?'

Praise if the child then gets the word right, but do not give a point.

Put the card down and choose another.

Ignore the child if he or she complains.

Show another card and repeat the process.

Continue presenting the words until the child recognises each one immediately it is presented. Remember to mix up the order of the words, otherwise the child may learn the words as items in a list.

Once he or she knows all the words immediately, introduce a new word. You may find that you are able to introduce several new words in each session. You should not introduce new words if the child does not instantly recognise the old ones. When the child has recognised the words immediately on three consecutive sessions the words can be discarded, to be reviewed at the end of the week.

Keep all the words together in a box.

(5) Just before the end of the 15-minute period, get the child to read the sentence from the back of some of the cards. Give one point for each one correctly read.

(6) Your child may have particular trouble remembering some words. For example, the words 'there, where, that, what' are often difficult for children to read. With these words your child keeps getting wrong:

Show the card and ask what it is.
If the child doesn't know, say: 'This word is . . .'
Pause, then show the card again: 'What is this word?'
The child says the right word, and is immediately praised *and* rewarded with one point.

(7) Children who do not read well often will not attempt to guess a word they are not sure of. If your child will not attempt a word he or she does not know, say that one point can be earned for *attempting* the word. You could help the child to do this, giving the sound of the first letter, or giving another word that starts with that letter.

(8) Once a week you should do some revision of the words your child has been learning. Mix up the cards in the box and select any that come to hand. Give your child one point for each word correctly read. If he or she gets a word wrong, ask him or her to read the sentence on the back.

If he or she still cannot read the word, put this word aside for learning. When you have four cards that cannot be read, teach these words as you do when learning the words.

The second and third meetings reviewed these points and clarified any particular problems.

Of the 30 parents invited, 23 attended the first meeting and four of the seven missing attended the second meeting. The remaining three were telephoned and home visits were made. Subsequently, at least two home visits were made to every family by the experimenter and the deputy head. These served to clarify any issues, and to ascertain that the programme was being accurately operated. The parents demonstrated with the child how they were carrying out the checking, reinforcing and recording. If their behaviour was very deviant, or if the parent expressed anxiety, the procedures were demonstrated with their child. In general, however, it was attempted to teach the parents by praising the more successful aspects of their demonstration.

After two months the children were reassessed and the parents were sent a letter telling them that the programme was now finished, thanking them for their help and co-operation, and telling them how much progress the children had made.

Design: Base-line Two

Two months after the conclusion of the experimental phase each child was reassessed by the experimenter.

Results

Gain or loss in reading age was calculated for the children at each of the three stages of the study (see Table 19.1).

Table 19.1: Change in Reading Age over Three Experimental Conditions

n = 30	Mean gain	Range
Base-line One	1.9 months	Minus 4 months to 16 months
Experimental	8.33 months	Plus 2 months to 16 months
Base-line Two	1.97 months	Minus 4 months to plus 7 months

The expected experimental effect was shown. There was a wide range of gains over the experimental phase. It should be noted that the child who scored 16 months' increase was not an isolated case, for seven children increased their scores by a year or more. Twenty-six of the 30 children showed the treatment effect. Two children showed gains in reading age for each phase, although these got progressively smaller; one showed an increase in gains over the whole project, and one showed a smaller gain during the experimental phase than during either base-line.

Discussion

The ability of parents to help their children learn word-recognition skills was demonstrated in this study. The treatment programme was carried out in busy homes, in many of which both parents were working. Many parents commented on the mutual enjoyment in the short sessions. The parental training was brief (one to three hours) in a large group of never less than 20 people, supplemented by two 30-minute sessions at home.

The results suggest that there was a strong parental interest and co-operation in carrying out the programme. The more limited gains shown during base-line two suggest that once professional support is withdrawn the programme may no longer be implemented in the home. Professional help was still available for the parents either from the school or the psychologist, but parents were themselves to request it. Some parents continued to avail themselves of this.

Ryback and Staats (1970) comment that 'The customary parent–child interaction in the context of complex skill acquisition is apt to be aversive for both participants. This situation is even more likely to occur with the child who has learning problems.' This observation was borne out by the parents in this study, several of whom initially expressed concern about their ability to overcome a history of unpleasant interactions with their children in the academic situation. It was felt, however, that this highly structured situation with emphasis on reinforcement for the child makes these problems less important. The situation also helps parents overcome their expressed feelings of inadequacy and impotence in coping with their children's problem. Furthermore, evidence of real progress in the child could be highly reinforcing to the parents.

Although the study was successful in demonstrating what could be achieved with limited resources, several issues need to be considered. The most serious is that word-recognition skills may show acceptable short-term gains, but the child will need more complex skills if further progress is to be made. It was found that once the children achieved a reading age of approximately seven and a half years they had mastered all the words on the Dolch List, but still had a long way to go to make up their deficit. Glynn (1980) taught parents a procedure described elsewhere in this volume (Chapters 18, 20 and 22), which was also successful but involved fewer children and considerably more professional time per family than the present study. Even so, the more complex skills taught may be more fruitful in the long term than sight vocabulary.

The second issue is the apparent lack of generalisation shown over the second base-line. The gains made during the experimental phase were durable in that few children lost ground in the next few months, but it was interesting to observe that the children who had made very large gains over the experimental phase (more than one year) were the ones who made comparatively large gains later. Possibly their parents were continuing the programme. Unfortunately, it was beyond the scope of the study to ascertain this. Had continuing support been offered the parents by the school, the parents might have had more impetus to continue.

A final issue is concern over the Burt Test as an assessment tool, which could be criticised on two grounds. First, it is essentially using the same form of reading (word recognition) as was being taught by the parent, and hence may have been influenced by this. Second, the test itself has been said to fail to tackle some critical functions of reading. Nevertheless, the studies reported here represent strong evidence for the effectiveness of a home-based token economy in accelerating reading skills.

References

Fry, L. (1973), 'Token Reinforcement and the Reading Ability of Retarded Readers', *New Zealand Journal of Educational Studies*, vol. 1, 165–76

Glynn, T. (1980), 'Parent–Child Interaction in Remedial Reading at Home', in M.M. Clarke and T. Glynn (eds), *Reading and Writing for the Child with Difficulties*, Education Review: Occasional Paper no. 8, University of Birmingham

Ryback, D. and Staats, A.W. (1970), 'Parents as Behaviour Therapy Technicians in Treating Reading Deficits (Dyslexia)', *Journal of Behaviour Therapy and Experimental Psychiatry*, vol. 1, 109–19

20 REMEDIAL READING AT HOME

Ted Glynn

This chapter describes two attempts to capitalise on the advantages of both home and school for providing remedial help to children with difficulties in reading. The programme was based on a model of reading which stresses the importance of children extracting a sequence of cues from printed texts and relating these, one to another, so that they understand the precise message of the text (Clay, 1979). These cues include the context of the story, the structure and pattern of the language in the story, as well as the letter and sound cues available within individual words.

Evidence for children's use of different cue sources is provided by analysis of their errors, particularly the kinds of substitute words they supply (Glynn and McNaughton, 1975). When children have learned to use all information sources available in a written text they frequently display the important behaviour of self-correction. Clay (1979) reported that self-correction was more closely related to reading progress in the first three years of instruction than either intelligence or reading-readiness scores.

Unfortunately, when children fail to make expected progress in reading they are frequently given less, rather than more, opportunities to read from text material. Children are frequently withdrawn from a regular reading programme and given remedial help of a kind that restricts the sources of information available to them in their reading. Furthermore, in the oral reading situation, the teacher may behave in such a way as to prevent children with difficulties from learning to use context or syntactic cues, and may even deny them the opportunity to self-correct. This might happen where a teacher, intent on giving remedial help to a low-progress child, in fact intervenes immediately the child makes an error, and supplies the correct word, and perhaps even praises the child for imitating this word. Such a remedial strategy is likely to reinforce dependence on the teacher as a source of cues for correcting errors, rather than to reinforce the child for using all cue sources available in a text, and to self-correct errors.

Previous research with teacher and paraprofessional tutoring of oral reading permitted the specification of the tutoring behaviours used in these studies (Glynn and McNaughton, 1975; McNaughton and Delquadri, 1978; McNaughton and Glynn, 1979). These tutoring behaviours are described in the introduction to this section. A fuller theoretical rationale for the selection of these tutor behaviours is provided in McNaughton (1978).

The Auckland Study (Mangere Home and School Project)

The Mangere Home and School Project (McNaughton, Glynn and Robinson, 1980) introduced a home remedial reading tutoring programme to parents of eight 8 to 12 year old boys with reading deficits of two to five years. This programme trained parents in their own homes to carry out the tutoring behaviours.

All parent tutoring sessions were tape-recorded at home by parents, both under base-line and trained tutoring conditions. The study had five aims. These were: to determine base-line levels of programme behaviours displayed by parents in the home setting; to demonstrate that the tutoring programme produced gains in these behaviours; to demonstrate that parents can maintain these behaviours without continued outside support; to demonstrate gains in children's reading at home; and to demonstrate that these gains would generalise to school. Independent measures of children's accuracy in reading text material at school were taken by graduate student observers.

Measures of Parent Behaviour

The following measures of parent tutoring behaviour were among those taken from the tape-recorded data gathered throughout the study.

Percentage Delay. This was a measure of the timing of tutor response to reading errors. Any instance of an interval of five seconds or more between a child and tutor response of any kind was scored as delayed attention. The percentage delay score for a given parent in a reading session was the percentage of instances of the total tutor error attention that were scored as delayed (rather than immediate).

Percentage Prompts. This was a measure of the type of parent response to a child's reading error. Prompts were scored as an instance of a parent responding to an error with a clue to or hint about the meaning of the word, or with a direction to look at the context of the story, or at the graphophonic features of a word. The percentage of instances of total parent error attention scored as prompts formed the percentage prompt score.

Praise. There were three types of parent praise tallied. All types of praise were contingent on independent reading. Total praise scores for each session included:

(i) praise for self-corrections;
(ii) praise for prompted corrections;
(iii) praise for other responses (e.g. praise for correct reading).

Parent Training Procedure

A parental booklet explaining this procedure has been produced (Glynn *et al.*, 1979). The procedure involves three components:

Written Instruction Sheet. A simple diagram was supplied to parents containing ten statements of what to do to assist a reader learning to read.

Weekly Training Sessions. Each week parent training was conducted during home visits. The visitor requested parents first to recall as many 'should' statements as possible without reference to the sheet. The visitor reinforced parents for correct recall and then read through the remaining 'should' statements with them. Parents were then instructed to conduct their own usual tutoring session carrying out as many of the 'should' statements as possible. Throughout the session, the visitor took notes detailing verbatim examples of reading responses and tutor behaviour in response to these errors. Immediately following the tutoring session, when the child was free to leave, the visitor spent a further few minutes with the parent going over the verbatim examples.

Weekly Feedback Sessions. In addition to the training session, another visit was conducted for a further detailed feedback session. This was based on an analysis of one of the tapes of tutoring sessions conducted in the absence of the visitor.

Changes in Parent Behaviour

Figure 20.1 presents summary data from each parent–child pair for baseline and training conditions. Data are shown separately for percentage delay, percentage prompts and praise.

The training sessions were separated into those in which tutoring took place with the visitor present (training) and those in which tutoring took place with the visitor absent (generalisation). The generalisation data reported by McNaughton *et al.* (1980) showed that all eight parents

Figure 20.1: Changes in Tutor Behaviour Across Untrained and Trained Tutoring Conditions for Eight Families (Auckland Study)

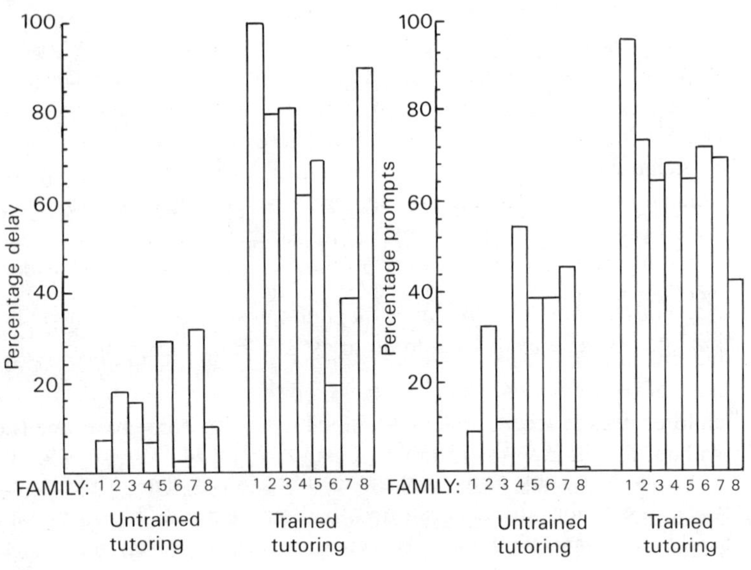

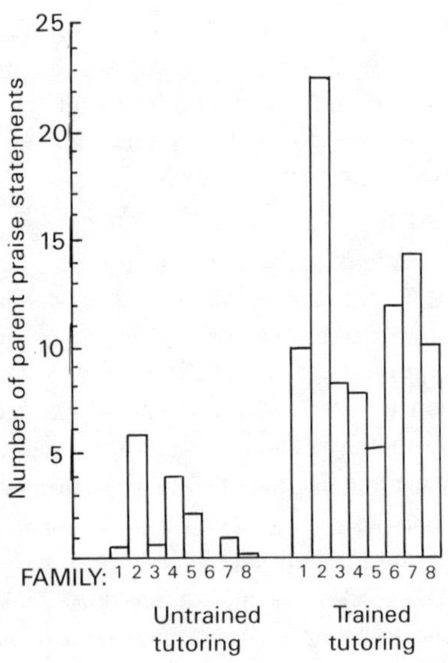

maintained their gains over base-line levels on all three tutor behaviours during tutoring sessions conducted without the presence of the visitor. Figure 20.1 indicates that the target behaviour for which all parents displayed lowest base-line levels was praise.

All children reached a criterion of 90 per cent accuracy on several successive book levels in their reading at home. Children averaged gains of 1.4 months in book level read at home over the one-month base-line, and 6.5 months over approximately 2.5 months of trained tutoring.

Achievement of the last aim, generalisation to school reading, was limited. For five of the children there were almost no opportunities for one-to-one oral reading from texts. Also, when written exercises related to reading were scheduled, these children, being considered non-readers, were occupied with filler activities. Some children, both at primary and intermediate schools, were withdrawn for individual reading instruction, but this instruction stressed phonics and word-identification skills, and not reading from texts. Hence, student observers were employed to hear children read at school under conditions similar to home base-line (i.e. without the tutoring programme).

Using this measure it was found that rapid gains within the graded series used to measure school reading occurred without the tutoring procedures for only two of the eight children. The tutoring procedures were then introduced into the school setting for five further children. With the support of the tutoring procedures in both settings, four of these five children gained an additional three to nine months in level of book read to criterion.

The Birmingham Study

In the second study, the identical programme was introduced to parents of four 10-year-old boys in an inner-city Birmingham school in England. These boys had reading deficits of between two years and two months and two years ten months. In the Birmingham school, unlike in the Auckland schools in New Zealand, all children had a classroom reading programme that included opportunities to read to their teacher from a graded text once or twice a week.

Changes in parent tutoring behaviours were very similar to those in the Auckland study. Delayed attention to errors and use of prompts occurred at low levels during base-line, except for one child.

All four parents increased their level of delayed attention and use of prompts with the introduction of the training programme. As was the case with the Auckland parents, the Birmingham parents displayed very low levels of praise under base-line conditions. Three parents did not praise *any* instances of children's corrections following a prompt. Praise for prompted corrections increased substantially with the tutoring programme, and praise for self-correction also increased, though not as substantially.

As in the Auckland study, all children showed marked improvement in reading at home. Over three months of home tutoring two children reached the criterion of 90 per cent accuracy on four different books, one reached criterion on three different books, and the fourth child on two different books. (In this study, books used at home were selected by the children, a procedure suggested by the study of Morgan and Lyon (1979; see Chapters 11 and 12 of this book) and so did not always form part of a graded series.)

Generalisation to school reading was more clear-cut than in the Auckland study. During the three months of home tutoring one child reached criterion of 90 per cent accuracy at school on seven successive books (from the graded series used by the teacher), one child reached criterion on five successive books, and the remaining two children reached criterion on two successive books. A standardised test of reading accuracy (Neale) showed that over the three-month period of home tutoring the four children made reading accuracy gains of four, six, seven and eight months (mean = 6.25 months).

It is possible that providing regular and structured opportunities for the child to read from books may itself prove beneficial for both child and parent owing to the reactive effects of experimental arrangements (Campbell and Stanley, 1967). This justifies the need for including an adequate base-line of untrained tutoring sessions prior to introducing the tutoring programme in studies of this kind, and of employing repeated measurement and small-N research designs which provide intensive data on behaviour change within individuals (Hersen and Barlow, 1976; Robinson and Foster, 1979).

The concurrent implementation of all four tutor behaviours may have altered the parent–child interaction in a way that would not have resulted had the behaviours been introduced sequentially. The child home-reading outcome data taken together with the parent behaviour data suggest a changed pattern of interaction to one which prompted increased independence of the child from the parent. This is supported by the increased proportion of errors self-corrected, the increased tutor praise for self-correction and increased praise for prompted corrections that occurred with the introduction of the training programme.

The generalisation to non-training sessions (demonstrated in the case of Auckland parents) may perhaps be attributed to the changed tutor–child interaction. Children's improved reading accuracy and marked increases in self-correction and prompted correction may both cue and reinforce parents for correctly implementing the tutoring programme.

One factor influencing the success of the programme was that it did not require parents to attend formal meetings away from home, with the added difficulties of arranging transport, and finding and paying for babysitters to care for other children. The programme provided regular feedback to parents on their performance of the tutoring behaviours with their own child. This might have been difficult to achieve in a group training setting outside the home.

These studies demonstrate that parents can successfully remedy their children's reading at home, even without the direct involvement of the teacher. However, generalisation of reading gains to school reading was more effective in the study where the teacher operated a reading programme which included oral reading from books of similar difficulty to those used in the home-reading programme. A close partnership between parents and teachers resulted in greater effectiveness.

References

Campbell, D.T. and Stanley, J.C. (1967), *Experimental and Quasi-experimental Designs for Research*, Rand McNally, Chicago

Clay, M.M. (1979), *Reading: The Patterning of Complex Behaviour*, 2nd edn, Heinemann Educational Books, Auckland

Glynn, E.L. and McNaughton, S.S. (1975), 'Trust Your Own Observations: Criterion Referenced Assessment of Reading Progress', *The Slow Learning Child*, vol. 22, 91–108

Glynn, T., McNaughton, S.S., Robinson, V. and Quinn, M. (1979), *Remedial Reading at Home: Helping You to Help Your Child*, New Zealand Council for Educational Research, Wellington

Hersen, M. and Barlow, D.H. (1976), *Single-case Experimental Designs: Strategies for Studying Behavior Change*, Pergamon Press, New York

McNaughton, S.S. (1978), 'Instructor Attention to Oral Reading Errors: A Functional Analysis', unpublished PhD thesis, University of Auckland, Education Department

McNaughton, S.S. and Delquadri, J. (1978), 'Error Attention Tutoring in Oral Reading', in Glynn, T. and McNaughton, S.S. (eds), *Behaviour Analysis in New Zealand 1978*, University of Auckland, Education Department

McNaughton, S.S. and Glynn, T. (1979), 'Effects of Timing of Tutor Attention to Errors on Reader Self-correction and Accuracy in Oral Reading', unpublished manuscript, University of Auckland, Education Department

McNaughton, S.S., Glynn, T. and Robinson, V.R. (1980), *Parents as Remedial Reading Tutors: Issues for Home and School*, New Zealand Council for Educational Research, Wellington, New Zealand

Morgan, R. and Lyon, E. (1979), 'A Preliminary Report on a Technique for Parental Tuition of Reading Retarded Children', *Journal of Child Psychology and Psychiatry*, vol. 20, no. 2, 151–60

Robinson, P.W. and Foster, D.F. (1979), *Experimental Psychology: A Small-N Approach*, Harper and Row, New York

21 PARENT-ASSISTED INSTRUCTION IN READING AND SPELLING

Jonathan Solity and Chris Reeve

Introduction

Parent-Assisted Instruction in Reading and Spelling (PAIRS) is a specific project developed within the Walsall Schools Psychological Service and subsequently extended to involve a number of Walsall schools. When the project started in 1979, we were not aware of Paired Reading as a specifically defined technique, and the confusion between PAIRS and Paired Reading is unfortunate, although the reader of this volume will be able to make comparisons between the two methods.

For the sake of brevity, we have not included discussion of our work involving parents in teaching spelling. However, the principles and methods of implementation are similar to those adopted to teach reading.

The Warnock Report (DES, 1978) provided us with the impetus to rethink our involvement with children who were failing in core educational skills like early reading and spelling. In considering our response to referrals made to the Schools Psychological Service we were particularly keen to explore ways of maximising contact with parents. This culminated in the PAIRS project.

The key features of the project emerged from existing work with pupils experiencing difficulties within mainstream education. The emphasis had been placed on curriculum-based assessment of children's educational needs which required the collection of detailed records to enable careful evaluation of pupil progress. This framework now underpins the main aspects of the project. These are:

(a) skill-based teaching;
(b) the use of precision teaching;
(c) curriculum-based evaluation;
(d) parents as teachers.

We will briefly describe each of these influences.

Skill-based Teaching

Teaching focuses on improving children's early reading skills. Initially, tasks are taken directly from the school's reading curriculum and emphasise teaching a basic sight vocabulary and phonic skills. As children acquire skills in these areas, teaching is extended to include oral reading and comprehension skills.

The skills taught reflect a 'direct instruction' view of teaching reading (Carnine and Silbert, 1979), whereby pupils are engaged on tasks which will lead to maximum generalisation from the specific materials used during teaching to a much wider content area. The approach stresses the need to teach skills to both high levels of accuracy and fluency. It is recognised that pupils will be more likely to maintain their performance levels over time when this can be achieved.

The Use of Precision Training

Our initial aim has been to show both parent and child just what progress is being made: this is particularly important for children and parents who may be poorly motivated as a result of previous failures. Daily probing and charting gives a quick and concise means by which improvements, even very small gains, can be recorded, observed and enjoyed.

The records are also essential in our discussions with parents about the effectiveness of teaching programmes. The time spent with them is more productive for having informative records which describe how well a child is progressing towards mastering a task. Probe data and charts also aid liaison with teaching staff as they too can see the improvements that are taking place.

Finally, by the very nature of precision teaching, information is collected not only on a child's level of accuracy but also on how fluently a task is performed. This ensures that children are not moved on to new tasks before they are ready and guarantees that they are given sufficient time to over-learn newly taught skills.

Curriculum-based Evaluation

Curriculum-based evaluation yields a wealth of detailed information on a pupil's progress on individual teaching programmes derived from the school's own curriculum. In particular we have been concerned to know:

(i) How many tasks have been taught?
(ii) How many days were required to teach each task?
(iii) Which were the most effective teaching methods?

(iv) Have improvements in sight vocabulary and phonic skills led to commensurate gains in oral reading and comprehension?

Parents as Teachers

Parents are taught how to teach reading skills to their children. In so doing we appreciated at the outset that we ran a risk in training parents to teach areas of the curriculum that had hitherto been the sole responsibility of the teaching profession. It has not been our intention to place parents in a position where they could take over the teaching role and replace teachers. Parents are reminded of this and they appreciate that the teacher remains in control of the curriculum and teaching methods used. The parent works under the guidance of the teacher and not as a replacement.

A final characteristic of the project is that to date it has only involved children who have been seen to experience difficulties in learning by either their parents, teacher or both. We have not yet extended PAIRS to the wider school population.

General Considerations

To ensure parents experience success we have tried to anticipate many commonplace pitfalls which can occur and to present management of the teaching situation in a factual, non-condescending manner. Specific details are available for reference in a set of ten booklets (Solity *et al.*, 1982) which list key issues for parents to consider. Good illustrations have helped break up the text and aided presentation of complex concepts. The injection of an element of humour has lightened as well as emphasised the message (see sample sheet in Figure 21.1).

The first of these booklets asks parents to think carefully about when and where they would work with their child. Conflicts with other parental duties must be thought through as carefully as conflicts with favourite TV programmes or playtimes. We have emphasised the need for praise and encouragement, the avoidance of recrimination and short daily sessions with no four-hour 'slogs' to catch up on Sunday afternoon.

We have also ensured that the core content of the PAIRS project is set within an acceptable and rewarding oral language and experience base. Parents have a keen awareness of their children's interests and the second booklet encourages them to capitalise on this in choosing and reading to their child appropriate topic and interest books selected from the school or local library.

Figure 21.1: Sample Sheet from PAIRS Booklet — 'Steps Involved in Administering a Probe'

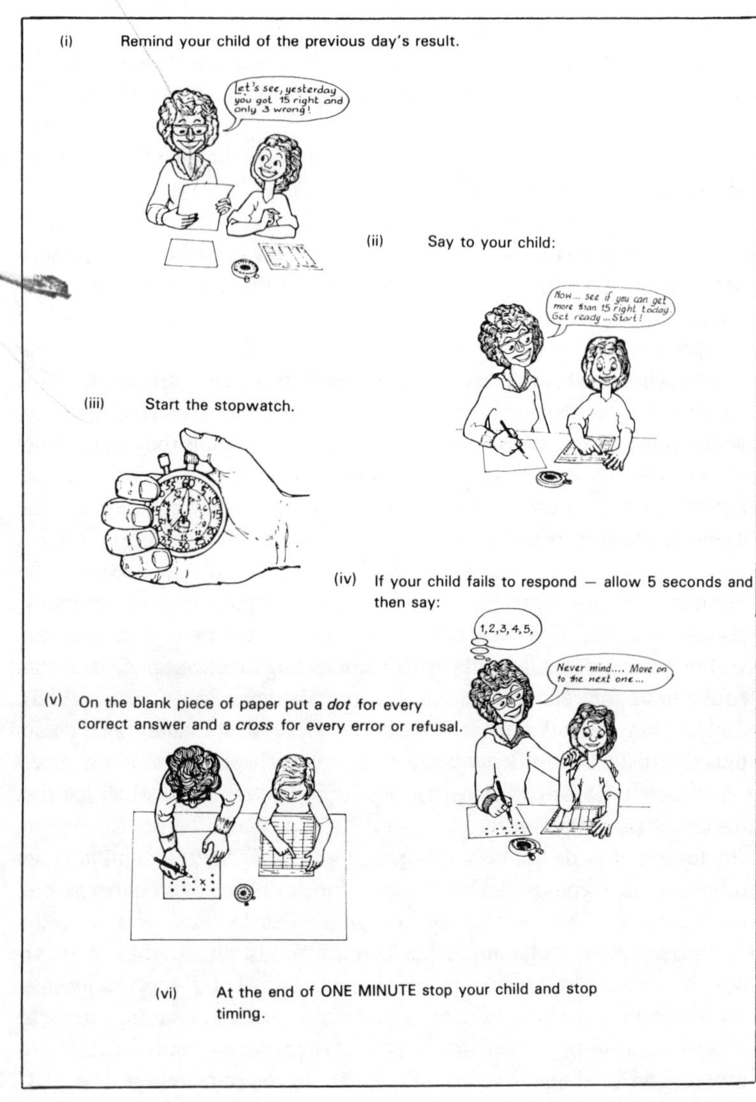

In the seventh booklet we consider the topics of comprehension and reading for meaning to show how a child can be assisted to establish purpose, anticipate events, review and question what he has read against his other knowledge and experience of the world. However much we encourage progress, we want to avoid the parent who rushes the child from the last word of the first book to the first word of the next one.

Deciding What to Teach

The reading instruction which parents provide does not occur in a learning vacuum. Children continue to attend schools where they are taught to read and it is necessary to ensure that these two teaching initiatives are compatible.

Many teachers work towards a reading objective of a reliable sight vocabulary, usually a combination of high-frequency, phonically irregular words (was, where, because, etc.), high-frequency nouns (boy, cat, school) and sight words selected from the school reading scheme, before introducing the child to a phonic-based programme or formal reading scheme. There is a high degree of concordance between teachers concerning which words occur with highest frequency, so something like the Ladybird Key Word List (McNally and Murray, 1962) can serve as an acceptable starting-point for many of our learners.

Placement probes were designed to establish which sight words a child could and could not read with respect to accuracy and fluency. The initial teaching targets aimed to give additional instruction and practice on those words which were not being read with sufficient accuracy or speed.

Similarly, some children were found to be attempting word-building or phonic teaching programmes before accuracy and fluency in recalling single-letter sounds had been properly established. Placement probes identified such difficulties, with home-based intervention provided to remedy the weakness.

Furthermore, the phonic placement probes can be used to determine how well each child can analyse words into individual letters, consonant blends and letter combinations, to determine the need for and elements of a word-building programme. Such a programme would typically progress from reading simple (VC. CVC) to more complex (CCVCC) phonically regular words. Teaching phonic skills has the advantage of introducing pupils to a generalisable activity which thus helps ensure that the gains in home-based teaching will subsequently be reflected in school performance.

When first encountered, many of our children already had a reading book from their school scheme. We have not entered debates about better or best schemes, nor advised schools on how to spend their resources. We have tried to stick with whatever scheme(s) the school was using, irrespective of its desirability. An oral reading probe can, however, quickly reveal whether a child's reading book is at an appropriate level of difficulty. We also see considerable value in encouraging silent reading to assist a range of comprehension skills (e.g. anticipation, use of context, etc.). Parents can still check on progress using oral reading probes and questioning techniques.

How to Teach

Teaching methods have been devised for the two aspects of skill-learning with which we are concerned: teaching reading skills to high levels of accuracy and fluency. The fourth and fifth booklets respectively describe activities for teaching sight words and letter sounds to accuracy.

The booklets illustrate the materials required and explain the steps to be followed in playing each game. The booklets are intended as an *aide memoire* and by no means provide an exhaustive list of possible teaching approaches. Parents invariably use them as a starting-point to build up their own confidence in teaching. Once this has been achieved we have often been impressed at the creativity and imagination of parents in designing their own methods.

During fluency-building, parents are encouraged to provide activities which offer their children opportunities to practice each new skill so that over-learning occurs. We have found that this is often the most difficult stage to teach as children are engaged on tasks which do not provide the same level of intrinsic motivation as the games in which they participated earlier. As a result it is particularly important that parents are generous in praising their children's efforts and emphasising how much progress has been made to help maintain interest and high levels of motivation.

Once children can read letter sounds fluently, they progress to blending phonically regular words. Here parents are introduced to a two-stage procedure which has been termed 'reading the slow way' and 'reading the fast way' to correspond with teaching each skill to accuracy followed by fluency.

While reading the slow way, children are taught to read aloud the individual sounds in a word (e.g. s + a + t), blend them together (s‿a‿t) and then say the word (i.e. sat). When reading words the fast way, the child reads the whole word without first of all reading the individual sounds or blending them together out loud. The child is, however, encouraged to internalise these two steps by being asked to do them in his or her head. This teaching method therefore aims to teach children to read letter sounds fluently, blend them together at speed and then name the words they make.

How to Record

At the beginning of the project we were apprehensive about our chosen method of recording progress. The procedures of probing and charting — although quite straightforward in themselves — were unfamiliar to parents and therefore likely to cause anxiety. Perhaps, though, it was the simplicity of the techniques and the way they were able to communicate progress that led to their success. The eighth booklet (sight vocabulary and phonics) and the ninth (oral reading) describe the steps involved in administering probes. Parents are reminded of the materials required, shown how to arrange them to maximum effect, given a set of instructions to give the children prior to probing and taken carefully through the steps involved in administering the probe (see Figure 21.1). After the probe results have been entered on a daily record sheet and chart, parents are encouraged to discuss the progress being made and to stress the reduction in errors when teaching to accuracy and to emphasise the increase in correct responses during fluency-building.

Parents have taken to probing and charting in a manner which exceeded our initial expectations. There are possibly three factors which account for this. The first is that the procedures can be administered quickly and help provide an exciting conclusion to a teaching session. Will yesterday's results be bettered today? Second, the charts provide a clear visual representation of progress which can readily be appreciated by the children: our failure-oriented children had probably become uninterested in conventional forms of feedback which showed them to be making little or no headway. On its own, a teacher's warm verbal praise and gentle encouragement may be thought of as 'a bit of a con' when the child knows he or she is still on book 1A. For most children, a clear indication of progress is sufficient to increase motivation and ensure further success.

The results place the parents in a position to which they are unaccustomed. In the past they have warily approached teachers and educational psychologists to be given news of how their children are doing at school. Now the roles are reversed. They are the people with the information on progress and it is the teachers and psychologists who are relying on them for details of improvements.

School-based Projects

In the development stage of PAIRS, parents visited the Child Guidance Centre which is situated near the town centre. Once confidence grew in the methods and appropriate materials had been prepared, it was decided that neighbourhood schools might act as a more convenient base for parent workshops.

Our first contact is usually a visit to the headteacher to outline the aims of the project, together with details of the likely demands that will be made on the school. During the meeting, the headteacher is urged carefully to consider his commitment to parental involvement. Although we help schools set up their first project they have to start subsequent ones on their own, so there must be a keen desire to involve parents in teaching reading in the school as a whole.

The school is encouraged to nominate a member of staff who will assume overall responsibility for co-ordinating the project within the school and for liaising with a member of the Schools Psychological Service. A difficult decision often relates to selection of parents. The dilemma to be faced is not unfamiliar to most teachers. Do you select the parents of children who are thought to have the greatest need when previous experience tells you that they would be unlikely to attend? Or do you plump for children whose need is not quite as great, but who have parents who are likely to participate? Our approach has been one of naive optimism, giving parents the benefit of the doubt and the opportunity to opt into the project without making too many assumptions about previous poor contact between homes and school.

Whichever parents are to be approached, the manner of approach is crucial. A letter home is easily misinterpreted and causes parental anxieties to increase. In general, a personal approach by the headteacher usually works best, perhaps a quick chat while a parent is waiting to meet another child from school.

The purpose and content of the workshops can be briefly explained and parents given the date of the first meeting. From then on it is left up to them to decide whether they feel they would like to participate in the project. By approaching parents individually one avoids making them feel embarrassed about not taking part as none of their friends or neighbours would know an invitation had been extended.

In reality, the headteacher and Schools Psychological Service are entering an informal contract with each other. The schools agree to guarantee the release of a teacher for each meeting, provide suitable accommodation, prepare teaching materials and arrange tea and biscuits for the beginning of each session. In return, the service makes available the PAIRS booklets and provides all the precision teaching materials. Both parties share the task of administering the placement probes to establish children's skill levels.

The first meeting the parents attend is usually fairly brief and designed to explain the nature of the project. Parents are given some realistic guidelines about what they might expect over the following weeks. They must then ask themselves the sort of question posed in the first booklet: will they have the time to work every evening at home under the necessary conditions? Will they be able to find a quiet room for 15 minutes? Will there be any interruptions? It is only following this meeting that the parents are expected to make a commitment and are given every opportunity to decline the invitation without loss of face. If anything, it is better to put parents off at this first meeting, by anticipating a variety of valid reasons which might soon preclude involvement, than to raise false hopes or expectations. We discuss possible advantages as well, but we want to avoid sales talk. Between the first and second meetings the parents are invited to contact the headteacher or teacher responsible for the project if they wish to be included.

During the second session, parents are encouraged to talk about their previous experiences of helping their children learn to read. We anticipate likely difficulties and attempt to find ways of overcoming them. Parents invariably find it reassuring to discover that they are not thc only ones who in the past have become short-tempered and frustrated when their children do not improve as they had hoped.

The following three sessions introduce parents to selecting teaching methods, probing and charting respectively and they follow a familiar format. First of all, the teacher and psychologist role play a skill — for example, how to administer a probe. The parents are then invited to practise on each other before finally getting their children out of their classrooms and administering a probe to them for the first time. During subsequent meetings, children's progress is reviewed and parents informally exchange ideas on how things are developing. The tasks children are given relate to their particular needs so they are not engaged in the same activities and we have rarely encountered situations where parents become competitive about their children's reading.

Evaluation

To date, there has been no large-scale formal evaluation of the PAIRS project. This is due to the nature of the principles and techniques adopted in curriculum-based assessment. Children have been on individually prepared programmes with their progress being compared to their previous performance levels, rather than those of either their peers or standardised populations through the use of normative tests of reading.

The project has acquired a momentum of its own based largely on the success parents have had in teaching their children, rather than the persuasive impact of 'hard data'. However, considerable information exists on the progress of individual pupils, some of which has been reported in White, Solity and Reeve (1984), Belcher (1984) and Peter (1984). What we can do here is give some idea of the current scale of the project and outline how we have tried to evaluate the project's effectiveness with respect to individual children.

So far, six school projects have been set up with between four and ten parents taking part in each. Psychologists are no longer involved and the schools have taken over responsibility for running and maintaining future initiatives.

When considering individual children we can begin to examine their progress through looking at: first, the number of tasks that have been taught; and second, the number of days required to teach each task. This can be extended and we can draw inferences by going back and checking that tasks taught previously can be remembered over time. Once a task has been mastered, a pupil is retested on a probe after an interval of several weeks during which no further teaching takes place. It is hoped that the child's performance levels have remained the same and have not deteriorated. This can be illustrated by looking at the progress of a pupil named Jane, shown in Table 21.1. It was felt that tasks SW1, SW2 and SW3 had been mastered once they were read at a rate of 50 correct responses with a maximum of two errors. Jane managed to do this on all three tasks in January 1983 and when given the same probes in July 1983 she had maintained her fluency levels, thus indicating that the words had not been forgotten in the intervening six months.

A further opportunity for evaluating progress occurs when tasks are taught from a related sequence of skills (e.g. a phonic teaching sequence). Over time it is expected that pupils transfer skills acquired in learning the earlier, easier skills in the sequence to the later more difficult tasks, on which teaching has not yet taken place. This can again be seen by looking at Jane's progress (see Table 21.2).

Table 21.1: Pupil Progress Monitored over Time

Skill	January 1983 Correct	January 1983 Errors	July 1983 Correct	July 1983 Errors
SWI: 12 most commonly occurring words in written English.	53	1	55	0
SW2: 20 next most commonly occurring words in written English.	54	2	54	0
SW3: 20 next most commonly occurring words in written English.	51	0	52	1

Table 21.2: Illustration of Transfer of Learning

Skill	September 1983 Correct	September 1983 Errors	December 1983 Correct	December 1983 Errors
Letter sounds	15	4	73	1
CVC	3	11	65	4
CVCC	Not attempted		53	2
CCVC	Not attempted		21	0
CCVCC	Not attempted		15	0

Between September and December 1983, Jane received tuition on three phonic tasks, reading letter sounds and blending CVC and CVCC words. No formal teaching took place to help Jane read CCVC or CCVCC words. However, examination of Table 21.2 indicates that her performance on these tasks improved. This happened because Jane transferred the blending skills she had learned through being taught to read letter sounds, CVC and CVCC words to the two later and more difficult activities.

Finally, we are also interested in longer-term evaluation and teacher reports on how effectively a pupil functions as a reader within the whole curriculum. It is always pleasing to hear that the collaboration between parents and schools has successfully resulted in a child no longer being seen as having 'special needs'.

References

Belcher, M. (1984), 'Parents Can Be a Major Asset in Teaching Reading', *Remedial Education*, vol. 19, no. 4, 162–4

Carnine, D. and Silbert, J. (1979), *Direct Instruction Reading*, Charles E. Merrill, Columbus, Ohio

DES (1978), *Special Educational Needs: Report of the Committee of Enquiry into the Education of Handicapped Children and Young People* (The Warnock Report), HMSO, London

McNally, J. and Murray, W. (1962), *Key Words to Literacy*, The Schoolmaster Publishing Company, London

Peter, M. (1984), 'How Parents are Helping Slow Learners to Read', *Junior Education*, vol. 8, no. 11, 25

Solity J.E. *et al.* (eds) (1982), *PAIRS Booklets*, Walsall LEA

White, P.G., Solity, J.E. and Reeve, C.J. (1984), 'Teaching Parents to Teach Reading', *Special Education: Forward Trends*, vol. 11, no. 1, 11–13

22 GIVING PARENTS A CHOICE: TEACHING PAIRED READING AND PAUSE, PROMPT AND PRAISE STRATEGIES IN A WORKSHOP SETTING

Sam Winter

Introduction

Paired Reading (PR) and Pause, Prompt and Praise (PPP) strategies involve very different error-correction strategies. The first provides immediate and total support in an attempt to minimise punishing events during reading. The second provides delayed and partial support in an attempt to encourage self-correction strategies, shown by Clay (1979) to be a powerful predictor of reading progress.

Despite the differences, a number of studies have shown both techniques to be effective when used by parents with their children (see Chapters 11–18 and 20; and Glynn, 1981; Grigg, 1984; Winter, 1984a and b). It is possible that each error-correction strategy works with a different population of children. If so, those differences are not yet apparent in the literature. Another possibility is that PR and PPP are effective because of a *common* component (perhaps positive reinforcement of correct reading) and that the precise error-correction strategy used is irrelevant. At this stage of research we really do not know.

Studies have usually been designed to instruct parents in the use of *either* PR or PPP methods. The psychologist or workshop organiser has chosen a technique for the parents and children involved. The clients themselves have been deprived of choice. And yet, as we have seen, there are presently no grounds for selecting one technique to the exclusion of the other. In this situation it seems fairer to instruct parents in the use of both methods, give them a chance to use each, and then ask them and their children to select the one they feel most comfortable using, and, if they have a view on it, the one they feel is working best for them. This workshop aimed to do all of these things. It was one of a series (Winter, 1984b) conducted during a period working as an educational psychologist in Hartlepool in the county of Cleveland, and involved the use of adolescent tutors to provide back-up in school for the work being done by the parents at home.

Preparation for the Workshop

Class teachers and the peripatetic reading teacher of the local authority junior school concerned were asked to make a list of all second, third and fourth years they felt would make *broader overall progress* were they to receive parental tuition in reading. They were expressly asked *not* just to consider children presently receiving remedial help, nor just to list children whose parents could be relied upon to provide tuition, or had previously shown an interest in their child's education. The school provided a list of 33 children (20 boys and 13 girls).

The parents of these children were then invited to a 30-minute introductory meeting in which this writer explained: (1) the reasons why they, and not other parents, had been selected; (2) our aim for them (that we should teach them skills they could use to help their child when reading); (3) the demands we would be making of them (that they should attend four one-hour training sessions to take place over a period of one month on the school premises and that they should use the methods they had been trained in for a period of around 20 minutes, six nights a week, with their child); and (4) the plans we had for peer tutors to provide back-up sessions in school during the period of the workshop. The meeting also provided them with an opportunity to meet the writer and ask questions about the workshop. Any questions they asked about the PR and PPP techniques were answered in very general terms. Parents were told that the detailed nature of each method would become clear in the workshop sessions themselves. At the end of the session parents who were interested in joining the workshop (and able to attend) signed on a slip of paper provided for that purpose. Fourteen parents signed, though only twelve were subsequently to attend the workshop.

In the period between the introductory meeting and Session One of the workshop proper, enrolled parents and relevant class teachers were asked to complete a short questionnaire indicating the child's performance in, and attitudes towards, reading. The questionnaire required them to tick boxes indicating the child's: (1) interest in reading; (2) accuracy when reading; (3) understanding of what he or she read; and (4) confidence when reading. For each of these there was a choice of five boxes marked 'very low', 'low', 'medium', 'high' and 'very high'. These questionnaires, when completed, constituted the pre-workshop teacher and parent questionnaires. Identical ones would be presented for completion at the end of the workshop.

Similarly, before the workshop actually began, this writer asked the children of each enrolled parent to read individually from a short (150 to 200 words) and manageable (error rate under 25 per cent) text of a predetermined readability level as measured on the Mugford Readability Index. Each child was taped as he or she read, and from those tape-recordings were later taken measures of reading rate, error rate, refusal rate (i.e. 'I don't know', 'Can you help me?') and rate of self-correction. These four measures together constituted an assessment of the child's pre-workshop reading fluency. Similar measures would be collected directly after the end of the workshop using completely unrelated texts of exactly the same readability level. Full details of the method, including instructions for scoring the tapes, are available from this writer.

This method of assessing changes in reading ability is hopefully more sensitive to relatively small improvements in reading skills over a short period, compared with more commonly used standardised tests such as the Neale Analysis of Reading Ability (whose smallest unit of measurement is one month of reading age). Equally important, it should not be characterised by test–retest practice effects (Netley *et al.*, 1965) or by problems of non-equivalence between supposedly equivalent parallel forms. This latter problem, under-reported in the literature and ignored by many action researchers, is readily apparent in, for example, the Neale test manual itself. Despite raw score differences between forms A and B of up to 2.5 on the accuracy scale and 2.37 on the comprehension scale in the age range that concerns us (Neale, 1958, pp. 13 and 14), both forms are given exactly the same norms (*ibid.*, pp. 38 and 39). These very norms show that under normal circumstances raw score differences of this scale would lead to differences of up to three and four months in accuracy and comprehension reading ages respectively. The conclusion is clear: the manual is thinly disguising a worrying level of non-equivalence in the two most commonly used forms of the test, itself perhaps the most commonly used method of evaluating PR and PPP gains.

The Workshop

During Session One the parents were first introduced to each other, then instructed in the use of PR (as originally developed by Morgan and involving both simultaneous and independent reading modes). This writer described what PR involved and explained what it was attempting to do. He then demonstrated it with a volunteer child, answered questions and then asked each parent to practise it with his or her own child who came into the training room for this purpose. During the 20 minutes of practice this writer, a student psychologist and the school's peripatetic remedial reading teacher observed and offered feedback on parents' performance. Parents were then given a handout summarising the elements of PR. They were asked to use it for the following week and complete a simple record sheet after each night's reading session. The record sheet involved page number (at start and end of session), session length (in minutes) and a space for comments and teaching notes to be used by the parent as and when he or she wanted.

During Session Two the group broke into three groups to discuss any problems that may have arisen during the first week. Parents then came together to learn PPP. The session followed the same instruction, demonstration, practice, feedback and written materials sequence followed in Session One. Parents were asked to use PPP for the next week.

During the period covered by Sessions One and Two, six fourth-year girl volunteers from the local comprehensive school learned how to use PR and PPP. It was hoped that they would be able to attend the parent training sessions and learn alongside them. Some were able to. However, others were taught in a small group on their own. Training followed the same pattern described for Sessions One and Two.

Session Three was given over to discussion, in two groups, of the parents' and children's experiences of and preference for PR and PPP. Of the twelve parents involved, six chose PPP and six chose PR. Since all of the latter subgroup felt their child preferred the independent reading mode, the division between parents became solely one of error-correction strategies used. The adolescent volunteers undertook to use the same technique as had been chosen by parents in their own work with the children, and to visit the school at an agreed time each week to give one 20-minute session to each of the two children they were responsible for.

Session Four, the last, was given over to a discussion between both parties — the parents and adolescents — of progress and problems using the preferred technique. Both sets of tutors were asked whether they wanted to carry on using the techniques for a second month. All parents except one said they would, although at a lower frequency. All the comprehensive school volunteers said they would continue. Post-workshop questionnaire forms were distributed for completion by parents and class teachers at an appropriate time — one month further hence. Arrangements were made to assess post-workshop reading fluency around the same date. The pre- and post-workshop measurement interval was therefore eight weeks.

The Results

Teacher Questionnaires (Pre- and Post-Workshop)

Teacher questionnaires before and after the workshop were available for nine of the twelve children whose parents took part. The end of term (and a move 7,000 miles east for this writer) prevented collection of the remaining three). It was possible to ascribe a numerical value to the ticks in the four boxes regarding interest, accuracy, confidence and understanding. The values were: 'very low' (1); 'low' (2); 'average' (3); 'high' (4); 'very high' (5). The questionnaire results are shown in Table 22.1. It will be seen from column 1 that, at pre-test, the children were generally judged to be below average (i.e. less than a value of 3) on all four characteristics. Columns 2 and 3 show that the average ratings for all four characteristics improved, albeit by varying amounts. Column 4 lends a note of caution to the preceding figures. It will be seen that only in one case, that of confidence, did the majority of the group improve. In every other case, the changes in mean figures were the result of a few children who were judged to have improved.

Table 22.1: Teacher Questionnaire Results (n = 9)

	Mean ratings			
	Before workshop	After workshop	Gain	Number showing gain
Confidence when reading	1.77	2.55	0.88	6
Interest in reading	2.33	2.55	0.22	2
Accuracy when reading	2.22	2.55	0.33	3
Understanding of what is being read	2.33	2.77	0.44	4

Parent Questionnaires (Pre- and Post-Workshop)

Arrangements were made for parents to mail their post-workshop questionnaire to this writer at a pre-arranged date. Like most postal ballots or surveys, this plan resulted in a poor response, one that could not be bettered for the same reasons as those outlined earlier for the teacher questionnaires. Those that were available revealed rather greater improvements than had been reported by teachers. This is in line with results from previous workshops run in four different primary schools (Winter, 1984b).

Reading Fluency (Pre- and Post-Workshop)

Analysis of each child's taped performance on texts of controlled

Table 22.2: Reading-fluency Results (n = 10)

	Mean figures Before workshop	After workshop	Change (%)	Number showing gain
Rate of reading (words per sec.)	1.24	1.45	+17	9
Error rate (% words read)	7.01	5.48	−22	7
Refusals (% errors)	15.45	11.21	−28	3*
Self-corrections (% errors)	21.27	21.34	0.0	5

* Three pupils made no refusals at pre-test, and so were incapable of improvement.

readability revealed substantial gains on three of the four measures concerned. The results are shown in Table 22.2. It will be seen that the majority of children ended the workshop period reading faster and making fewer mistakes. In addition, three of the seven children who were able to improve their refusal rate (see note to table) did in fact do so, bringing the average for the whole group down by 28 per cent. The least conclusive figures are those for self-corrections, where five children improved, while five did not, thereby leading to an unchanged average for the group.

Discussion

Taken together, the workshop results indicated an improvement in children's reading skills and attitudes as a result of parent tuition backed up in school by cross-age tutoring. Teachers' reports indicated substantial improvements (predominantly in confidence) that were confirmed in higher reading speeds, lower error rates and, to a lesser extent, lower refusal rates.

The teacher questionnaire results are of particular interest when considered in relation to the back-up provided in school. Previous studies (Winter, 1984a and b) have shown that both standardised reading test scores and reading fluency figures improve subsequent to parent tuition, regardless of whether tutoring also occurs at school. By contrast, teacher questionnaires show positive improvements only where back-up has been provided. Where it is not provided, one often observes a dramatic discrepancy between parent and teacher opinions as regards pupil gains (teachers can even report that the children have deteriorated). Where it is provided, both parents and teachers agree with each other (and with the objective data) that gains have been made. Furthermore, it is not necessary for class teachers to provide the back-up, nor for it to be provided in the classroom. Peripatetic reading teachers, other parents, volunteers, or headteachers can successfully provide back-up anywhere in school. This study offers supportive evidence for the value of back-up, and adds adolescent pupils to the list of those who can provide it. We know that peers of the same age as the target pupils can act as successful main tutors (Winter and Low, 1984). No doubt classmates could also act as back-up tutors.

Finally, fine analysis of the data reveals no significant differences between gains made by pupils under PR versus PPP. This provides support for the notion that we may as well let parents and children choose (rather than choose for them) which technique they use — at least until we have a fuller understanding of which methods work best, when and for whom.

References

Clay, M. (1979), *Reading: The Patterning of Complex Behaviour*, Heinemann Education, Auckland

Glynn, T. (1981), 'Behavioural Research in Remedial Education: More Power to the Parents', in K. Wheldall (ed.), *The Behaviourist in the Classroom: Aspects of Applied Behaviour Analysis in British Educational Contexts*, University of Birmingham Educational Review Offset Publications

Grigg, S. (1984), 'Parental Involvement with Reading: An Experimental Comparison of Paired Reading and Listening to Children Read', unpublished MSc (Educational Psychology) dissertation, University of Newcastle-upon-Tyne

Neale, M. (1958), *Manual to the Neale Analysis of Reading Ability*, Macmillan Education, London

Netley, C., Rachman, S. and Turner, R.K. (1965), 'The Effect of Practice on Performance in a Reading Attainment Test', *British Journal of Educational Psychology*, vol. 35, no. 1, 1–8

Winter, S. (1984a), 'A Short-term Paired Reading Workshop for Parents: A Controlled Study', (unpublished paper)

Winter, S. (1984b), 'Programming for Transfer with Parent Workshops', paper presented to the 1984 Cleveland County Psychological Service Conference

Winter, S. and Low, A. (1984), 'The Rossmere Peer Tutor Project', *Behavioural Approaches with Children*, vol. 8, no. 2, 62–5

23 PARENTAL INVOLVEMENT AT MOWBRAY SCHOOL

Pauline Holdsworth

This chapter describes the involvement of parents in the teaching of children with specific reading difficulties who are admitted on a short-term basis to Mowbray School. It is in four sections:

(1) A consideration of the school, its function as a centre for short-term placement, its liaison with mainstream education, and its use of direct instruction programmes.
(2) A description of the development of a working partnership between school and parents.
(3) An analysis of the nature of the groups and the results which they have achieved.
(4) An examination of the effects of long-term follow-up and of their implications for future work.

The School

Mowbray School was purpose-built to accommodate children with a wide range of special educational needs. Since its inception it has catered for the needs of groups of children with specific reading difficulties, moderate learning difficulties, language problems, and emotional and behavioural problems. The school serves a large rural area in North Yorkshire which imposes practical constraints on parental involvement schemes.

The Short-term Placement System

The first group of children with specific reading difficulties was admitted to school in November 1981, and the demand for such places meant that further groups were established subsequently. The staff involved with these were very aware of remedial intervention programmes which dramatically accelerated reading development initially, but the long-term effects of which were negligible. The aim of the staff was to attempt to design a short-term placement system which would have effective long-term implications. It was envisaged that there would be three different but interlocking types of intervention which would continue when the child returned to the mainstream, and thus span approximately a two-year period.

Design of the Intervention System

(1) The initial stage which is offered at Mowbray School is a restricted curriculum, biased towards literacy.
(2) The second stage, which is developed alongside the first, is the parent training. This attempts to ensure that parental involvement will help produce and maintain accelerated reading gains.
(3) Stage three involves the liaison between mainstream schools, Mowbray School and parents, and operates for three terms after the child has completed its placement at Mowbray. The aim is to ensure the generalisation and maintenance of reading skills acquired at Mowbray.

Selection Procedure

Children are identified as having specific reading difficulties by the special education advisory service and educational psychologists. All children thus identified are then tested using the placement test for the Corrective Reading Programme.

The majority of the children are of junior school age. They are said to be of average or above average ability and most have had remedial help in their own school, but have made little or no progress over a period of a year or more. Characteristics of children in these groups include short attention span, distractability, attention-seeking, high levels of anxiety, memory deficit and reversal problems.

Parents are encouraged to visit the school, initially to assist them in deciding on the desirability of the placement and later to attend workshops where the nature of their involvement in the programme is explained.

Liaison with Mainstream Schools

Once a place has been accepted, the mainstream school is asked to complete a brief report on the child's level of performance in the basic subjects, and their staff are invited to visit Mowbray to observe the groups at work.

The child's contact with the feeder school is maintained by encouraging attendance at its special functions (sports days, etc.), and by a return to the school for the last week of each term. The progress of the children is reviewed termly and a report is sent to mainstream schools and the parents.

At the end of the final term a liaison meeting is held. It aims to give an overview of the reading programmes completed; to describe the parental involvement, including precision teaching; to identify ways in which progress may be generalised and maintained.

It was anticipated, and indeed experience has shown, that the last crucial aim is difficult to achieve. In order to move towards solving this problem a number of procedures have been established:

(1) An information sheet is distributed, outlining the teaching points which need to be covered and listing material which may be used.
(2) The children are all placed on reading schemes available in their schools.
(3) A record system, involving the noting and checking of errors and a weekly timed read, is started. Parents are fully involved.
(4) Liaison visits are made — twice in the first term and once in the following two terms. Additional visits are made and may continue beyond the agreed three terms on request.
(5) All the children are tested at the end of each term by the headteacher of Mowbray and the results are then discussed with the mainstream staff.
(6) Mainstream staff are invited to courses held at Mowbray School.

The Introduction of Direct Instruction

Eclectic methods of teaching reading were found to be not entirely suited to the needs of the short-term placement group. The teacher recognised that a programme was required: (i) which was highly structured and would accelerate learning, making short-term placement feasible; (ii) which had an objective measure to help the selection of children for the groups; (iii) which could predict the intervention period required to assist in forward planning; and (iv) which was new with regard to method and material — an important consideration when working with children who have experienced failure.

It was found that the Corrective Reading Programme: (i) was certainly highly structured, and research in the USA and Australia supported its claim to accelerate learning; (ii) provided a placement test to aid the selection of groups; (iii) made possible an estimate of the time needed to achieve a given objective through its division into three levels with a stated number of lessons in each; and (iv) offered a teaching method which was different in that the teacher used scripted lessons, the group was required to respond on signal, and materials were presented in an unusual form.

Two groups were identified by use of the placement test — one in need of the first programme and the other at the second level. Initially, one lesson was taught per day, but the weekly sessions were increased from five to nine once the staff and children had become accustomed to the method and format of the lessons.

Parental Involvement

Mowbray School aims to develop a partnership with all parents in the education of their children. It was recognised, however, that parental involvement would be especially important if rapid progress was to be made and maintained with children on a short-term placement. At first, many of the parents were found to be extremely anxious, but this seemed to decrease as they discovered that they had an active role to play in their child's reading programme — and that they would be trained, given clear directives and placed in an important position with regard to monitoring the development of their child's fluency through the use of precision teaching.

Initial Reservations and Revelations

Although the Corrective Reading Programme seemed to meet the criteria identified by the teacher, it was not embarked upon without reservation. The tendency of the teacher to view the design of the programme too simplistically generated many of the initial apprehensions which evaporated as knowledge of the programme increased and positive feedback was received from the group.

The sessions were very teacher-orientated and initially it appeared that only rote learning was taking place. In time, it was in fact found that basic rules were taught which could be generalised giving the children greater independence.

The scripting and signalling superficially appeared to be very constrictive and mechanistic. It was found, however, to free the teacher to attend to the children's learning, once the teacher and the group were familiar with the format.

The fact that it was an American programme posed the question 'Would the Americanisms and cultural bias be outside the experience of the group?' Actually, it was found that the influence of American television programmes and comics made the language more acceptable to the children than to the teachers. It could also be used positively to develop comprehension skills as teacher and children searched the text to illuminate unfamiliar words and phrases.

The programme emphasises decoding and the teacher was concerned that comprehension might not keep pace with the development of decoding skills, thus leaving a child 'barking at print'. However, the gains in comprehension have often been remarkable.

It was impossible to predict if the children would be able to work as intensely as required, as many were described as having a short attention span, while the programme demanded full attention for a period of approximately 45 minutes. In fact, it was found that the essential rapid pacing and pupil–teacher interactions were very motivating and held the attention of the group.

The programme was intended for senior remedial pupils and it was not known if the material would appeal to younger children. However, these junior-age children found the stories both interesting and amusing.

Development of a Working Partnership

When the decision was taken to use a direct instruction programme it was obvious that if parents were to play an active role in their children's learning they would need to be trained. The programme introduces some sound/symbol associations which are unfamiliar and the teaching of signalling and blending all needed to be covered. Parent training should then ensure that school and home work together with the child in a way which is consistent, encouraging and successful. The outline of the contents of the workshops is given in Table 23.1.

Pamphlets have been prepared for use in each of five workshop sessions. These are used in training the parents, but also provide a record of the ground covered and an available prompt, if necessary, when working at home.

The Structure of Workshop One

Parents are taught the sound/symbol associations used in the programme, as a group, using the direct instruction method of model–lead–test. They are required to answer on signal working from the blackboard with the teacher. No individual responses are asked for, otherwise they are taught like their children, with generous praise for effort.

Attention is then drawn to the two signals used by the teacher when teaching the sounds: the point–touch for continuous sounds and the quick tap for short sounds. This blackboard work session continues until the group is reasonably firm. There is then a role play. First the teacher plays the part of the child and all parents present a sound with the appropriate signal. Then the script is also practised, 'What sound?' being accompanied

Table 23.1: Parent Workshops

Workshop	Time	Programme level	Content
One	Term 1: week 1–2	'A'	(1) Introduction to the programme (2) Sound/symbol association (3) Signalling — tap and touch (4) Parental Involvement I
Two	Term 1: week 2–3	'A'	(1) Sequencing, blending sounds and signalling (2) Reading the fast way (3) Correction procedures (4) Parental Involvement II
Three	Term 2: week 1–2	'B'	(1) Introduction to precision teaching (2) Role-play session (3) Parental Involvement III
Four	Term 2: week 3–4	'B'	(1) Correction procedures (2) Firming (3) Preview of extra support materials (4) Parental Involvement IV
Five	Term 3	—	(1) A review of progress (2) Preparation for Stage Three (3) An introduction to 'Shared Reading'* (4) Parental Involvement V

* Simultaneous or synchronised reading.

by the signal. Next the parents work in pairs, presenting sounds to each other with the appropriate signal.

Parents are then taught the correction procedure to use if their child makes an error — model, lead and test. The need to correct immediately and not impatiently is stressed! There is then a further role play. First the teacher plays the part of a child making an error, and all the parents correct, then the parents work again in pairs.

A final session from the blackboard concentrates especially on sounds which are found difficult by the children, and the unusual sounds such as 'qu' (pronounced 'coo') and 'y' ('ye').

Parental Involvement I

Parents are requested:

(1) To hear their child read the sounds in the first lessons of the workbook each evening and to use the appropriate signals.

(2) To use the correction procedure taught if the child makes an error and to underline that sound so that the teacher is also alerted.
(3) To give extra attention to sounds already underlined by the teacher.
(4) To initial each lesson they have checked and to make any comments they feel necessary, e.g. 'Joanne is still reading "e" for "a" '.
(5) To give praise liberally!

The structure of Workshop One and the methods used provide the basic format for all the training sessions. The material covered in each session can be seen in Table 23.1. However, the developing involvement of the parents requires more detailed description.

Parental Involvement II

Parents are requested to check reading of words:

(1) To check their child reading the words from the worksheet(s) that have been completed that day (the parent's script is contained in the pamphlet).
(2) To underline words the child misreads.
(3) To return to errors at the end of the session, including the words underlined by the teacher, and to teach to these errors.
(4) To initial lessons checked and make any necessary remarks.
(5) To give their child encouragement.

Parents are also asked to check reading of sentences:

(1) To check the reading of the sentences.
(2) To record the errors.
(3) To time the read.
(4) To teach to the errors.
(5) To complete the record sheet at the back of the child's workbook and many any comments necessary.
(6) To give praise.

Parental Involvement II

As part of the precision teaching procedure, parents are requested (for day one):

(1) To hear their child read for exactly one minute from the probe sheet. (This consists of a passage of approximately 200 words taken from lessons ending in 4 or 8 from Corrective Reading

Programme Level B. There are 28 probes in all.)
(2) To note any errors by scoring through the words misread.
(3) To record the total number of words read correctly and the errors on the ratio graph.
(4) To make a list of error words and teach to the errors.

For day two parents are asked:

(1) To teach to the errors.
(2) To let the child practise reading the probe sheets.
(3) To time the child for one minute, again noting any errors.
(4) To record the data on the graph.
(5) To make a list of error words, as in day one.

This procedure is repeated until the criterion has been reached. Then the probe sheets are returned to school. The criterion for this programme is 100 or more words to be read in one minute on two consecutive days, with two or fewer errors.

All sheets are returned to school once per week for the child's progress to be checked and for help to be given if necessary.

Parental Involvement IV

Parents are requested:

(1) To continue with the precision teaching.
(2) To use the correction procedures taught.
(3) To make use of any supporting material sent home. (This could be preparation for lessons or probe sheets concentrating on a specific difficulty with words, e.g. moping/mopping or b/d confusion.)
(4) To give their child every encouragement.

Parental Involvement V

Parents are requested:

(1) For an initial eight-week commitment to use Shared Reading. (A folder, record sheets and a guide are provided. It is stressed that this technique, which consists of parent and child reading together in synchrony, is one which they will be able to use to help their child read a variety of material after the initial project ends.)
(2) To continue to use the record system with books from school.

(3) To continue to give their child every help and encouragement on reintegration.

Practical Considerations

The first and main difficulty is imposed by the large catchment area which means that some parents have to make journeys of over an hour to reach the school. This drastically reduces the number of workshops it is practical to run.

Second, the sessions have to be very concentrated. It is not always possible to spend sufficient time for all parents to be as confident as is desirable. If parents do have difficulties these have to be resolved by letter or telephone.

Third, at least one child in each group has had parents who have been unable to attend the workshops for a variety of reasons, including the fact that they were illiterate, they worked at night, they were single parents with younger children, or had no transport. The last problem can usually be solved through the school. If parents are unable to help the child with the homework or precision teaching this is covered as far as possible by the teacher and volunteer helpers in school.

Fourth, parents are not always able to attend all the workshops. Depending upon the reason for non-attendance and the workshop missed, the pamphlet for that workshop is sent home and a phone call or letter sent to help explain what has been covered. If possible, an alternative meeting is arranged.

Fifth, precision teaching is used to improve the child's fluency of reading, to provide valuable daily feedback to all concerned and to enable children to reach their maintenance of skill level more quickly than if the direct instruction programme was solely relied upon. It is regretted that time does not allow for parents to be trained to use this method in a more sophisticated way.

Sixth, it is not always easy to maintain all the parents' high level of involvement. Initially they are very conscientious but some spend less time working with their children towards the end of the placement.

The parents are asked for different kinds of involvement as time passes and positive feedback is given to attempt to maintain their involvement.

A group record sheet is kept so that praise and encouragement can be given, not only by the teacher, but by the group. This often urges the group on to complete the probes with their parents.

Monitoring Parental Involvement

A record of parental involvement is now available from:

(1) a check of all lessons initialled;
(2) the reading record sheets completed;
(3) the probe sheets returned and the ratio graphs;
(4) The 'Shared Reading' record sheets.

The Characteristics of the Groups

The actual teaching groups consisted of 11–13 pupils of both junior and senior age (some part-time), with a wide span of ability and, as reported earlier, a variety of problems. The data presented in this paper cover only the children of junior school age. Across-group comparisons may be very misleading as the groups were in no way homogeneous. The wide ranges of results often defy adequate description when encapsulated in a 'mean score'.

Results from Standardised Tests. The first group was tested using Daniels and Diack Standard Test of Reading Skill. The results may be unreliable as there was only seven months between the tests (see Table 23.2). The group all made progress in reading accuracy of between six months and 1 years 5 months. All other groups were tested using the Neale Analysis of Reading Ability, as this seemed to be the most appropriate test available, despite doubts raised with regard to the actual cross-reliability of the so-called 'parallel' forms A, B and C.

The results at the end of the Corrective Reading Programme support a number of observations.

(1) Test results show that *all* children have made progress in both reading accuracy and comprehension.

(2) Comparison of total mean gains across groups is inappropriate as these are contaminated by a varying time factor. For a clearer picture, the range of ratio scores (months of reading age gain per month elapsed) is presented in Figure 23.1. A wide range of progress can be seen from this table, 0.7 to 3.6 months of ratio gain, in fact.

(3) It has become apparent that the Corrective Reading placement test alone is not a fine enough measure to select homogeneous groups. At present the placement test is the only measure common to all groups, no allowance is made for variable background factors, and so the groups cannot be regarded as 'matched'.

(4) Children admitted for the Corrective Reading Programme Level B would be expected to have higher entry skills, and the majority have

Table 23.2: Reading Test Results

(a) Four months between tests (Group H)

n	Sex	Mean C.A. (yrs)	Mean Retardation (yrs of R.A.)	Mean Reading Age (yrs): Neale Analysis Forms A-B					
				Pre-test		Post-test		Gain	
				Acc.	Comp.	Acc.	Comp.	Acc.	Comp.
8	F 1 M 7	10.07	2.15	7.92	8.39	8.87	9.79	0.95	1.40

(b) Seven months between tests
(i) Group HO

n	Sex	Mean C.A.	Mean Retardation	Mean Reading Age (yrs): Daniels & Diack Test 1		
				Pre-test	Post-test	Gain
9	F 1 M 8	9.85	2.82	7.03	8.07	1.04

(ii) Group H2b

n	Sex	Mean C.A.	Mean Retardation	Mean Reading Age (yrs): Neale Analysis Forms A-B		
				Pre-test Accuracy	Post-test Accuracy	Gain Accuracy
5	F 1 M 4	9.92	2.58	7.34	8.93	1.59

(c) Ten months between tests
(i) Group H2a

N	Sex	Mean C.A.	Mean Retardation	Mean Reading Age (yrs): Neale Analysis Forms A-B					
				Pre-test		Post-test		Gain	
				Acc.	Comp.	Acc.	Comp.	Acc.	Comp.
6	F 2 M 4	8.88	2.09	6.79	6.9.1	8.12	8.65	1.33	1.74

(ii) Group H3

N	Sex	Mean C.A.	Mean Retardation	Mean Reading Age (yrs): Neale Analysis Forms A-B					
				Pre-test		Post-test		Gain	
				Acc.	Comp.	Acc.	Comp.	Acc.	Comp.
10	F 2 M 8	8.99	1.57	7.42	7.42	8.63	9.21	1.21	1.79

(iii) Group H4

N	Sex	Mean C.A.	Mean Retardation	Mean Reading Age (yrs): Neale Analysis Forms A-B					
				Pre-test		Post-test		Gain	
				Acc.	Comp.	Acc.	Comp.	Acc.	Comp.
8	F 1 M 7	8.97	1.83	7.14	7.01	8.49	8.83	1.35	1.82

Figure 23.1: Comparison of Ratio Gains in Reading Accuracy

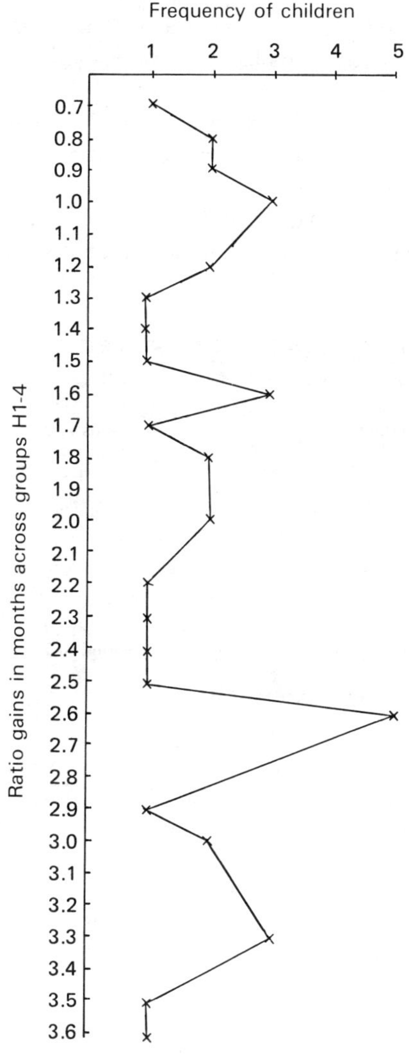

(Mean ratio gain = 1.997)

made greater gains over time than children admitted for Level A. The mean ratio gain for the children placed on Level B is 2.76 months and for those on Level A 1.5 months.

(5) An examination of the ratio gains across all groups (Figure 23.1) shows that 79 per cent of the children have made gains in excess of the 'normal rate'.

(6) In the highest-scoring group only one child had parents who were described as being spasmodically involved in their child's programme. On the other hand, in the group scoring one month or less, all but one were described as having spasmodic, little or no help at home. Parental involvement in the programme as a whole is therefore seen as a significant factor.

Subjective Feedback: from Parents. This has been collected in three ways: (i) from a record kept of any comments made by parents; (ii) from parents' comments on the termly report sheets; and (iii) from interviews with parents at the end of the placement.

Information collected from these three sources naturally covers a wide spectrum, but certain themes were found to recur.

(1) Changes in the children's general behaviour were observed. Parents reported that children had 'blossomed', or were more confident in themselves and much happier about going to school.

(2) Parents reported their satisfaction with their children's improved reading ability, which often seemed to them more than that indicated by the gain on the reading test.

(3) Parents observed their children not only choosing to read more but making more of their reading. They were reported as reading a variety of printed matter — television programmes, signposts, advertisements and books — many bought several years earlier. They then used their reading to recommend television programmes to the family, for example, or to read a story to a younger child or to help navigate a new route.

(4) The parents' anxiety about reintegration into the mainstream school was very obvious. The majority have asked for a longer placement, usually until secondary transfer.

Subjective Feedback: from Children. This has been collected from: (i) observed behaviour; (ii) a record of comments; and (iii) a semi-structured interview conducted by a voluntary helper well known to the group. Four main themes are discernible.

(1) The children think that they have made progress and are much better readers or 'better at doing things at school'.
(2) They are very happy at Mowbray School and the majority would like to remain.
(3) They all thought their parents were pleased with them because they were better readers.
(4) They liked being able to read things for themselves 'instead of just hanging around waiting for somebody else to tell you what it says'.

Long-term Follow-up

Feedback from Schools

The majority of schools have reported satisfaction with the placement and reintegration. Most of the children are reported as making good use of their reading and joining in classroom activities with their peers. Of the 35 children reintegrated, only two are perceived by their schools as having acute reading difficulties which prevent them joining in class activities. Schools have usually been very surprised if the end-of-term results have indicated regression or, at best, slow progress.

After the initial direct instruction groups were reintegrated, schools reported difficulty replacing children on more traditional material. This is now covered by Mowbray staff. Some schools asked if more attention could be paid to written work, and again the programme at Mowbray was modified. Advice and materials on writing and spelling have been distributed to both schools and parents.

Follow-up Test Results

No data are available for the first group (H0). Table 23.3 shows the results for Group H1. The top half shows the results for a subgroup (a) formed by three pupils from Mowbray, plus two more from the junior school, where a mini-experiment was run for ten weeks. This group was taught twice per week Corrective Reading Programme Level C. The results were very encouraging. The second subgroup (b) received a normal primary programme, with some modifications depending upon the resources of the school. The results were very uneven, but the rate of progress had fallen for the majority of the group.

The follow-up results for the other groups, who returned to primary school, were disappointing. At follow-up varying from three to five months later, the mean ratio gains were less than one for all groups on reading

Table 23.3: Follow-up at Ten Weeks (Group H1)

(a) This subgroup was taught Corrective Reading 'C'

		Mean Reading Age (yrs): Neale Analysis Form B-C					
	Mean	Pre-test		Post-test		Gains	
n Sex	C.A.	Acc.	Comp.	Acc.	Comp.	Acc.	Comp.
5 F 2 M 3	10.25	9.01	9.34	10.08	10.79	1.07	1.45

(b) This subgroup returned to primary school

		Mean Reading Age (yrs): Neale Analysis Form B-C					
	Mean	Pre-test		Post-test		Gains	
n Sex	C.A.	Acc.	Comp.	Acc.	Comp.	Acc.	Comp.
4 M	10.28	8.97	10.12	9.21	10.56	0.24	0.24

accuracy, and for four out of six groups on reading comprehension. One group actually showed a (very small) loss on both accuracy and comprehension. A variety of forms of the Neale Analysis were used, and this did not seem to affect the results in any systematic way.

It was acknowledged from the outset that continuation of progress after return to mainstream would be difficult to achieve. This outcome raises a number of questions.

Were the children selected by suitably sensitive screening procedures? Were they returned to mainstream too early in the programme sequence? What would be the effect of completing Level C before return? In view of individual differences in rates of learning and levels of self-motivation, is the plan by which pupils are returned to the mainstream after a fixed period of instruction too rigid? What other criteria could be used? Is the climate in the receiving school conducive to continuing progress on the part of the pupil? Do teachers regard the 'Mowbray experience' as 'a complete cure'? Is the communication system effective in relaying appropriate information on individual cases? Does sufficient supportive and developmental expertise exist? Is the organisation structured to capitalise on such expertise? Is the school geared to involving and channelling the enthusiasm and assistance of parents?

Future Plans

It is vitally important that stage three of the intervention is given special consideration by everyone involved, so that the chances of success are enhanced.

First, reintegration might begin earlier, so that the teacher from Mowbray could spend several half-day sessions working alongside the class teachers and assisting in:

(i) the development of a structured programme of work, using materials available in the school, or which could be borrowed from the resource centre;
(ii) the introduction of a record system, incorporating fluency and error checks;
(iii) the encouragement of parental involvement with the record system and with Shared Reading.

Second, it is envisaged that in the first term a liaison 'surgery' may be arranged at Mowbray when time could be given to a consideration of problems encountered in individual schools and an exploration of possible solutions.

Third, it is planned to focus attention upon the importance of parental involvement in children's learning by running a day conference in conjunction with the special education support team.

Fourth, a retiming of the admissions is also being considered so that children are not returned to schools in the summer term which appears to be very unsettling.

Fifth, a change in timing would mean that the two groups would run in parallel and it may be possible for one to work slightly more slowly for children who need extra practice.

Sixth and last, the encouraging nature of follow-up results from children who have participated in a Shared Reading project suggest that it might be beneficial for all the children to be involved with their parents in a similar venture.

Experiences to date of involving parents as partners in developing their children's reading has certainly shown that rapid progress can be made, and if this involvement is encouraged and continued, such progress may be maintained.

Further Reading

Ainscow, M. and Tweddle, D.A. (1979), *Preventing Classroom Failure: An Objectives Approach*, Wiley and Son, Chichester

Greening, M. and Spenceley, J.M. (1984), 'Shared Reading: A Review of the Cleveland Project', *In-Psych: Bulletin of the Cleveland County Psychological Service*, vol. 11, no. 2, 10–13

Levey, B. and Emsley, D. (1982), 'Involvement of Parents in the Teaching of DISTAR Reading to Slow Learning Children', *Occasional Papers of the Division of Education and Child Psychology, British Psychological Society*, vol. 6, no. 1, 43–6

Matthews, C.F. and Booth, S.R. (1982), 'Precision Teaching: Or How to Find Out If Your Teaching Is Effective without Waiting a Term or Even a Year', *Remedial Education*, vol. 17, 4–7

Muncey, J. and Williams, H. (1981), 'Daily Evaluation in the Classroom', *Special Education: Forward Trends*, vol. 8, no. 3, 31–4

Raybould, E.C. and Solity, J.E. (1982), 'Teaching with Precision', *Special Education: Forward Trends*, vol. 9, no. 2, 9–13

PART 2:

PARENTAL INVOLVEMENT IN READING IN ACTION

D. VARIATIONS

24 AN INTRODUCTION TO VARIATIONS

Sheila Wolfendale

It was a difficult task for the editors to decide upon categories of parental involvement in reading which appear to be hard and fast.

A number of schemes are exclusive and 'pure', their intention overall being to explore a particular method, to build in controlling factors and to evaluate the effects and effectiveness of that method. Schemes are included in the previous sections on the criterion that a certain method is demonstrably the dominant one.

Projects in *this* section are characterised by their heterogeneity in terms of a mix of teaching methods — for example, the chapter by Trevor Bryans and his colleagues, who describe a combination of parent reading (child listening) and paired reading. Colin Tyre and Peter Young describe the adoption of a holistic approach, wherein a number of contributing components can be identified, such as general support for the children and parents in the scheme over a prolonged period of time, and the provision of 'holiday schools' to maintain motivation and progress. In the study by Lorraine Wareing, the intention was to compare concurrent use of different methods. Tessa Cooknell describes a project which included team work as a core component, as well as a variety of teaching methods.

The Fox Hill school-based reading workshops provide a demonstration of the potential for maximising in an organised and concerted way the contribution of parents coming into school 'to help'. The work of Sue Buckley with young Down's Syndrome children and their parents has caught the attention of the media, of professionals' and parents' associations, and again demonstrates the value of the 'method' in promoting measurable progress, as well as providing parents with techniques to play a crucial part early on in their child's development and skill-acquisi tion.

Strictly speaking, then, this section outlines work which is not only a *variation* of a 'one method' approach, but which in some instances intentionally *combines* methods and approaches. The importance of this section lies in the fact that we are still at an early and exploratory stage.

It may be too early to gauge which of a number of 'techniques' of intervention designed to bring teachers and parents together in a common cause is the 'best buy'. It may finally be invidious to view parental involvement in reading in these terms, in the expectation that we could ever evolve one formula — especially when the context into which it falls, that of the teaching and learning of reading itself, has been riven by competing and conflicting theories and their derived practice.

Accordingly, while it may not be right and proper to be prescriptive, it is possible, having identified methods and schemes that demonstrably 'work', to identify further a number of requisites that can be built in to promote, if not to guarantee, success. We aim to provide guidelines and planning considerations in Chapter 32.

This introduction will round off by reference to variations on the theme which are not included in this book, but which are written up elsewhere and which provide further proof as to the potential of model-building in this area.

(1) 'Shared Reading' may legitimately be regarded as a variation on Paired Reading, but one which has its own intrinsic rationale. It is in fact described by its authors (Greening and Spenceley, 1984) as 'a simplified version of the Paired Reading technique'. They examine presumed disadvantages of the independent-reading mode (cf. Chapter 11), which is borne out by a little evidence, and endorse simultaneous reading.

The reading gains made by second-year junior children after the eight-week long study using the simultaneous-reading mode only convinced Greening and Spenceley that the approach was worth while. A further aspect built into the programme was the instruction to parents to pay no attention to mistakes, but to continue reading with the child even if he or she could manage only a few words of the text. An eleven-page teachers' manual has been produced by the authors.

(2) Although the bulk of parental involvement in reading work has appeared in print between the late 1970s and the present time, an article in the journal *Reading* (Coulson and Howells, 1975) heralded this upsurge of interest. Their account of a project which involved four infants' schools showed the multifaceted nature of parental involvement in reading, and that the perceived benefits are various. The main aim was to create or recreate interest in books.

Parents of infants who were poor readers were asked to read aloud to their children using books from school (picture books, story and factual books). The parental training and the consequent activities seem from a contemporary vantage-point to be fairly blunt, which is inevitable in innovative work that is then replicated and developed from the embryonic idea.

The study was a valuable precursor of later work, and indeed turned out to have an immediate influence on local schools. The dearth of pre- and post-test measures has an interesting and relevant bearing on the work reported in this book. Issues are highlighted which relate to whether some planning considerations are optional, or should be a mandatory part of any involvement in a reading project that seeks to test hypotheses.

One view is that work that is evidently part and parcel of educational provision and routinely available within a school need not be evaluated so stringently, using the parallel that school lessons *per se* are not thus evaluated. Another view is that hypothesis-testing exercises ought by definition to be amenable to the acccepted features of experimental design, in so far as is feasible within a 'real life' situation. Questions pertaining to evaluation are considered in Chapter 31.

(3) One particular variation and expression of parental involvement in reading was described in 1978 by Obrist (1978) in a piece entitled *How to Run Family Reading Groups*. Parents and their children meet (in local libraries, schools, community centres) to read and review books. A review form was devised for parents to record their own and their children's reactions to the material.

Waites and Swindon (1981) adopted this model for school-based family reading groups. Margaret Swindon provides a parent's view of the value of reading for information and pleasure at home, and in particular of the tremendous benefits of family reading. Thorpe (1982), a schools librarian, extended the idea to include secondary-aged children and their families, and this example illustrates the applicability of family reading to 'pre-readers', to beginning readers, and to older children who are developing higher-order literacy skills. The prime aim is to establish a habit in children (and their parents?) of 'voluntary reading' (Irving, 1980) which will be sustained in later life.

It will be seen that some projects described in this book include measures by which to gauge pre- and post-project attitude change by the participants, usually via questionnaire. Few studies have attitudes as the main focus, however. In studies where investigating attitude to the exercise is ancillary, the index is crude and in the form of a 'yes/no/comments' questionnaire. More elaborate investigations would require more complex exploration into attitudes to reading teaching and learning as well as the perceived effectiveness of the parental involvement. Two studies that have attempted to delve into this little-investigated phenomenon are those of Ayres (1984) and English (1983).

The work characterised in this section as being 'variations' provides yet further confirmation of the sheer vitality and viability that is the hallmark of parental involvement in children's reading.

References

Ayres, J. (1984), 'Parental Involvement with Remedial Reading', unpublished MSc dissertation, Institute of Education, University of London

Coulson, N. and Howells, R. (1975), 'Parental Involvement in Children's Reading', *Reading* (United Kingdom Reading Association), vol. 9, no. 3, 9–13

English, A. (1983), 'A Study to Measure Attitude Change Following a Parental Involvement with Reading Scheme', unpublished MSc dissertation, North East London Polytechnic

Greening, M. and Spenceley, J. (1984), *Paired Reading Made Easy*, Cleveland County Psychological Services

Irving, A. (1980), *Promoting Voluntary Reading for Children and Young People*, UNESCO, Paris

Obrist, C. (1978), *How to Run Family Reading Groups*, Occasional Publication, United Kingdom Reading Association

Thorpe, D. (1982), 'Family Reading Groups: The Beginnings of a Community Experience in West Hertfordshire', *Reading* (United Kingdom Reading Association), vol. 16, no. 3, 143–52

Waites, T. and Swindon, M. (1981), 'Family Reading Group', *Reading* (United Kingdom Reading Association), vol. 15, 41–7

25 THE KINGS HEATH PROJECT

Trevor Bryans, Anne Kidd and Marie Levey

This four-phase project, based at the Kings Heath Child Advisory and Psychological Service, Birmingham, was carried out over a period of more than two years during which time 46 children and their families participated. The first two phases of the project were located in a secondary school, the last two in a primary school. As the project progressed, a number of modifications were made because the authors wished either to generate new hypotheses or to respond to the needs of a new situation.

In this chapter it is proposed to describe the four phases of the Parental Involvement in Reading Project, with a short summary on the issues arising from each phase.

Phase One: Selection of Children

At the time when the first phase of the project was set up (May 1982) most of the reported studies of parental involvement in reading had been carried out at the infant and junior school stages. The authors wished to try out a parental involvement programme using a group of secondary age children, partly because of the schools' request to the attached educational psychologist for some form of specific intervention with first-year children who had acknowledged difficulties.

The comprehensive school was a five-form entry, 11–18 age group, banded into three groups from the first year. Approximately 60 children in the third band were placed in three classes in order to have only 20 pupils in each class. These first-year 'bottom' sets are made up of children with a history of lower performance in junior school, based on lower standardised test scores and teachers' reports. In general, these children in the third-band classes moved through the day as a group from lesson to lesson, experiencing the full range of the curriculum — with the exception of French.

At an initial meeting with staff from the school a list of names was drawn up. All these children were in the third band of the first year of the school. The main criterion for inclusion on the list at this stage was that children should have reading ages of around nine years in order to facilitate progress and minimise the number of difficulties, hesitations and errors experienced when reading with their parents. In practice, however, the range of reading-attainment scores on the Neale Analysis of Reading Ability was much greater than this.

Second, only children whose parents were thought to be able to support their children (for whatever reason) in monitoring and maintaining all aspects of the programme were included.

Letters were sent to 13 sets of parents with a tear-off slip for return to the school. Nine parents expressed interest in becoming involved with the project.

Paired Reading: A Variation

The choice of any one technique or method of instructing pupils in any curriculum area is usually a combination of faith and experience to date. Hewison and Tizard (see Chapter 4) noted that a parent listening to the child reading aloud regularly was in itself the most important variable in the child's subsequent success. The work of Miller *et al.* (see Chapter 13) had begun to demonstrate that children with difficulties may need a more specific type of intervention, namely Paired Reading.

In the present study, because the pupils were known to have learning difficulties, the method of parental involvement in reading chosen was a variation of the Paired Reading technique as described by Morgan and Lyon (see Chapter 12). This technique is already noted elsewhere in this book and involves a simultaneous phase of reading together and an independent phase, where the child signals her or his intention to read alone. It was decided to simplify and extend this technique to the following three-stage format.

In Stage One, the parent would have to read a selected passage of eight to ten lines of print with the child following the text. Stage Two could involve the child and parent simultaneously rereading the same passage with the parent either correcting errors or supplying the word if the child hesitates or 'refuses' for five seconds. Finally, Stage Three would involve the child attempting to read the entire passage on her or his own. Persisting errors occurring at this point were to be corrected by the parent and reinforcement in the form of praise given on correct completion of units of the passage, usually a sentence.

The main reason for adopting this variation of Paired Reading was that a short pilot using two children on the Morgan and Lyon method indicated that the error rate was very high when the reading material, chosen by the child primarily for interest, was difficult. Frequent pauses and stoppages in order to correct the child — no matter how sensitively executed — did tend to reduce both flow and comprehension of passages. So the choice seemed to be between using the Morgan and Lyon method with a carefully controlled range of books in terms of difficulty — or to use a simplified version of their technique which undoubtedly was more repetitious but would give parents and children access to a wider range of books.

Preliminary Meeting with Parents

The initial meeting was held in the staffroom of the school with all of those attending sitting in soft armchairs in a circle. Tea and biscuits were served by the teachers at the start of the meeting. The purpose of the project was briefly explained and then the precise requirements of the parents' involvement was explained. This included a discussion of what to encourage and what to avoid in helping a child to read, as well as an explanation of how the record form was to be used and filled in after each reading session with the child. Most of the questions posed at that preliminary meeting with the parents were to do with the practical difficulties of organising times to hear reading when, for example, the parent worked shifts, or specifying who would hear reading when English was not spoken at home. By the end of this meeting all of the nine parents agreed to participate in the programme, and times were agreed for the training session.

Materials

The record sheet to be filled in by the parents after each reading session was, apart from books, the only other piece of material required. This record sheet included details about the materials and page numbers read, as well as the time of reading. The record sheet also had space for comments by the parent about the reading session. The record sheets were returned to school every Monday morning in order to note parents' and children's responses to the programme. Another feature of the record sheet was the use of a triangular symbol which the parent placed under the comments column to indicate that the three stages of the reading session had been succcessfully carried out.

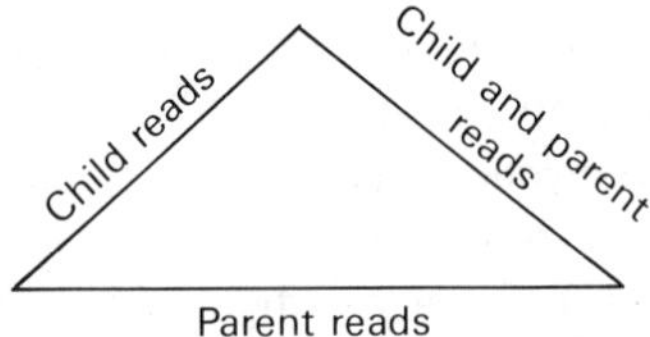

A bulk loan of 250 books was arranged from the children's section of a local library to supplement the range of books already available within the school. These books and readers were chosen by the remedial staff of the school and offered a wide range of both interest and content to the pupils. All reading schemes were excluded from the range of books on offer because it was felt that they too often bore a resemblance to school-based (and often tedious!) routines. The reading materials were placed conveniently in one of the remedial rooms where they could be chosen, exchanged and returned during the lunch-hour.

The Training Session

A single training session of approximately 30 minutes' duration was organised in school, usually during the afternoon, for all participating. The main aim of the individual training session for the involved educational psychologists and teachers was to help the parents and pupils to adjust to the requirements of the Paired Reading format, given that it is an essentially unusual reading mode which, as it turned out, none of the parents had experienced previously.

Two facets of the paired-reading method were emphasised and practised during the training session. First, parents were encouraged to reinforce the child's efforts verbally during Stage Three. Second, parents were given explicit instructions on how to correct errors.

Returning briefly to verbal reinforcement, it was observed that at the outset of the training session, in every single case, parents were quite unused to reinforcing the child's often successful attempts at reading the passage alone at Stage Three and so rarely did so. Indeed, several parents were enthusiastic 'over-correctors', waiting to pounce on errors at Stages Two and Three particularly, despite the guidance offered beforehand and the exhortations given in the handout.

The correction procedure practised was extremely simple. If the child made a mistake the parent corrected the word, asked the child to repeat the correct word, and went on. Similarly, if the child hesitated or could not identify the word the parent waited for five seconds, said the word aloud, the child repeated the word and then they went on.

Although, again in all cases, the parents and children had no difficulty whatsoever in synchronising their voices at Stage Two, there was a tendency for parents to read the passage too quickly at Stage One. It was also recommended to parents that each reading session should be for no more than 15 minutes per day on six days per week.

At the time of conducting the project (June 1982) there was little literature available on what the optimum period for a project of this sort should be. As the project required a considerable degree of commitment from both the school staff and the attached educational psychologists, it was agreed that in order to maintain a high level of motivation a period of five weeks — between early June and mid-July 1982 — would be most appropriate.

A follow-up meeting at the end of the five-week period was arranged between the parents and the professionals involved in the project.

Pre- and Post-testing

The nine children included in the project were tested at the outset of the five-week period by the head of the Remedial Department using Form 'B' of the Neale Analysis of Reading Ability. All three scores of accuracy, comprehension and rate were used. No other member of the project group knew the results of the pre-testing until after the post-testing had been carried out by another member of the project group. The testing was therefore carried out 'blind' to help minimise some of the experimenter effects which can occur in projects of this type.

Results

On average, reading accuracy for the group increased by almost ten months over the period, reading comprehension decreased by an average of four months and the reading rate decreased by an average of four months. Analysis of these results showed that of the three reading indicators sampled, only reading accuracy exhibited a statistically significant change (p 0.01 Wilcoxon Matched Pairs Test). The reading accuracy pre- and post-test scores were converted into quotients enabling age effects to be taken into account. Analysis of the accuracy quotients again indicates that the results are significant beyond the 0.01 level Wilcoxon Matched Pairs Test.

As in the case of most projects of this nature, the group trends mask very considerable variations evident with individual children. Two of the children of Asian origin presented some testing problems in that their pronunciation of individual words in the reading-test material made accurate scoring difficult for the testers in both the pre-test and the post-test, so that the large measured gains of both children in reading accuracy must be treated with some caution (child PS, 27 months; child ND, 19 months). Either leniency or excessive strictness on the part of one or other of the two testers could be responsible for some of the very high reading-accuracy gains in their cases. However, one other child (MM) whose mother was very interested in the project and who carried it out with great thoroughness, gained 14 months in reading accuracy over the course of five weeks. Another child was hospitalised for two weeks during the programme because of a broken leg and so missed a considerable, but unknown, number of reading sessions.

One very significant finding was that there is considerable evidence from the results that as reading accuracy improved, the children's reading rate in almost all cases tended to decrease, thereby casting doubt on some investigators' practice of accepting that improved rate of task performance is almost invariably to be taken as a significant indicator of improving task performance. In effect, the opposite may be true in that children's reading errors reflect poor attention to detail and minimal decoding effort with an accompanying increase in both reading rate and reading errors. It is also possible that the observed drop in comprehension may be related to this same factor (i.e. that as the pupils' reading accuracy improved, it was at the expense of comprehension).

Follow-up Meeting

A follow-up meeting was arranged for parents at the end of the project. At this meeting the parents were asked to fill in a brief question sheet on aspects of the programme. This meeting, in fact, was poorly attended with only five of the nine children represented by their parents. In general, the parents reported positive gains in their children's reading attainment, confidence and attitude to reading. One parent in response to question five ('Did you notice any differences in your child's reading?') noted:

Punctuation	—	improved
Fluency	—	improved
Accent on words	—	improved
Speed	—	decreased
Overall confidence	—	improved

These comments were fairly typical of the five parents sampled on this question. To question seven, on the desirability of running the sessions for more than five weeks, one parent recorded: 'I would wish it to be carried out for four weeks — have a break of a week or so, then continue for another four weeks'. Two other parents also suggested an intermittent approach like this over a longer period.

Most parents, as the record card shows, tended to settle into a routine of reading with the child at a particular time of the day. However, the time chosen varied from parent to parent. In some cases, the reading sessions were carried out straight after school, in others after a mid-evening snack or after watching television.

In this final meeting the parents were told about the test results of the group as a whole and not individual scores. Only by doing this could feelings of inadequacy or anxiety be reduced if comparisons were made with other children.

Summary

There was general agreement that the project, small-scale though it had been, confirmed that parental involvement in the form of Paired Reading at the secondary level was a powerful, time-inexpensive and cost-effective means of helping children with a history of reading failure at the secondary level. The staff at the school resolved to incorporate parental involvement in reading into the overall remedial provision for children in the early years of the school.

However, the authors were still concerned to explore in greater detail the kind of positive educational changes observed at Phase One.

In particular, two questions remained unanswered. For example, using children as their own controls in a rival situation such as that outlined above clearly sets up a whole range of uncontrolled 'Hawthorne effects' — including novelty change of routine within school, being selected for special attention by teachers and visitors to the school, as well as what is often a sudden upsurge in parental interest.

First, it was proposed to have a base-line observation period over which changes in attainment could also be measured. Second, the authors wished to have much more information about precisely which reading and reading-related skills change as a consequence of a period of Paired Reading intervention. So a much more comprehensive range of pre- and post-test assessment was proposed for Phase Two.

Phase Two

Phase Two of the project began in January 1983 when invitation letters were sent out to 22 parents of first-year children in the same secondary school selected by teachers as having a reading problem. Eleven parents agreed to join the project which was scheduled to run over the period of the Easter term, and to use the same Paired Reading method, record sheet and training procedure as had been employed in Phase One of the project. The reading material was chosen by the children as before from home or school, supplemented by a stock of local library books.

The design of this project was to test the eleven children on a range of tests at the beginning and end of the five-week non-intervention/base-line period and yet again at the end of the five-week intervention period.

The tests used were: the Neale Analysis of Reading Ability, Accuracy, Comprehension and Rate; Jackson Phonic Sheets 3–11; Dolch List of 89 Commonly Occurring Words; the Daniels and Diack Spelling Test.

The results of this project provided at least partial answers to some of the questions and issues posed at the outset.

First of all, there were no significant differences between the pre-intervention and base-line scores on any of the four test measures indicating that no measurable gains occurred on any of the tests used to assess reading competence during the five-week base-line period.

Reading accuracy, as measured on the Neale Analysis, improved on average by six months over the intervention period (*p*.005) Wilcoxon Matched Pairs Test. Similarly, the spelling scores of the children assessed by the Daniels and Diack Spelling Test improved significantly over the five-week intervention period (*p*.025).

Neither the scores of the children on the Jackson Phonic Sheets nor on the Dolch List showed any significant changes over the intervention period, although incomplete data giving the rate of reading on the Dolch test suggested tht if this had been used as a timed test these might have shown a positive result.

Only four of the parents were able to attend the post-intervention meeting; although all four thought the project worthwhile, two parents were unsure as to whether their children's reading had improved, while the other two thought that their children were definitely making fewer sorts of errors, particularly those of omitting or inserting words. A questionnaire given by school staff to the children at the end of the project indicated that they, too, had found reading at home extremely helpful and that they all enjoyed reading more by the end of the five-week period.

Phase Three

The next two stages of the project were conducted by Anne Kidd in a local primary school. The 15 poorest readers in the first-year junior class were selected for inclusion in the project, which was to run for five weeks during the period March–May 1983. Eleven children's parents agreed to participate. The format was identical to that described above for the secondary school. The Neale Analysis of Reading Ability and the McNally Key Words List were used as the pre- and post-test measures of children's progress.

During the two months between tests the children gained between one and five months on the Neale accuracy score with the pre- and post-project differences significant at the 0.5 level (Wilcoxon Matched Pairs Test). When corrected for age by using quotients, however, these differences were not significant. On the Key Words List all the children improved, although three children were near the ceiling score on the pre-test so could only show an improvement of between two and four words by reading all of the 200 words accurately at the post-test. For the other eight children, the number of new words read from the list ranged from eleven to 55.

The feedback from parents was considerable both during and after the project. All the parents would have wished to drop Stage Two of the three-stage format (i.e. the simultaneous-reading phase), some after one or two weeks, others right from the beginning. Eight of the parents recorded that their children's reading definitely improved — the most frequently observed improvements were expression and observation of punctuation. Two parents commented that their children read more from newspapers and other materials outside of the reading session.

Phase Four

Phase Four of the project was conducted a year later during the spring of 1984, and involved 15 first-year junior-age children using the, by now, well-established procedures. However, this time parents were given the choice as to whether or not they wished to maintain the three-stage paired reading. The overall positive results were again achieved — this time with three parents who adopted the three-stage format throughout, three parents who began by using it and four parents who dropped the simultaneous reading from the outset.

The school has now incorporated the parental involvement in reading into the school's practice.

To summarise then:

(1) Parental involvement in reading in primary and secondary schools requires a high level of planning in terms of presentation to parents and teachers in the participating school. The project is likely to be more successful if there is willingness on the part of the involved staff to meet with the parents and discuss issues of common concern, such as reading.

(2) The problems of maintaining good contact between and among parents, teachers, advisory teachers or educational psychologists are considerable, such that explicit commitments or even contracts are necessary to ensure that a project of this sort is maintained.

(3) A simple, easily taught technique such as Paired Reading is more likely, in our view, to meet with success because many involved parents either listen to their children read or evolve their own modelling, feedback and correction techniques.

(4) Parents appear to be very unused to reinforcing positively their children's efforts, and need help to overcome the tendency of 'waiting to correct errors'.

(5) Our observations lead us to assert that both primary and secondary age children's accuracy when reading aloud improves considerably as a result of Paired Reading help by their parents. However, it may be that gains could be a direct function of 'time on task'.

(6) Children who have been on Paired Reading programmes seem to display more confidence than previously.

(7) Story books and adventure stories were more frequently chosen by both primary and secondary age children.

(8) The three-stage format of paired reading used in this project did enable pupils with reading difficulties to tackle a range of books.

(9) To maintain progress over a long period it seems advisable to run the parental involvement periods at intervals throughout the school year (e.g. for one month per term).

(10) There continues to be a dearth of appropriate test/assessment materials which can be used to evaluate children's progress in reading. Most of the tests used in this series of projects gave information about single aspects of reading performance but professional judgement still played a part in this evaluation.

26 A COMPARATIVE STUDY OF THREE METHODS OF PARENTAL INVOLVEMENT IN READING

Lorraine Wareing

Preparation and Implementation

This study set out to investigate three aspects of a home-reading project; the benefits to be derived from a short-term, low-level intervention; the relative superiority of any one of three methods of parental involvement to be used; the practicalities of including (and possibly benefiting) children of non-English-speaking parents.

Three primary schools took part, each implementing one of the three methods to be described. The project team was established to include at least one teacher representative from each school. As the organisation within each school differed, selection of the parent group to be invited to attend the initial training session was at each headteacher's discretion, on the understanding that ultimately it would be possible to select from each school a group of five children from the third and fourth year juniors whose parents would be likely to commit themselves to completing the project. One parent training session was held at each school. Each followed a similar format differing only in the description of the particular home-reading method to be employed. Illustrated notes were distributed to reinforce training. Parents were then asked to consider the commitment involved and return a signed contract to confirm their willingness to participate. The use of a record card, which was to pass between home and school daily, was explained. Column headings included: 'Day', 'Time' (of session), 'Title of Book', 'Pages Read', 'Source of Book' (e.g. home, school library, etc.), 'Parents' Comments', 'Teacher's Comments'. In addition to the meeting each family was visited once during the third or fourth week of the project to help resolve difficulties and generally encourage parents to continue with the work.

Selection of subjects was limited to those who had returned their contracts by the appointed day. Control subjects were selected from those whose parents had not attended the training session nor shown any subsequent interest. Control and experimental subjects were matched approximately on age and reading ability as recorded on existing school records. Each subject (experimental and control) was then assessed by a member of the project team for reading accuracy and comprehension by means of the Neale Analysis of Reading Ability (Form B). For the following eight weeks, parents of experimental subjects helped their children to read at home according to one of the three methods outlined below.

(1) Paired-reading Method (PRM)

This method has been well documented (see Morgan and Lyon, 1978 and Chapter 12; Bushell, Miller and Robson, 1982 and Chapter 14) further accounts appear elsewhere in this volume.

(2a) Reading-aloud Method (RAM (Eng.))

Parents allocated to this method group were directed to listen to their children reading. Variations of this method are described elsewhere in this volume. In this instance a particular strategy for dealing with mistakes and unknown words was suggested whereby a short period (ten seconds) was to be allowed for the child to self-correct or 'work out' difficult words. After this pause, praise was to be given for effort or achievement, the word supplied if necessary and no further attention given to the event.

(2b) Reading-aloud Method (RAM (Non-Eng.))

Parents without a reading knowledge of English were similarly asked to hear their children read on the assumption that although they could not offer specific help with corrections or unknown words, their interest and involvement would prove motivating to the children.

(3) Linguistic Method (LM)

This, the most complicated of the methods, consisted of four different phases. In the first, the parent was to read a short but meaningful section of a book. Second, the parent and child were to talk about what had been read, the parent stimulating the child's powers of verbal expression. Then the child would retell the story in his or her own words while the parent committed it to paper. Finally, the child would read this version of the story aloud, the parent adopting the same strategies for mistakes and unknown words as used in the RAM method.

The post-tests of reading accuracy and comprehension (Neale Analysis of Reading Ability, Form A) were administered to all subjects during the week following conclusion of the project.

The intervention was intentionally 'low key', making use of school resources where possible and causing minimal disruption to school routine. On cessation of home reading a questionnaire was issued to parents to investigate the perceived usefulness of various components of the project and thereby provide information for future research.

Results

Comparison of mean group differences between pre- and post-test scores showed that: (i) greater improvements in reading accuracy had been made by the experimental groups in all conditions other than PRM; and (ii) greater gains in reading comprehension had been made by the experimental group in PRM and RAM (Eng.). However, a statistical analysis of the results using a two-way crossed ANOVA showed the differences to be insignificant. Nor did any one method of intervention prove significantly more effective than the other two.

Results from the RAM (non-Eng.) subgroup were not included in the statistical analysis, but these children appeared to derive no less benefit than the other children in the study. Average gains over the period of the project in reading accuracy and comprehension respectively were 0.16 and 0.24 years for the RAM (Eng.) group and 0.76 and 0.36 years for the RAM (non-Eng.) group.

Discussion

There are a number of possible explanations to account for why statistical analysis of the results did not show any significant gains made by children in the experimental groups.

The simplest explanation is that parental intervention of this nature, on a short-term basis, does not confer the benefits other studies lacking a control condition have suggested. It is of note here that two studies which have used a control group — namely those by Friend (1981) and Ashton and Jackson (1982) — were obliged to consider the same possibility.

An alternative explanation may be sought in the form of assessment used to measure progress. Reading is a complex process and the reading behaviour sampled in the administration of a single test may neglect areas of progress. This question of validity of reading tests is raised by Ashton and Jackson (1982). Similarly, regarding test reliability, in the absence of a test with 100 per cent test–retest reliability, conclusions drawn on the basis of test results could be used to overcome the inadequacies of a single test, but for schools attempting to involve whole year groups in parent-reading schemes the amount of time required might justifiably be considered disproportionate to the perceived usefulness of the exercise.

Moving on from reading tests, two less formal methods of evaluation did suggest that the children involved sustained benefits for which no simple measuring instrument is available. First, the school in which greatest staff enthusiasm and participation were evident used the project as a basis for generally developing home–school links and extended the scheme to include over 80 children in addition to those taking part in the research. Second, sampling of parents' opinions by means of the questionnaire confirmed that a majority of parents considered the project to have been a worthwhile undertaking and had noted an improvement in their children's attitude to reading over the period of intervention.

The comparative superiority of any one of the methods may be considered in terms of: (a) improved reading ability; and (b) simplicity of method, including case of administration and training.

Information concerning parents' implementation of the methods was gained from checklists administered at home-visit sessions. This indicated that in all but one case of PRM and two cases of LM parents had quite independently adopted methods approximating closely to the simplest method of hearing their children read aloud (i.e. that described earlier as RAM (Eng.)). The lack of a significant difference between improvements in reading across the three experimental conditions therefore probably reflects the finding that a similar method was being used by almost all parents regardless of training. The case for making use of a simple RAM technique is discussed by Dyson and Swinson (1982, and see Chapter 6) and it would seem that in the absence of costly and time-consuming training this may be the method most generally suited for use by parents.

To conclude and summarise: although improvements in the children's attitude to reading were noted by parents and teachers, no significant gains in reading as measured by a standardised reading test could be identified over the period of the project.

Experiences in other parts of the country — such as Rochdale (Jackson and Hannon, 1981 and see Chapter 5) and Haringey, London (Tizard, Schofield and Hewison, 1982 and see Chapter 4) — have shown that long-term, low-level, interventions using simple techniques can be easily integrated into school routines and can enlist and maintain parents' support over long periods. The Haringey project also showed significant improvements in reading scores on the basis of such an intervention. As the efficacy of short-term intervention is still in doubt, for schools wishing to undertake projects of parental involvement without the support of a research team and considerable additional resources, these are perhaps the most profitable way forward for the time being.

References

Ashton, C. and Jackson, J. (1982), 'Lies, Damned Lies and Statistics', *Journal of the Association of Educational Psychologists*, vol. 5, no. 10, 43–8

Bushell, R., Miller, A. and Robson, D. (1982), 'Parents as Remedial Teachers', *Journal of the Association of Educational Psychologists*, vol. 5, no. 9, 8–13

Dyson, J. and Swinson, J. (1982), 'Involving Parents in the Teaching of Reading', *Journal of the Association of Educational Psychologists*, vol. 5, no. 9, 18–22

Friend, P. (1981), 'Backing up the Parents', *Times Educational Supplement*, 30 October

Jackson, A. and Hannon, P. (1981), *The Belfield Reading Project*, Belfield Community Council, Rochdale

Morgan, R. and Lyon, E. (1979), 'Paired Reading: A Preliminary Report on a Technique for Parental Tuition of Reading-retarded Children', *Journal of Child Psychology and Psychiatry*, vol. 20, no. 2, 151–60

Tizard, J., Schofield, W.N. and Hewison, J. (1982), 'Collaboration between Teachers and Parents in Assisting Children's Reading', *British Journal of Educational Psychology*, vol. 52, 1–15

27 AN INNER-CITY HOME-READING PROJECT

Tessa Cooknell

Background

This project began in 1981 when Rod Parry was appointed head of St John's Primary School, in Ladywood, an inner-city area of Birmingham. He had had a lot of experience as a home–school liaison teacher in a priority area, and came determined to develop good relationships with the parents of his new school.

The need to use what resources there were as effectively as possible was very great, and the idea of setting up a home-reading project appealed to the teachers because it appeared to provide a powerful tool to tap parental help. Ideas came from other studies done in similarly difficult circumstances, all of them well known and described in this book. The major ones were the Haringey study (Tizard, Schofield and Hewison, 1982 and Chapter 4), the Belfield project (Jackson and Hannon, 1981 and Chapter 5), the Derbyshire project on Paired Reading (Bushell, Miller and Robson, 1982 and Chapter 14) and Ted Glynn's work, begun in Birmingham, on methods for parents to help their children read (Glynn, McNaughton, Robinson and Quinn, 1979 and Chapter 20).

The research design had to be flexible because it had no extra staff resources except a little time from the educational psychologist and remedial adviser. It had to be planned to evolve through various rough stages, adapting to changing circumstances.

This did not mean that design was to be left to chance. The phases were quite carefully timed and structured, and various types of evaluative mechanism built into each. Some parts followed a classical research design or objectives model, other parts an illuminative model (Lawton, 1980).

However, there was initially no extra money for equipment and teacher time had to come out of the normal timetable.

The project had a planning team of four teachers and two advisers.

Stage One: the Blueprint

After circulating of several discussion papers on research background, methods for parents to use and structure of a homework 'system', a 'blueprint' for a one-year project was drawn up to include both top infants' classes (44 children, aged 6–7 years). The choice of these two classes was no accident because they were taught by the head of infants and the home–school liaison teacher.

The project was planned as a pilot, to extend upwards and downwards if it worked.

The team performed a variety of functions, all contributing to each in varying degrees. The teachers took the major part in co-ordinating the homework scheme and in workshop planning and home visiting, but the remedial adviser contributed a tremendous amount to curriculum development, and she and the author masterminded much of the project design and evaluation.

Everyone was therefore able to feel that the project was theirs, but the head's skill of facilitation also contributed to the fact that there were no disputes over 'ownership' and that a team developed that communicated effectively and shared the work.

Stage Two: Curriculum Assessment

The remedial adviser set out to assess the children's reading skills and pinpoint instructional needs. She used the Neale Analysis of Reading (also a pre- and post-test measure; Neale, 1965), the Clifford Carver Word Recognition Test (Carver, 1970), and the Caerleon Assessment of Phonic Skills by Hughes (no date).

Stage Three: Curriculum Development

As a result of her findings, the adviser set to work with the staff to extend and reorganise the reading curriculum of the infants' school, a process which had started a term or two previously. Books were borrowed on block library loan, basic readers were purchased and discussions among the teachers organised on how to teach 'phonics'.

Without this basic foundation, it would have been very difficult to build up a parent curriculum.

Stage Four: Initial Meetings

Initial meetings were then held to apprise the parents of the plans for a project. Contacting some parents proved to be very difficult, and was only achieved by the teachers writing a lot of letters home and visiting the non-cooperative, some of whom remained uninterested. Nevertheless, about 90 per cent came to the meetings.

Stage Five: Workshops and Methods

A three-session workshop was run for the parents; 37–44 families were represented.

A behavioural checklist was drawn up to be used to evaluate teaching outcomes.

After an initial 'shock session' consisting of two short sketches entitled 'How Not to Do It' (i.e. hear reading) and 'How to Do It' there was discussion of teaching points and circulation of a list of 'Do's and Don'ts'. The parents were then shown and practised several techniques which they tried out on their own children, who were called in for the occasion.

These techniques were hybrids of various research techniques and the teachers' own ideas:

(1) A 'simple method' for hearing reading, where the parent learned to praise regularly, wait five seconds if a child made a mistake, to allow for self-correction, and then tell him or her the word.
(2) A 'complex method' for hearing reading taken from Ted Glynn's work (see Chapter 20), which gave different ways to correct specific types of mistake.
(3) 'Paired Reading' taught as described in the original research (see Chapter 12).
(4) A comprehensive technique in which parents were first asked to talk about the pictures and then play a game in which both parent and child took turns to formulate questions about the story.

We designed the behavioural checklist to evaluate parents' use of these techniques. Although we did use it during the workshops, it was too difficult to combine objective observation with helping parents all the time, so intervention usually took priority.

In retrospect it could be that we asked too much of the parents. Many could not read very well themselves and many spoke a Caribbean dialect or Punjabi and were not ready for refinements of technique. I was satisfied if they could establish a good rapport with their child, praise him or her and treat reading as an enjoyable task which could be practised together. I did not find that parents found praising easy, and many did not take to Paired Reading because they thought it made the child's task too easy. They did not understand the purpose of the comprehension game, which was to get the children to formulate their own ideas about a story, and often would just ask questions but not vice versa. I found this particularly so with one or two stern fathers from Pakistan who had a formal, almost Victorian, view of instruction.

However, the coaching of parents during these sessions provided some very valuable opportunities to give assistance to one or two parents or were unable to communicate with their child, without making them feel singled out for help.

Stage Six: Home Visiting

We then made a systematic attempt to follow up the workshops with home visits, behavioural checklist in hand. This continued for a month or two but then, regrettably, the remedial teacher's time was cut and she could not cover the two teachers' classes while they went out, so home visiting ceased and evaluative data were left incomplete.

Stage Seven: Homework Scheme

Meanwhile, a 'homework scheme' based on the Belfield project (see Chapter 5) went into operation, with work set five nights a week for 10–15 minutes a night using a two-way record card. This appeared to work well. However, the head of infants deservedly got promotion and left two-thirds of the way through the year. The new head of infants then inherited the unenviable task of getting to know a group of children who did not react well to new people, and the setting of homework suffered and went down to two or three nights a week.

During this time the homework library was extended from basic readers to a much broader-based, newly catalogued and classified one, and the parents then had to be introduced to a refinement of Paired Reading and record-keeping systems (Bryans and Kidd, 1982; and see Chapter 25) to cope with a wider range of reading material.

A great deal of creative work also went into devising a set of boardgames to teach 'beginning readers' word-recognition and phonics skills (adaptation of Ludo, Snakes and Ladders, Snap, Pelmanism, etc., were used — see Nichols, no date).

These games proved well suited to parents' needs because they already knew the rules and the games lock combatants into a structure that ensures taking a turn and two-way talk. On the other hand, they may lead parent and child to treat reading like a competition and place stress on acquiring surface skills (Arnold, 1983) to the detriment of reading comprehension.

Stage Eight: Evaluation

The project was evaluated, in the main, at the end of the year:

(1) Reading gains were measured by the Neale Analysis of Reading.
(2) Record cards were checked to see how often parents said they had heard a child read.
(3) A meeting was called on parents' night to discuss parents' experiences of the project and administer a short questionnaire.
(4) The teachers gave their impression of the project.
(5) We looked at parents' responses in terms of helping in school.

Summary of Results

Reading Skills and Reading Gains

Table 27.1 describes reading levels in July 1983 and reading gains made between November 1982 and July 1983 (nine months) using the Neale Analysis of Reading, Accuracy and Comprehension, Forms A and B.

Table 27.1

	Accuracy July 1983		Gains Nov 1982–July 1983		Comprehension July 1983		Gains Nov 1982–July 1983	
Class	3F	3S/4T	3F	3S/4T	3F	3S/4T	3F	3S/4T
Median	7y 3m	7y 5m	8m	5m	6y 9m	6y 11m	no change	2m
Range	6y 7m	6y 3m	2m	−1m	no score	6y 3m	−1y 9m	−7m
	9y 5m	8y 5m	1y 7m	1y 2m	8y 7m	8y 7m	10m	2y 0m

Comments. Both classes made bigger gains in accuracy. Analysis of the skills involved revealed the need for further phonic work and the detailed phonics scheme was finally introduced into the school in September 1983.

The poor comprehension scores were a cause for concern because the children did not seem to be using what they read very well. This tied up with teachers' comments that the pupils regarded reading as a competition to get through the reading books, and also with parents' comments that only a small proportion ever used the public library.

Over the next year this imbalance in the curriculum was tackled in school by developing a different approach to teaching reading (see page 353).

The Connection of Homework and Reading Levels

Table 27.2 shows the amount of parental help in reading each child received compared with reading levels (total number of weeks in which child could be heard = 29).

Table 27.2

Class	3F	3S/4T
Number of children in full scheme	22	22
Total weeks in which heard read once or more by parent	304 weeks	343 weeks
Average number of weeks in which each child heard by parent	14 weeks	16 weeks
Range	2–28 weeks	0–29 weeks
Number of children heard in 18+ weeks	8	11
Number of children heard in 18+ weeks with reading-age accuracy of 7.0 yrs +	8	7
Number of children heard in 18+ weeks with reading-age comprehension of 7.0 yrs +	8	6

Comments. Despite a problem with lost or damaged record cards, we were able to ascertain that the children, on average, had been heard reading at home at least once a week for 14–16 weeks. The amount of help given ranged very widely.

The results were complicated by the fact that some children who received little help at home, received compensatory help from the one parent, an African father, who volunteered to hear reading in school, but they appear to show that the smallish number of good readers in each class were those who had received more than average help at home.

The Parents' Response to the Scheme

Table 27.3 shows the parents' response to a questionnaire (number of returns = 30).

Table 27.3

	Yes	No	No answer
Do you plan to carry on working with your child?	28	1	1
Would you like other children to join the scheme?	22	3	5
Do you get enough help from the teachers?	21	6	3
Would you like to help your child with other work?	28	1	1
Do you and your child visit the library?	9	20	1

Comments. It seemed that the majority of parents wanted to continue helping their child with reading, maths or other work.

Roughly two-thirds wanted other children to join the scheme and felt they had had enough help from the teachers.

Only a very few parents took their children to the library.

Two comments illustrating a range of attitudes:

> Basically, the scheme is a very good idea. The only problem I have is time. Time to get to reading evenings and time to sit with my child to hear her read or do homework. However, when any *specific* homework is given I try to make sure she does it.

> My child attends school from the hours 9.00 a.m. until 3.15 p.m. at the age of 7 . . . and the hours they attend should be sufficient. Not many children want to be cooped up in this weather to do homework . . . I didn't have homework at his age and I can read quite well at the age of 35.

The Teachers' Response

Both teachers liked the scheme and said the children had become more interested and competitive about reading, and some parents more confident about helping.

Their main criticism was of the amount of time it took to set and check homework, and chase record cards lost and destroyed, issue games, check library books, and that the scheme had not been able to run as it should for lack of resources.

Epilogue: September 1984

From interest, I interviewed the headteacher a year later, and a year after both the remedial adviser and I had left the area. I wanted to see what had happened to the home-reading scheme and what other developments had occurred.

A great many changes had taken place. There had been a 50 per cent turnover of the project's original personnel and new teachers and advisers had appeared with other ideas and projects.

The home-reading scheme had continued in a less tightly orchestrated form with the children with whom it originated. Books went home but no record cards, and results had not been evaluated in any particular way.

Meanwhile, the staff of the infants' section had noticed that the children's use of reading was poor and their creative writing stilted and unadventurous. Accordingly, staff had been switching teaching emphasis from hearing children read individually, to small-group oral work and reading, and to developing creative writing that was done in rough first, and not marked heavily for punctuation and spelling. They had involved the parents in this new approach.

The head's commitment to forming good links with parents had continued, but was being operated in other ways.

This might seem a quiet end for a home-reading project whose results were not spectacular, but it proved to have been an early phase in a cycle of developments. For me the project was an adventure from which I had learned a lot about curriculum design and evaluation, and for the teachers it had started a process of curriculum development and a partnership with parents that had survived various changes and is still going on.

Acknowledgements

Thanks are due to Rod Parry, Rob Davis, Teresa Furey, Sally Hutchins, Jan Spooner and Tina Townsend who 'owned' this project as much as I, and contributed so much to it, and to John Hughes for his unstinting support.

References

Arnold, H. (1983), *Listening to Children Reading*, Hodder & Stoughton, London

Bryans, T. and Kidd, A. (1982), *Parental Involvement in Reading*, Child Advisory and Psychological Service, Birmingham

Bushell, R., Miller, A. and Robson, D. (1982), 'Parents as Remedial Teachers', *Journal of the Association of Educational Psychologists*, vol. 5, no. 9, 71–13

Carver, C. (1970), *Word Recognition Test*, Oxford University Press, London

Glynn, T., McNaughton, S., Robinson, V. and Quinn, M. (1979), *Remedial Reading at Home — Helping You to Help Your Child*, New Zealand Council for Educational Research, Wellington

Hughes, John M. (no date), *Caerleon Assessment of Phonic Skills*, Gwent College of Higher Education, Caerleon

Jackson, A. and Hannon, P. (1981), *The Belfield Reading Project*, Belfield Community Council, Rochdale

Lawton, D. (1980), Open University Course P234: The Politics of Curriculum Evaluation, The Open University, Milton Keynes

Neale, M. (1963), *Neale Analysis of Reading*, Macmillan, London

Nichols, R. (no date), *Helping Your Child to Read*, Centre for Teaching of Reading, University of Reading

Tizard, J., Schofield, W.N. and Hewison, J. (1982), 'Collaboration between Teachers and Parents in Assisting Childrens' Reading', *British Journal of Educational Psychology*, vol. 52, 1–15

28 'HAVE YOU A MINUTE?' THE FOX HILL READING PROJECT

Hilda Smith and Margaret Marsh

Fox Hill Nursery and First School is in the middle of a large council estate on the north side of Sheffield. The area has a significant rate of unemployment and there are many one-parent families. The school qualifies for the Education Priority Area Allowance. The staff of the school are committed to parental involvement. In October 1981, after months of discussion, we started the Fox Hill Reading Project, which includes all the children and parents in our school.

The Workshops

We started our project with a group of 25 children (middle infant) aged five and six years. We chose this age group because we felt they were well settled into school and extra help could be given to them before any of the children experienced failure with reading. We invited the parents to a meeting during school time to discuss the workshop and the methods we use to teach reading. The parents were asked to take part in a variety of reading activities with their own child such as listening to their child read, playing reading games together, helping with a sound sheet, talking about books and pictures and looking at books. The parents came into school for one hour each week to 'work' alongside their child in the classroom.

After the first year the project was so successful that we decided to extend it. The parents who had been attending continued and we invited the parents of the new 'F2' children to take part. At that time the number of children involved was 85. We had four separate workshops at different times in the week involving four classes and their teachers.

In January 1983 we started a language workshop for the 'F1' children aged four and a half to five and a half years. These parents take part in pre-reading activities such as talking together about a picture, simple boardgames, fine motor-control work, reading to their child, visual-discrimination activities and simple sound sheets.

All the workshops are held in the mornings from 9 a.m. until 10 a.m.

During that time, parents have a cup of coffee or tea and are given a sheet with suggestions of activities for their child to do. The activities vary from week to week, but each activity chosen reinforces or practises a skill already taught by the teacher. We use a great variety of reading games and worksheets which have been designed for parents to use with their child. The children enjoy working alongside their parents and they all look forward to 'workshop'.

Reading at Home

We started this project in the autumn term of 1982. The workshops for the 'F2' and 'F3' children were becoming well established and we felt we needed some way to extend the parental involvement to include the 'F4' year. Some of the parents had been involved for nearly two years and they were starting to ask, 'What will happen in "F4"?' Thus we started the reading at home, based on the Belfield project, but different in that our children take their books home two or three times each week. These parents became very involved and every 'F4' parent participated. Each child was given a waterproof folder and a booklet containing instructions and a space for parents' comments. We have found that reading regularly at home has improved the level of reading. Reading at home is continuing in our middle school.

Comments from Staff

> Having carried out a reading workshop for a year, I can now see a great improvement in the reading. The progress the children have made could not have been achieved in any other way. The individual attention received by each child is something which could not be carried out in the normal classroom situation.

> In all, the reading workshops and reading at home have three-fold benefits, for parents, teachers and children alike. We are a team pulling together for the same ends and we, as adults, have experienced success through the success of our children.

> Listening to, and enjoying lively discussions about the contents of the books the children read and seeing the higher standard of work they produce makes me feel that 'We should have done it sooner!'

Comments from Parents

Each week there is a variety of work to do. It has given me a feeling of involvement in David's school work.

I have read many comments about how the workshops have improved the children's reading standards and have given parents an insight into the methods of teaching reading, but I cannot help thinking that the social aspect of the venture is equally important. It is nice to think you are actually welcome to come to school and take an active part in your child's education. I, for one, welcome the opportunity and it is rewarding to feel that you are actually contributing something.

The atmosphere is relaxed and I feel most of the mums who come are friendly, personally; it's just a good feeling you get helping your own child and getting results.

Advantages of the Project

We are now in the third year of our project and it is a continuing success. The workload for all the teachers has been tremendous but we feel it is worth while, and as a staff we are committed to parental involvement. The level of reading throughout the school has improved. We have no test results to substantiate this statement, but we do not feel we need to have that kind of 'proof' of our success.

We have better relationships with our parents — they have become our friends. We feel that working closely with parents has improved our working relationship with the children in our classes. Many parents have told us that the workshops have improved their relationships with their own children. The workshops have helped many isolated parents to make friends. Our parents have gained a great deal of confidence in themselves and their abilities, and they understand more about their children's education. Attitudes towards reading have been improved and parents have realised that reading is fun and is something to be enjoyed.

Additional Comments

We feel that it is necessary to mention a few points concerning the organisation and running of the project.

The attendance at the workshops has been between 90 and 95 per cent of all parents. Most parents have attended every week. A few parents have never attended because they work and a small minority (about ten) are not interested at all, despite home visiting. We have managed to find other adults to work with the children concerned.

We provide a crèche at every workshop to cater for the 'little ones'. We feel that this is important because it leaves the parent free to spend time exclusively with the older child. Parents run the crèches voluntarily and they do a marvellous job.

We are fortunate in that our school is of open-plan design with two classes in one area. This has meant that we have enough space and furniture to seat a class of children and their parents.

It is possible to start and run workshops without any extra staff or funding. Complete co-operation among the staff has ensured the success of our project.

We cannot stress too much the amount of time involved in setting up and running a workshop. It should be started in a small way involving one class or group of children and then extended. We have spent a lot of time discussing workshops and making apparatus to be used.

Expansion of the Idea

In February 1984 we started an 'F4' games morning. The parents of these children asked if we could find some way of involving them in school as well as reading at home. They have been coming into school to play reading games with a group of three or four children. This has only been running for a short while and we recently had a meeting with the parents to discuss how they felt.

The main points from the meeting were: first, they felt it was better to work with their own child as they had been doing at the workshops; and second, they expressed a wish to start using number games as well as reading games. As this latter is a new idea, we realise that it will possibly take us at least six months to discuss the aims and structure of such a venture, and time will be needed to make the necessary apparatus.

We have also started a language workshop in the nursery involving the full-time children who are due to come into school. We feel it is too early to comment on the success of this project, as there is still a lot of input needed and it is constantly being reviewed and discussed.

In many cases we have asked our parents to undertake a big commitment, but they are willing to become involved. The success of the project is due to the consistent enthusiasm of the parents of Fox Hill. One of the most important aspects has been the confidence which our parents have derived from working alongside the staff:

'It is like going into a friend's home,' commented one parent.

We must emphasise that our ideas work well in our situation, but that each school and community has to decide how to involve parents (for details of booklet see Chapter 33).

29 PARENTS AS COACHES FOR DYSLEXIC AND SEVERELY READING-RETARDED PUPILS

Colin Tyre and Peter Young

Introduction

Despite considerable published evidence that the majority of parents make good partners in the education of their children, there remains a reluctance on the part of many professionals in LEAs to employ this much under-used resource. The extent of this reluctance — and in some instance, outright refusal — to accept parents as partners was brought home to the authors when they took evidence from parents of children with severe reading problems, some of whom had been classified as dyslexic.

Whereas research has frequently shown that parents can help the generality of children to read, our research demonstrated that children who have been assessed as dyslexic and as severely reading-retarded can be given considerable help by their parents. We would recommend that all LEAs which have no effective provision for children with specific reading difficulties, should consider introducing some form of parental involvement. The partnership with parents and the methods we applied proved effective in ameliorating the problems of this minority group of pupils who had not responded to normal remedial methods; it did not require considerable additional resources in terms of materials, time and personnel. This suggests that, particularly in these times of financial restrictions, it is foolish not to take advantage of a resource which can be utilised with comparative ease.

Account of the Project

In a DES-funded action research project managed by the Education Department of University College, Cardiff (1981–2), parents of 30 children from three LEAs in South Wales were encouraged to work with their children for half an hour a day for a year (Young and Tyre, 1983).

Fifteen pupils, aged 8–13 years — Experimental Group E1 — who had been diagnosed as dyslexic by recognised independent clinics or specialists, were each matched with two pupils of the same age, sex, reading ability and non-verbal reasoning quotients. The matched group of 30 pupils was selected from a sample of approximately 300 pupils identified by their headteachers as having severe difficulties in learning to read. The matched pupils were allocated randomly to Experimental Group E2 and to a control group. Experimental Groups El and E2 took part in a programme of daily instruction by their parents and attended three holiday schools over a period of one year from June 1981. The aim of the project was to improve the reading ability of the pupils in the two experimental groups.

Parents of children in Experimental Group El and E2 were given a one-day training session in which they were familiarised with the technique of Paired Reading and with game-playing activities based upon what they had been reading. Paired Reading, a description of which is provided elsewhere in this book, is particularly suitable for use with younger pupils barely able to read (e.g. children aged ten and under who are two or more years retarded in reading) so an approach to Paired Reading was found to be particularly effective.

The Five-stage Approach to Paired Reading

Having first read the passage, the parent then:

(1) Talks about the passage, the pictures, characters, the story so far, with the child for two or three minutes.
(2) Reads the passage aloud as naturally and with as much expression as possible, while running a finger along under the lines of print, for three minutes.
(3) Reads the passage aloud with the child joining in, in unison (i.e. Paired Reading) for three minutes.
(4) Reads the passage aloud with the child in unison, but this time pausing occasionally for the child to provide the next word or phrase at points in the text where the parent is reasonably certain the child will be able to carry on; three minutes.
(5) The child reads the passage aloud. Should the child hesitate, the parent supplies the word or phrase; three minutes.

We regard 'Paired Reading' or 'response reading' as making a significant contribution to the marked progress of many pupils. But some parents and some pupils disliked it; clearly, semi-literate parents find it difficult; some pupils regard it as childish. Yet we have found — and the evidence supports this — that it can be a very sophisticated and demanding activity (in terms of articulation, expression, etc.) which makes a unique contribution to the automatisation of reading in severely retarded readers. We recommend that 'instructors' of parents and teachers thoroughly familiarise themselves with the technique.

For older pupils who read above the eight-year-old level, Paired Reading may be modified to what we have called 'prepared reading'. Here the passage to be read is discussed before being read aloud to the pupil, who is then asked to read the passage silently and seek further help, if necessary, before reading it aloud.

The parents are also trained to give writing and spelling activities and provided with Portage-type support. The Portage Scheme (Cameron, 1982; Dessent, 1984) is an attempt to provide educational and development aid to preschool handicapped children and the technology was imported into the UK from Portage, Wisconsin, USA. A major feature of the Portage home-visiting service is that it enables parents to teach their own children in their own home. It is a highly sophisticated service-delivery model that brings all the powerful teaching techniques of behavioural psychology to parents. A teacher–researcher was, therefore, employed on the project to visit the parents' and, in consultation with the authors, to advise and support the parents in their day-to-day work with their children.

Initially, books were selected for each pupil, which were two years *below* the child's reading ability. This was in order to ensure immediate success in Paired Reading and to reduce stress in both parents and pupils.

For many years the authors, as a result of their previous researches, have insisted that only a holistic model of reading could provide an adequate base for the satisfactory acquisition of written language skills. By a holistic model of reading we mean a model which embraces reading, writing and spelling as activities which should be developed hand in hand, as well as a model which places reading firmly in the context of language and meaning. The holistic approach to reading included, therefore:

reading for meaning;
learning to read by reading;
activities which focused attention on the components of the reading process;
writing and spelling of what had been said or read;
meaningful memorisation of texts and verses;
comprehensible language in spoken and written forms;
a natural learning experience in which on-task instruction could be

given by parents in a style with which they were comfortable and free of anxiety.

Parents were encouraged to acknowledge their children's successes in the ways in which they tackled and accomplished tasks, but to avoid criticism.

Throughout the year parents were supported by frequent and regular home visits by the teacher–researcher appointed and trained for this purpose. Parents also met together to discuss with the project team progress and difficulties. No distinctions were made between the parents of the children in the Groups El and E2.

The three holiday schools attended by the pupils in Groups El and E2 were run by the project team and staffed by six experienced remedial teacher advisers who were trained in the use of the same methods and activities as those used by the parents. The aims of the holiday schools were: to monitor pupils' progress; give the children a successful and enjoyable experience of education alongside peers with similar reading difficulties; and to complement and supplement the work of the parents. The first holiday school, in the summer holiday, demonstrated that the majority of pupils had made progress in reading and were thoroughly familiar with the procedures and activities. They had acquired sound study habits, were task-orientated and eager to work. All three holiday schools were fully and enthusiastically attended by pupils from both experimental groups.

Results

Pre- and post-testing using the Neale Analysis of Reading Ability and the Salford Reading Test as indicators showed a significant improvement had been made. The true gains of the children — who, it should be remembered, had long experience of failure — varied between one and four years' progress in reading in the project year. The true difference between Experimental Groups El and E2 was not significant. However, the true differences between the experimental groups and the control group were significant at the 0.0001 level. With one exception, all experimental group pupils made more than one year's progress in reading, eleven made between 2 and 3 years' progress, ten made between 3 and 4 years' progress, and one made 4 years' progress. The estimation of the amount of change was calculated by taking the difference in pre- and post-test results, but was also calculated using a formula recommended whenever the effects of remedial or other special treatment are to be evaluated and the gains thus measured were referred to as 'true gains' (Davies, 1970).

In contrast to these significant gains made by the majority of the 'dyslexic' and matched group pupils, only two pupils in the control group had made more than one year's progress in the year and the remainder were found to be further retarded in reading ability than they were a year earlier.

However, although the gains of the experimental groups are gratifying, it was the unique contribution made by the parents working alongside and supervised by the project team that is of particular interest. Although the major aim of the action research project was to help those children classified as dyslexic to learn to read, there is no reason to believe that a similar system would be any less effective for helping other specific learning difficulties, for dyslexia or specific reading disability/difficulty is regarded as particularly difficult to remediate. Whatever had been done had proved to be appropriate to the needs of the two groups of children.

Although, as described above, we had used a variety of reading tests in parallel versions, we also monitored the children's progress on the books they were able to read and in the changes in their reading behaviours. We did this by direct observation of pupils during holiday schools; by recording the information collected by the teacher–researcher; and by asking the parents and children. By the end of the year ten of the children were able to read and understand adult texts. Parents and pupils independently reported an overall, and in some cases dramatic, improvement in schoolwork. Books, newspapers, magazines and comics were being read for pleasure in bed or in free time. The majority of parents considered their children, and the majority of children considered themselves, to be adequate or good readers. Spelling had improved, though not as markedly as reading, and many children were expressing themselves efficiently and fluently in writing for the first time. All parents reported that their relationships with the children had improved or remained good throughout the year.

When we designed the project we were authoritatively advised that all the research evidence pointed to the fact that we were unlikely to succeed to any significant extent. Our depressed expectations, therefore, may have affected the progress the children made. When some children made early progress in their reading — in the first quarter — we were reluctant to advance them. We can only state that had we had more confidence in what we and the parents had been doing, and in the models of reading instruction we used, many of the pupils would have advanced more rapidly to more difficult books or might well have made even greater progress in the year.

Discussion of the Results

Perhaps the most significant lessons we learned from the action research project were the following.

(1) That children who have been assessed as dyslexic and as severely retarded can be given considerable help by their parents.

(2) Parents who are prepared to help their children to overcome severe learning difficulties need sensitive guidance, reassurance and skilled training in methods appropriate to the parent–child relationship.

(3) For those helping children with reading difficulties a comprehensive concept of the reading process is required.

(4) The approach to the teaching of reading needs to be readily understood by parents, comparatively easy to use and so effective as to reduce their anxiety and their children's feeling of failure.

(5) If parents are to be invited to help their children, it is important to assure them that they have taught their children a wide range of social skills and to walk and to talk. Similarly, they had demonstrated their abilities as instructors or coaches in helping their children to swim, ride bikes, skate, etc. Parents need this reassurance if they are to be expected to help their children learn the skill of reading which the schools and their teachers had failed to teach them. The approach to reading was therefore presented as an extention of parents' role as instructors in skills such as cycling, when they were essentially supportive both psychologically and physically.

(6) Paired Reading is particularly suitable for use with younger pupils barely able to read, for example, children aged ten and under who are two years or more retarded in reading; the five-stage approach to Paired Reading is particularly effective.

(7) For older pupils who read at the eight-year-old level, Paired Reading may be modified to what may be called 'prepared reading'.

(8) It was found particularly important to select books which respected the maturity of interest of the pupils but which were about two years below their tested levels of reading ability; *this regression to security combined with Paired or prepared Reading greatly enhances chances of success.* For this reason, many books from the Trend Series were used. The older children accepted the cover illustrations as in keeping with their age.

(9) Parents who are prepared to help in these ways also need to be trained to praise and reward their children — whether verbally or gesturally — and to avoid criticisms of and confrontation with them. 'Warm fuzzies are preferable to cold pricklies.'

(10) Parents who wish to help their children but find themselves, for whatever reason, unable to do so, should be given the opportunity of having another member of the family, or an acceptable substitute, trained to carry out the reading and other activities.

(11) If parents are to undertake and be trained in language, reading, writing and spelling activities, they should be given Portage-type 'precision teaching' support materials.

(12) Parents should also be given regular weekly support from a specially trained professional. In our main project, fortnightly home visits were made and for the demands that were being made on the parents and children this we consider was often insufficient. However, where fewer demands are made or the system is based in a school, as in some of the minor projects which we introduced, access to help when required can suffice.

The training skills for reading showed that they can be easily assimilated and thereafter easily supervised and monitored. The training required by parents for the associated writing and spelling activities needs to be more comprehensive, the practice more carefully supervised and the outcomes more carefully monitored. Although examples of writing and spelling tasks were given in the hope that parents would generate their own activities, parents felt more comfortable and secure with 'activities material' prepared by the authors. There was a greater variation in the performance among parents in teaching handwriting. To correct poor handwriting and retrain those who had failed to learn correct letter formation, particularly of secondary aged pupils, is expecting a lot from parents. Lack of skill in correct formation of letters was a major problem among the project sample. The parents found it very useful to employ 'Write and Spell' Series which showed, by flicking the corners of the books, the way in which to form letters and write common letter combinations. The provision of booklets — *Notes for Parents* — which backed up material given in the in-service sessions was essential. For those unused to periods of fairly concentrated instruction a recapitulation in the privacy of their own homes was reported by parents, and confirmed by the teacher–researcher, as being most helpful. The training of parents is a particular skill where a suitable language of instruction is imperative. No base-line of knowledge can be assumed and invariably the parent group is 'mixed' in background and motivation. The slightest use of jargon or specialist language may make a discourse incomprehensible to some parents and it was found particularly helpful to call upon parents' own experience and knowledge in an informal discussion situation. Daily activities should not exceed half an hour and they should be on-task — that is, have as their source the reading book being used — and should take account of the children's performance in reading activities. In the project, 15 minutes were spent on Paired Reading and 15 minutes on the language activities. For most parents to carry such a routine of daily doses — come what may — for a year was too much. We hesitate to recommend any ideal length of time for group schemes of parent participation with demands similar to those of the project. So many factors have been shown to affect efficiency and new ones come to our attention with each minor project. Were we planning a further group project which demanded a similar parental commitment, we would plan to run between a minimum of three and a maximum of six months with perhaps a second phase after an appreciable break.

Holiday schools can well supplement and complement the work of parents and ordinary school teachers, they can be thoroughly enjoyable so far as the children are concerned and improve both their skills and their self-esteem. They are best organised separately for primary and secondary aged pupils. They are excellent users of idle educational plant and their organisation and costing are matters with which most LEAs are familiar in the context of holiday schools for the gifted, for musicians, for students of English as a second language or for children with severe learning difficulties.

The implications for teacher training, in the light of this project, are that many initial and remedial methods of teaching reading used by teachers over-emphasise subskills at the expense of meaning; that inadequate attention is often given to the teaching of handwriting; that writing and spelling are rarely taught hand in hand; and, as evidenced by the results of pupils in the control group, that normal remedial techniques and measures do not effectively meet the educational needs of the majority of reading-retarded pupils.

Reading-retarded pupils and their parents should continue to receive help and support until the pupils' level of functional literacy — that is, their performance in reading, writing, spelling and written expression — is at least appropriate to their levels of attainment in other subjects across the curriculum.

Further Projects

As a result of experience gained in working with parents outside the school situation, it was decided to explore the possibility of modifying the procedures of the project design for use in schools. To this effect, a series of minor projects have followed. The series started with two similar projects in two primary schools.

The success of the two minor projects, and other variations on the original design since, have indicated some ways in which the ideas and practices of the main project may be adapted and disseminated.

Conclusions

In the light of the experience gained in the main and sub-projects, we consider a carefully planned and centrally directed school-based scheme will provide the most practical and appropriate model. Parents need to see that they are assured of professionally skilled support and that resources and books have been specifically provided for their children. The headteacher and members of staff also need encouragement and support and to be convinced that the contribution of the LEA and of parents are additional resources which will benefit the pupils and enhance the education provided by their school and classes in both the short and the long-term.

The main project design has proved particularly successful in the treatment of individual children. Amendments to the basic design can readily be made and tailored to meet the needs of the child, the abilities of the parents to act as coaches, the family circumstances and the school curriculum. The experience with the individual treatment has highlighted the need for further research into the relative effectiveness of different strategies and their interactions with the wide variety of children who fail to acquire written language skills and whose parents vary greatly in their ability to act as coaches. While we agree that usually 'Irrespective of socio-economic background or conceptualised area of concern, the parent(s) of any child is in a position to optimise and enhance the functioning and well-being of that child' (Wolfendale, 1983), we must, if we are to mobilise this considerable resource and use parents in the role as coaches effectively, further refine the models of parental intervention and continue to develop the skills needed in training both teachers and parents to make the most of this essential partnership. Effective parental intervention, particularly if children have severe learning difficulties, is a complex process. We need to know a great deal more than how to encourage co-operation if we are to utilise parents as full partners in the business of educating their children: we need, above all, effective methods of intervention and amelioration to meet special educational needs. Our experience in pursuit of that aim has benefited immensely from working with parents as partners.

References

Cameron, R.J. (ed.) (1982), 'Working Together: Portage in the UK', NFER-Nelson, Windsor

Davies, F.B. (1970), 'The Assessment of Change', in Farr, R. (ed.), *Measurement and Evaluation of Reading*, Harcourt, Brace and World, New York

Dessent, T.C. (ed.) (1984), *The Imperative of Portage*, NFER-Nelson, Windsor

Wolfendale, S. (1983), *Parental Participation in Children's Development and Education*, Gordon & Breach Science Publishers, London

Young, P. and Tyre, C. (1983), *Dyslexia or Illiteracy?*, The Open University Press, Milton Keynes

30 TEACHING PARENTS TO TEACH READING TO TEACH LANGUAGE: A PROJECT WITH DOWN'S SYNDROME CHILDREN AND THEIR PARENTS

Sue Buckley

Introduction

This chapter describes a rather unusual reading project involving mentally handicapped children born with Down's Syndrome and their parents. The work described is unusual in two ways. First, because very young mentally handicapped children are being taught to read by their parents and, second, because reading skills are being used to help their language development.

The Portsmouth Down's Syndrome Project began in 1980 as the result of the initiative from Leslie Duffen in which he described the progress of his Down's Syndrome daughter, Sarah. Sarah began to learn to read at the age of three years using a 'look and say' flashcard approach. She had only a small number of single words in her spoken vocabulary when she began to learn to read. Her father taught her a large sight vocabulary in a systematic way and for a number of years her reading age was ahead of her chronological age (Duffen, 1976). In all areas of her development, Sarah made exceptionally good progress for a child with her condition and completed her entire education in the normal school system. Her father was convinced that her advanced development stemmed from her early reading programme. Specifically, he felt sure that all her understanding and use of spoken language had been built up from reading — i.e. that she found it easier to learn new words and sentences when she learned them from print than when she simply heard them spoken.

Sarah's progress with reading and language skills and her father's hypothesis that reading had been a 'way in' to spoken language aroused considerable interest. A search of the relevant literature on Down's Syndrome revealed a number of other accounts of reading skills in preschool-age Down's children. Some of these accounts were single case studies describing the achievements of individual children (e.g. Hunt, 1966; Smith, 1974; Orme *et al.*, 1966). Other references to early reading in this group of children were found in reports of major early-intervention projects in the USA and Australia (Hayden and Haring, 1977; Rhodes *et al.*, 1969; Pieterse and Treloar, 1981). These projects were reporting that some of the Down's children were mastering a useful sight vocabulary at the age of three to five years, confirming the individual case reports.

The suggestion that teaching reading might improve the spoken language skills of Down's children was of particular interest as delayed and deficient language development is a major problem for most of these children throughout their lives.

Support for Duffen's view that spoken language could develop from reading was provided by Saunders and Collins (1972) in an article describing the work of a private school for Down's children in Sussex:

> It would be true to say that through our work we have taught some children to speak through teaching reading. We do not wait for children to speak before we start teaching language and reading. One can ask, which card says 'tree' and which says 'house' and the child can look and find them.

The reports of some of the early-intervention projects indicated that they also recognised that teaching reading could be an integral part of a language programme (Rhodes and Gooch, 1969; Pieterse and Treloar, 1981). In both these projects, children were being taught to read words that they did not necessarily understand; comprehension exercises and games were included to teach meaning as a separate step.

Usually, children learn to talk from listening to adults talking. They learn the meanings of words, then phrases and sentences from listening. The implication of Duffen's and others' work was that Down's children found it easier to understand and to remember words which they say in the printed form more easily than if they only heard them spoken.

The research into cognitive deficits in Down's Syndrome may provide some explanations for the apparent advantage of visual over auditory language input for these children.

A range of difficulties in auditory perceptual function have been reported, ranging from peripheral deficits to deficits in central processes. A number of studies report high percentages of Down's children with significant hearing losses (e.g. Rigordsky *et al.*, 1961; Cunningham and McArthur, 1981; Keiser *et al.*, 1981).

Studies of Down's children learning to sign indicate problems in the discrimination of similar-sounding words such as egg/leg, cat/pat, dish/fish, boy/ball, toes/toast and cat/clap (Le Provost, personal communication, 1984).

The fact that Down's children are reported to be using signs appropriately as early as 18 months — much earlier than they usually begin to use spoken words — suggests particular deficits in the listening and/or speaking channels rather than a cognitive inability to learn to use a language (Le Provost, 1983).

Deficits in central brain processes necessary for language are implied in various studies (Rempel, 1974; Nakamura, 1965; Bilovsky and Share, 1965; McDade and Adler, 1980), and it has been suggested that the overall pattern of deficits may well be considered in practical terms to result in problems for the Down's child similar to those of the deaf child (Scheffelin, 1968). If this is the case, then the Down's child will have considerable difficulty learning to understand and will use language solely from listening to adults and may be helped by the use of visual forms of language such as signing and reading.

Whatever the underlying reasons for normal or even advanced reading skills being displayed by a group of children assumed to be moderately to severely retarded, the phenomenon itself and its implications for language remediation seemed to merit further study and so the project described here was established in 1980. It was inspired by the work of a parent and the project rested on working with parents.

The studies published up to 1980 established that word-recognition skills are present in some Down's children at an early age. A whole range of questions follow from this and need careful evaluation if the real significance of such skills is to be established. The following are some of the important questions:

(1) What proportion of Down's children show early reading skills?
(2) Are there any characteristics which differentiate readers from non-readers?
(3) At what developmental point should the teaching of reading begin?
(4) Which teaching methods should be used to teach reading?
(5) Can the teaching of reading assist the development of language and speech in these children?
(6) Will the Down's child be able to develop these early reading skills to a level of reading competence that is either useful or pleasurable or both?
(7) Is the time and effort needed to teach reading reasonable in terms of final outcome or should the time be spent on enhancing some other area of development?

The Project: 1980–3

The Sample

In order to begin to answer some of these questions, a sample of preschool age Down's children was established. To study their reading skills, it was necessary to be able to teach reading to a representative sample of Down's children. The effect of the genetic fault on the child's development varies widely and the sample needed to reflect this range to be representative.

In order to teach a preschool age sample and in order to ensure that the children benefited from involvement in the research, working with parents at home and fitting the reading work into a comprehensive early education programme seemed the best way to proceed. Letters were sent to all parents of Down's children between two and four years of age in two local health districts. The letters briefly explained the nature of the research and then each family willing to participate received a visit to discuss the project in detail and to ensure that they knew what they were taking on.

Fourteen families agreed to participate. This sample comprised all the families approached. The only child not included at the outset was in the care of the local authority. The developmental quotients of the children at the outset (see Table 30.1) suggest that the sample represented the usual range for such children. One child has a severe hearing loss, one a minor loss, one additional brain damage and another a visual problem — again, these are the usual range of additional handicaps found in this condition.

Home Teaching

Each child received regular home visits. Simply on the basis of travelling distances these visits were weekly for half the group, fortnightly for the remainder. The teacher and parent used the materials of the Portage programme for early education as a basis for a comprehensive remedial programme for each individual child. The reading activities were introduced only as part of this wider educational programme when the parents and teacher felt it appropriate.

Parents and teacher kept weekly records of the child's progress on all the tasks set.

Reading Programme

From the outset, it was felt that the teaching of reading should be related closely to the language development activities for each child. Therefore, the 'core curriculum' was designed to teach the child to understand and to use words. Consequently, tasks were developed to teach the child to understand the *spoken* word from picture-card activities first. The same procedures were then used to teach the child to understand the *written* word.

A behavioural approach was used, with an emphasis on analysing the task into component stages, teaching each stage using errorless techniques and ensuring that each step had been mastered before moving on to the next.

The choice of core vocabulary for the picture-card and flashcard work was based on: (i) the vocabulary development of normal children; and (ii) the interests of the individual children.

Parents selected vocabulary from the words known to be common in children's early speech and supplemented this with words in which they felt their children were interested. This produced some interesting early vocabularies which included not only family names but words such as 'hulk', 'Coca-cola', 'harbour', 'chimney' at an early stage to reflect the child's interests and recent experiences.

For each new word the child was learning, picture activities usually came first. The child learned to match, then select and then name the picture cards. Matching simply requires the child to identify identical pictures visually. Selecting requires the child to point to or pick up the correct picture when the adult asks for it by name. Naming requires the child actually to name the picture. Exactly the same steps are repeated when flashcards are introduced.

Initially, no flashcard work was introduced until the child was using about 50 simple words appropriately and spontaneously in speech. The child was then taught only to read words that formed part of his or her spoken vocabulary (i.e. words that were already understood and used). For the children who found this early reading easy, they later did learn to read new words — i.e. words they did not understand or use when first introduced in the printed form. Comprehension of the words was then taught after flashcard recognition had been mastered.

Other authors also suggest that it is not necessary to wait for any speech from the child before embarking on this early word recognition (e.g. Saunders and Collins, 1972; Pieterse and Treloar, 1981; Rhodes and Gooch, 1969).

Once a small vocabulary of single words was mastered, then two-word phrases were built with flashcards as a child at that stage of language development would say them — 'car gone', for instance.

From this stage a flashcard vocabulary was built up steadily, introducing words needed to build phrases and practice given at reading and saying a variety of phrases. Activities to teach and test comprehension were included for each new word or phrase. Eventually, the reading can be used to teach the child normal sentence construction and grammar. Until this stage is reached, infant books are not suitable. The child may be able to read aloud from such texts because of an ability to recognise each individual word, but may not understand the sentences if the grammar and syntax are beyond his or her level of language development.

This means that for each child, individual flashcards, phrases and books have to be made to reflect individual vocabulary, experience and interests.

At every stage in the language and reading work, the importance of generalising the child's knowledge from the card activities to everyday experience was emphasised. Parents were encouraged to take every chance of using words being learned throughout the day in their normal context and to play other kinds of games and activities with pictures, words and objects to extend the child's experience of and use of words. Only in this way can the meanings of words be expanded appropriately and their use for communication be demonstrated to the child.

A booklet and video-tape illustrating the methods used in the Portsmouth project in more detail and showing the children at work may be obtained from the author (address on page 328).

Results

The main findings of the study are set out in Table 30.1 and may be summarised as follows.

The Extent of Reading Skills

The results confirm those of earlier studies. *Some* Down's Syndrome children are able to learn to read single words at a very early age.

Of the final sample of eleven children, two children (1 and 3 in Table 30.1) were able to read words from flashcards with amazing ease at 2 years 7 months and 3 years respectively. Both children enjoyed the task, required only a few repetitions of each new word in order to master it and rapidly built up an extensive vocabulary.

A third child (2 in Table 30.1) mastered his first sight words at 4 years and two further children (4, 5) at 5 years 4 months and 5 years 10 months respectively. These three children required more carefully structured teaching as outlined in the reading programme and much more practice before words were mastered.

In all, five (45 per cent) of the sample show reading skills equal to

Table 30.1: The Relationship between Age, IQ, Language and Reading Skills (years:months)

Child	Chronological age	Griffiths DQ	Age at which first words spoken	Language development (August 1983)	Age at which first words read	Reading progress (August 1983)
1	5: 4	93.9	2: 0	7/8-word sentences	2: 7	700 words simple books
2	7: 0	66.2	1: 3	5/6-word sentences	4: 0	70 words/sentences beginning books
3	5: 6	81.9	2: 1	7/8-word sentences	3: 0	50 words
4	5:10	53.4	2:10	100+ single words	5: 4	8 words
5	6: 2	58.7	2: 6	100+ single words; 2-word phrases	5:10	4 words
6	5: 2	74.6	2: 2	80+ single words; 2-word phrases	—	Matching 4 words
7	5: 6	65.1	1:10	100+ single words; 2-word phrases	—	Matching 4 words
8	5: 6	57.2	2: 4	100+ single words; 2-word phrases	—	Matching 3 words
9	5: 3	72.1	2: 6	100+ single words; 2-word phrases	—	Matching 3 words
10	5: 1	50.9	2: 6	20 single words	—	Matching, selecting and naming pictures
11	5:11	37.8	—	3 Makaton signs	—	—
12	5: 5	61.2*	3: 2	Profoundly deaf child		
13	5: 7	76.7*	2: 1	Left study May 1981		
14	5: 8	63.3*	3: 1	Left study June 1981		

* DG 1981.

Three children (12, 13, 14) were not included in the reading programme. The mother of the profoundly deaf child (12) did not wish to continue to participate in regular teaching, though kept in touch and received visits as requested. The remaining two children had to leave the study on starting school placements at the request of the school headteacher. Child 11 has not yet started the reading programme.

or better than those expected in a normal sample of children of this age range, despite considerable retardation in speech and language skills.

Can 'Readiness' be Predicted?

For the sample as a whole, the emergence of such reading skills cannot be predicted on the basis of chronological age, DQ scores or stage of language development. Some Down's Syndrome children (numbered 1–5 in our sample) are able to begin to read when still at the 50 single-word stage of speech and language development. No criteria which would predict 'reading readiness' for this sample were apparent.

However, for children 1 and 3, the really precocious readers, certain common features are apparent. They have DQ scores in the low–normal range and considerably more advanced language and speech development. While their present level of functioning may well be a *result* of the reading programme and its 'language teaching' emphasis (particularly for Child 1), they were the most able children in the sample at the outset. The reading and language programme may have prevented the expected decline in DQ for Down's Syndrome children of this age (Ludlow and Allen, 1979). In fact, for Child 1 DQ has *increased* each year (85.7 in 1980).

The ease with which these two children have learned to read suggests that the process is in some way different for them. Child 3 would probably now be reading as extensively as Child 1, who reads to herself for pleasure, but his teaching has been severely disrupted by the birth of another child in the family.

The video-tape sequences of the children clearly illustrate a qualitative difference in the reading of these two children, which is difficult to define.

The Nature of this Reading Process

Analysis of the types of errors made by the three most able readers may have some important implications. While the teaching process aims to reduce errors to a minimum, some are inevitably recorded. The majority of such errors were, as one might predict, *visual* errors, confusions resulting from the visual similarity of words (e.g. Child 1 initially confused hair/rain and this/shoe). Something entirely unexpected was the appearance of *semantic* errors, where the child produces a word similar in *meaning* to the target word (e.g. Child 3 produced the following errors — for sleep, go to bed; harbour, ship; baby, Paul (the name of his baby brother)). Such semantic errors are characteristic in the residual reading skills of deep dyslexics and it has been suggested such patients are using right-hemisphere processes (Coltheart, 1980). (The video includes sequences of children spontaneously producing both types of errors.)

The nature of the language deficits in Down's Syndrome — particularly the immature syntax and tendency to 'telegraphic' speech (Evans and Hampson, 1969; Gibson, 1978) — suggests that they may be heavily dependent on the right-hemisphere components of language (Day, 1977; Moscovitch, 1976; Zaidel, 1978) and support for this hypothesis comes from studies suggesting that Down's children show right-hemisphere dominance for language (Hartley, 1981; Anderson and Barry, 1975; Reinhart, 1976). For a more detailed discussion of the significance of these issues see Buckley (1985).

The Success of 'Look and Say' Teaching

All the teaching has been of the 'look and say' whole-word-recognition type. None of the children has any phonic skills. As Child 1 clearly demonstrates, it is possible to build a very large reading vocabulary in this way. She discriminates plurals and derivatives with no problem whatsoever. This implies that Jorm (1983) is correct in suggesting that phonic skills are useful but certainly not essential for reading.

Conclusions and Comments

The results of the intensive phase of the project described begin to provide answers to some of the questions outlined in the introduction. These questions all relate to the extent and sigificance of reading skills for the children's development. The children's progress provides partial answers to some of the questions, leaves some unanswered and raises new questions, and so the research in Portsmouth is now developing in new ways to take up some of these issues.

In addition, in the context of this book, the involvement of parents and the advantages and disadvantages of relying on parents to teach their children in these circumstances needs some comment in the light of the experience of working so intensively with the parents over three years. New and different ways of working with parents are currently being explored in the next phase of the project.

The Significance of the Research for the Children

The progress of the children in the Portsmouth project confirms the findings of earlier studies. There are some Down's children who are able to begin to learn to read as early as three years or even earlier. About half the children were making progress by five years of age, but a large sample needs to be studied to make confident predictions about the extent of such skills in this group of children as a whole. It would be reasonable to suggest that the progress of this group is an under-estimate of what could be achieved with optimal teaching.

In this sample, three children were lost from the group before attempting reading. On a number of occasions family events, such as moving house, illness and births, disrupted the teaching programmes considerably. The kind of tight supervision and control of teaching possible in a nursery school setting cannot be imposed on parents teaching their children at home.

The language development of the reading children suggests that the language has benefited from the reading. However, a more controlled study of a larger group of children will be needed to confirm this suggestion. On a number of occasions parents commented that they noticed their children using words in their speech after learning to read them more quickly than words learned from listening.

Certainly, the reading has been worthwhile for its own sake for three of the children, who were able to read books by the end of 1983. Longer-term follow-up of the whole group is needed to determine the full extent of their reading development and to decide for which children the teaching required has been worthwhile in terms of achievements.

On the question of methods, the ones described here seem to be effective, but comparison with other methods would be needed in order to be sure that this is the most effective approach to reading for Down's children.

The Contribution of the Parents

This entire project depended on working with parents at all stages. The parents, under the guidance of the researchers, carried out all the actual teaching of their children. All the parents learned the behavioural teaching techniques and became most effective at using them in a controlled manner. They were enthusiastic and almost always highly motivated to work with their own children. Of course there were times, in individual families, when parents became depressed or despondent — but these were not frequent.

The families varied widely in terms of social circumstances and parental education and experience. However, all became highly competent teachers and learned a great deal about all aspects of child development.

The factors that prevented some parents being as effective in teaching as they might have been were not issues of competence, they were almost always issues that prevented them from having enough *time* to work with their children. During periods of family disruption, teaching progress was often minimal, sometimes for quite long periods. This was as frustrating and worrying for the parents concerned as it was to the researchers. The disruptive effect on the child's programme could have been reduced if the project had been partly school-based.

The other significant factor felt to reduce the effectiveness of the parent as teacher was the acceptance of the child's handicap and consequent emotional relationship with the child. If the parent still felt an element of rejection of the child, this would produce tension between parent and child and reduce the parent's motivation to teach. If the parent needed to scc the child's progress in order to deny the reality of the child's handicap, then again the anxiety would create tensions between parent and child in the teaching situation. In addition, if the child's handicaps were severe then slow progress might disillusion the parent.

However, none of these factors operated in a simple or predictable way. Some of the best teachers — whose children showed the greatest overall developmental gains — were parents of the most severely handicapped. Conversely, one parent of a more able child was to some degree rejecting and therefore less effective.

Overall, the parents became expert teachers of their children in quite a short time. Some had more to learn than others at the outset, but all were willing to learn. A relationship of *equal partnership* with the home teacher was emphasised from the outset. She had skills and expertise to share with the parents, who in turn were experts on their own child. Parents were always involved in deciding what to teach and how to teach in discussion with the teacher.

On several occasions, the research might have taken different directions but for the initiative of parents. The first child to begin on the reading programme was unwilling to learn to match words — so instead of following advice and not proceeding to the next step, her mother taught her simply to name the cards. She loved this and so we discovered she could learn to read with ease, thanks to her mother using her intuition and ignoring our advice.

Another child seemed to be making such slow progress that we suggested that reading was not for him and that mother concentrate on other activities. She ignored us and quietly persevered with practice on a small vocabulary — he now reads simple books.

Unfortunately, not many fathers took an active role in teaching. The mothers did almost all the work. This may have been partly because home visits took place in the day-time, excluding most fathers from participating each time the teacher came. Fathers who were on shiftwork and so met the teacher and could actively contribute to decision-making were more likely to be actively involved with the child's teaching.

Future Developments

The initial results of the first three years' work received substantial publicity early in 1984. The project team then began to receive many letters from parents and professionals and to receive invitations to lecture.

From the letters and audience comments at lectures, it has become clear that many Down's children up and down the country are making similar progress to the research children. Parents and teachers have given us many case histories to illustrate this fact and also indicated a willingness to collect longitudinal data for us, so we are moving into a new phase of parental involvement.

A national sample of families is being established from volunteer families and professionals who are willing to maintain accurate records of their children's progress. They will record language development as well as reading progress if relevant.

The validity of parent diary records as a means of studying language development has been established in the field of normal child language (Snyder, Bates and Bretherton, 1981; Barrett, 1984) and the accuracy of parents' observations of their handicapped children's language has been confirmed in a recent study in Manchester (Cunningham and Sloper, 1984). The major difference in this collaboration with parents will be the type of contact that can be maintained with families.

In the home-teaching situation, families have regular contact. This probably helps to monitor the teaching procedures closely, to maintain motivation and to check on the accuracy of parents' records. With a national sample, this type of contact will not be possible. A subsample may be studied more intensively to check on the reliability and validity of data and parents will be asked to return record sheets at frequent intervals, in order to maintain some kind of regular contact, if only by mail.

As an intermediate strategy, local co-ordinators are to liaise between parents and project to provide some face-to-face contact and a source of advice on teaching problems and practice. In this way, it should be possible to collect longitudinal data on a large sample of children in a relatively inexpensive manner.

References

Anderson, A. and Barry, W. (1975), 'The Development of Cerebral Dominance in Children Attending Regular School Classes, Special Classes for the MR and Special Schools for the MR', unpublished PhD thesis, Carlton University

Barrett, M.D. (1984), 'Early Semantic Representations and Early Word Usage', in Kuczaj, S.A. and Barrett, M.D. (eds), *The Development of Word Meaning*, Springer, Berlin

Bilovsky, D. and Share, J. (1965), 'The ITPA and Down's Syndrome', *American Journal of Mental Deficiency*, vol. 70, 78–82

Buckley, S. (1985), 'Attaining Basic Educational Skills: Reading, Writing and Number', in Stratford, B. and Lane, D. (eds), *Current Issues in Down's Syndrome*, Holt-Saunders, in press

Coltheart, M. (1980), 'Reading, Phonological Recoding and Deep Dyslexia', in Coltheart, M., Patterson, K. and Marshall, J.C. (eds), *Deep Dyslexia*, Routledge and Kegan Paul, London

Cunningham, C. and McArthur, K. (1981), 'Hearing Loss and Treatment in Young Down's Syndrome Children', *Child: Health, Care and Development*, vol. 7, 357

Cunningham, C.C. and Sloper, P. (1984), 'The Relationship between Material Ratings of First Word Vocabulary and Reynell Language Scores', *British Journal of Educational Psychology*, vol. 54, 160–7

Day, J. (1977), 'Right Hemisphere Language Processing in Normal Right-handers', *Journal of Experimental Psychology: Human Perception and Performance*, vol. 3, 518–28

Duffen, L. (1976), 'Teaching Reading to Children with Little or no Language', *Remedial Education*, vol. 11, no. 3, 139–42

Evans, D. and Hampson, M. (1969), 'The Language of Mongols', *British Journal of Communication*, vol. 3, 171–81

Gibson, D. (1978), *Down's Syndrome*, Cambridge University Press, Cambridge

Hartley, X.Y. (1981), 'Lateralisation of Speech Stimuli in Young Down's Syndrome Children', *Cortex*, vol. 17, no. 2, 241–8

Hayden, A.H. and Haring, N.G. (1977), 'The Acceleration and Maintenance of Gains in Down's Syndrome School Age Children', in Mittler, P. (ed.), *Research to Practice in Mental Retardation*, vol. 1, University Park Press, Baltimore

Hunt, N. (1966), *The World of Nigel Hunt*, Finlayson, Darwen, Lancs

Jorm, A.F. (1983), *The Psychology of Reading and Spelling Difficulties*, Routledge and Kegan Paul, London

Keiser, H., Montague, J., Wold, D., Maune, D. and Pattison, D. (1981), 'Hearing Loss of Down's Syndrome Adults', *American Journal of Mental Deficiency*, vol. 85, 467–72

Le Provost, P.A. (1983), 'Using the Makaton Vocabulary in Early Language Training', *Mental Handicap*, vol. 11, no. 1, 29–30

Ludlow, J.R. and Allen, L.M. (1979), 'The Effect of Early Intervention and Pre-school Stimulus on the Development of the Down's Syndrome Child', *Journal of Mental Deficiency Research*, vol. 23, 29–44

McDade, H.L. and Adler, S. (1980), 'Down's Syndrome and Short-term Memory Impairment: A Storage or Retrieval Deficit?', *American Journal of Mental Deficiency*, vol. 84, 561–7

Moscovitch, M. (1976), 'On the Representation of Language in the Right Hemisphere of Right-handed People', *Brain and Language*, vol. 3, 7–71

Nakamura, H. (1965), 'An Inquiry into Systematic Differences in the Abilities of Institutionalised Adult Mongols', *American Journal of Mental Deficiency*, vol. 69, 661–5

Orme, J.E., Fisher, F.J.S. and Griggs, J.B. (1966), 'The Big Words', *New Education*, vol. 2, no. 12, 25–6

Pieterse, M. and Treloar, R. (1981), *Down's Syndrome Program*, Progress Report 1981, Macquarie University

Reinhart, C. (1976), The Cerebral Lateralisation of Speech Processes in Down's Syndrome and Normal Individuals, Canadian Psychological Association 37th Annual Meeting, Toronto

Rempel, E.D. (1974), 'Psycholinguistic Abilities of Down's Syndrome Children', in *Proceedings of the Annual Meeting of the American Association of Mental Deficiency*, Toronto

Rhodes, E. and Gooch, B. (1969), *A Language Stimulation and Reading Programme for Severely Retarded Mongoloid Children*, Research Monograph no. 11, State of California Department of Mental Hygiene

Rigordsky, S., Prunty, M. and Glovsky, G. (1961), 'A Study of the Incidence, Types and Associated Etiologies of Hearing Loss in an Institutionalised Mentally Retarded Population', *Training School Bulletin*, vol. 58, 30–44

Saunders, J. and Collins, J. (1972), *Teaching Mentally Handicapped Children*, Penny Gobby House School, Hove

Schefflin, M. (1968), 'A Comparison of Four Stimulus Response Channels in Pained Associate Learning', *American Journal of Mental Deficiency*, vol. 73, 303–7

Smith, W.W. (1974), *Teaching a Down's Child*, East Grinstead Society for Mentally Handicapped Children

Snyder, L.S., Bates, E. and Bretherton, I. (1981), 'Content and Context in Early Lexical Development', *Journal of Child Language*, vol. 8, 565–82

Zaidel, E. (1978), 'Lexical Organisation in the Right-hemisphere', in Buser, P. and Rougel-Buser, A. (eds), *Cerebral Correlates of Conscious Experience*, Elsevier, Amsterdam

PART 3:

IMPLEMENTATION

31 REVIEW AND PROSPECT

Keith Topping

Comparison and Contrast of Techniques

All the projects described in Part 2 of this book have some outcomes in common. All resulted in positive change in children's attitudes to reading and in parental perceptions of their children's reading competence, and provided a foundation for the further development of home–school co-operation. Where they differ is in terms of the 'harder', supposedly more 'objective', evidence for improvement in the reading skill levels of the children involved.

In the subsection on 'Parent Listening', only three of seven contributors provide 'hard' evidence of this kind. This reflects the great variety of approaches adopted under this heading, often representing fairly minimal and inexpensive interventions. A meta-analysis of the data which *are* available suggests that a mean ratio gain of twice 'normal' rates of progress in reading is a typical outcome for parent listening projects.

For what is often a lightweight intervention, these results are most encouraging and represent high cost-effectiveness. However, it is necessary to conduct further careful research into the actual process of such interventions, particularly into what parents and children actually do during the project in relation to any training or advice they are given. Ted Glynn's work (see Chapter 20) is exemplary in this respect. Much of the advice given during parent listening projects tends to be vague and not operationalised, and training ensuring skill-acquisition is not common. Guidelines need to be clear, and not too various, for it would be difficult satisfactorily to test the effectiveness of the technique in a situation where every school was proliferating idiosyncratic approaches. Reference to Chapter 33 should help schools produce clear, thorough, sensible formats, which do not differ greatly from school to school while remaining locally relevant.

What is also far from clear is the extent to which parent listening is effectively applicable to children with severe reading failure.

By contrast, all six contributors to the subsection on 'Paired Reading' offer hard data. In Chapter 11 it was noted that typical mean ratio gains for Paired Reading projects were of the order of three times 'normal' rates of progress for reading accuracy and five times 'normal' rates for reading comprehension. That these are not merely exceptional results from seminal projects is becoming increasingly clear as results accrue from a multitude of schools in LEAs adopting the technique on a broad front (e.g. Topping, 1984b). There is also evidence from meta-analysis on this substantial scale that mean ratio gains in reading accuracy are typically five times base-line (pre-project) levels.

Paired Reading projects may be more expensive in terms of professional time than parent listening projects if home visiting on a regular basis is incorporated. With some target populations, home visiting is essential to secure the viability of the project, and there is evidence that home visiting increases the absolute effectiveness of projects (Topping, 1984b). However, with target populations which are more diverse and less pre-selected, additional gains accruing from the incorporation of home visits might be small. Thus automatically including home visits might actually reduce *cost*-effectiveness.

Readers will have noted that the Paired Reading contributors exhibit very much greater homogeneity of technique than is the case for authors in the subsection on 'Parent Listening'. This makes it very much easier and quicker to answer important questions about the Paired Reading approach.

The contributions to the 'Behavioural Methods' subsection are very various, but four of the five contributors cite hard data, and the fifth has not done so owing to difficulties of summarisation — a problem of too much data rather than too little.

For many of the behavioural techniques, it is still early days. The results reported in these pages are most encouraging, but many of the techniques await wider usage in schools before teachers will feel competent to disseminate the skills to parents.

Although the evidence to date is sketchy, it seems as if typical mean ratio gains from Pause, Prompt and Praise projects are of the order of two and a half times 'normal' rates. The precision teaching results are very difficult to quantify in this way, but there is some initial indication that typical mean ratio gains are of the order of two times 'normal' rates with both precision teaching and direct instruction approaches. Of course, these latter techniques are commonly employed with highly specific target populations with severe reading failure, and so these ratio gains are not directly comparable to those cited for other techniques.

It is clear that both precision teaching and direct instruction approaches to parental involvement are likely to be more expensive in terms of professional time than other approaches (with the possible exception of the 'workshop' approach). At first glance it might seem that their *cost-*effectiveness to date might be in question. However, deployed as they usually are — as a relatively 'heavy' intervention for children who have failed to progress using other means — they can hardly be criticised on these grounds.

Despite the variousness of the contributions to the 'Variations' subsection, it is pleasing that five of the six contributors give hard data. The 'workshop' approach described in Chapter 28 is clearly heavy in its consumption of professional time, and in this area, most of all, detailed research work is needed on tangible outcomes.

Many of the approaches described in this subsection are so diverse, constituting combinations of methods as well as variations on other techniques, that it becomes extremely difficult to distinguish the outcome of each component of the total methodology in isolation. Even where the components have been proved effective separately, no summative effect can be assumed when using them together.

However, one or two fascinating trends emerge fairly clearly. An example of this is the way the Bryans, Kidd and Levey variant of Paired Reading (see Chapter 25), with its emphasis on rehearsal and repetition, seems to accelerate reading accuracy much more than reading comprehension — exactly the opposite of what pertains with the original format of Paired Reading.

Sue Buckley's contribution inspires several important messages: that parental involvement in reading can be extended to the most improbable populations; that there are no barriers, except in our own minds; and that progress is not necessarily faster through charges on multiple fronts — it may prove better to do one or a few things intensely and well.

Weaknesses and strengths are to be found in every technique of parental involvement in reading. Some of these were delineated for some of the methods in Chapter 2. We now have adequate evidence on the effectiveness of Paired Reading (and the beginnings of evidence on its cost-effectivenesss), some evidence on the effectiveness of parent listening, and a little evidence on the effectiveness of a range of behavioural methods and variations in the UK.

A rough estimate can be made of the relative professional time-cost of establishing typical projects under the various categories, and this can be drawn up into a 'cascade' of increasingly expensive interventions (see Figure 31.1).

The implication here, simplistically, is that there is no point in using a more expensive intervention unless a less expensive one has been tried and has failed with the target population in question, assuming that the

Figure 31.1: Cost Cascade of Parental Involvement in Reading Techniques

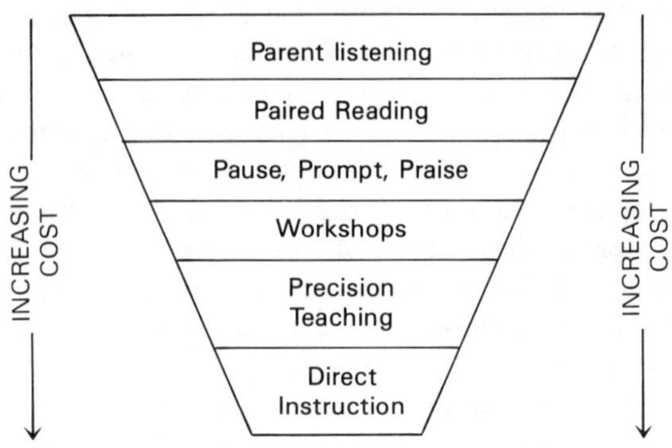

absolute effectiveness of the techniques is equivalent (which, of course, in reality it is not likely to be).

It seems improbable, from evidence in other fields (Topping, 1983), that when we have enough data to construct a parallel cascade of absolute effectiveness, it will match the cost cascade exactly. Given the likelihood of differential effectiveness of some techniques with different target populations, the eventual construction of a global cascade of cost-effectiveness may never prove possible.

Further research may articulate which techniques work best for which target populations, variously defined in terms of chronological age, degree of reading retardation, past learning histories, and so on. It is likely to become commonplace to have different structured techniques operating from the same school for different target groups. Chapters 17, 22, 26 and 27 foreshadow this development.

Compatibility and Similarity of Techniques

It is worth reiterating that the various techniques of parental involvement in reading are as similar as they are different. Indisputably there are strong theoretical tensions between some of the methods. For instance, Paired Reading specifically instructs parents to intervene if the child cannot successfully read a word within five seconds at the most, while Pause, Prompt and Praise specifically instructs parents *not* to intervene until the child has failed to read the word for at least five seconds. It is true that Glynn's contention that the former practice results in over-dependency and inhibits development of self-correction strategies can be seen to apply to a small proportion of children in Paired Reading projects. In practice, the parents of these few children usually resolve the dilemma by only remodelling the error word, rather than by returning to simultaneous reading, and very few such parents adopt the Pause, Prompt and Praise tactic of delaying longer or giving more complex prompts (they have not been trained to do so, of course).

The fascinating thing is that, despite these inherent contradictions in the two techniques, they both produce very positive and quite similar results. Perhaps there is evidence here that it matters less *how* parental behaviour is shaped by structured training, than the fact that it is shaped, by structured training of one sort or another.

As was outlined in Figure 2.3 (page 30), possible interactive links between different techniques are increasingly evident. Schools may soon have projects using different techniques running simultaneously for different groups, but may also come to offer projects based on different techniques to run consecutively for the same group. Thus, it may become possible for families to follow up a parent listening involvement with a curriculum-based workshop, to move from the second phase of Paired Reading on to Pause, Prompt and Praise, or from Precision Teaching of sight vocabulary on to either Paired Reading or to the first stage of direct instruction. What a plethora of good things schools will have to offer the community — and this takes no account of the *new* methods which will be invented during the next decade.

Whatever new techniques are developed, the influence of the general factors underpinning the effectiveness of all methods of parental involvement in reading will remain strong. In Chapter 2, it was proposed that the four most important of these were: modelling, practice, feedback and reinforcement. The first of these merits further consideration here.

Merely exposing children to books is not enough — demonstration of appropriate reading behaviour by adults markedly raises the independent *usage* of the books by children (Haskett and Lenfestey, 1974). There is evidence from Bronfenbrenner (1970), Bandura (1977) and Clarke-Stewart (1978) that modelling is maximally effective when the model is:

(1) available and prominent in the life of the child;
(2) sharing substantial life experience with the child;
(3) powerful and in control of resources;
(4) prestigious and of high status;
(5) perceived as competent by the child;
(6) seen to enjoy the modelled behaviour;

(7) gaining some reward from the modelled behaviour;
(8) warm and accepting in emotional tone;
(9) replicated by multiple similar models;
(10) demonstrating a behaviour which yields entry to a group.

The implications of these for the power of parental involvement will be largely self-evident to the reader. The implications for the active involvement of fathers in parent involvement projects, particularly where a majority of the target group is likely to be boys, is perhaps worth dwelling upon. In far too many families, it is mother who provides the input, does the work, and is the major if not the only model of reading behaviour. Special efforts to bring in fathers from the shadows are likely to yield substantial benefits.

Of the ten conditions for effective modelling, the fifth has particular implications for the design of parental involvement projects. While it is often easier to train children in a technique than their parents, the importance of the parents' ability to demonstrate competence in the technique must not be under-estimated. Here, the briefer and simpler techniques have a considerable advantage — they are less likely to generate confusion resulting from information overload, and arguably maximise the probability of demonstrating competence in the technique for a wide range of parents.

Certainly, techniques should not be very time-consuming, and it is desirable that they come to seem as 'natural' as possible to the families involved, although most will appear novel to the project participants at first. All parents are interacting with and thereby 'teaching' their children something every day, and the project technique should be compatible with the natural tempo of family life.

The emphasis must be on *enjoying* learning, since if the activity does not become self-reinforcing, the project effects will not endure or generalise. The 'little and often' formula for parent–child activity is valuable in that the activity ends while it is still fun, it tends to elicit spontaneous generalisation of related behaviour (such as the child continuing to read the book silently alone), and it fits more easily into the demands and stresses of everyday family life. It is essential to *avoid* making home more like school. For many children in parent involvement projects, school has already largely failed. Making school more like home is likely to prove a more fruitful avenue for exploration.

Evaluation

Given that parent involvement projects operate in very complex environments (i.e. family homes), evaluation of the effects of specific techniques is something of a researcher's nightmare, let alone the efects of the more general underlying factors. Yet an evaluative exercise should be an integral part of every project, even where it is a school's second or third venture in the same format. Every school needs to be sure that it has found the structure that works best for its own catchment and organisation. Even then, times change, and without inbuilt regular evaluation, the danger is that the school will not change with them. Evaluation is also important in convincing sceptics of the value of this kind of work. Schools will also find that parents and children are very eager to be told how they have got on, so it is as well to have something concrete to tell them. Having said this, one of the great advantages of parental involvement projects is their cost-effectiveness — so it would not make sense to spend more time evaluating the project than actually running it.

Some thought about the design of the evaluation is essential. If you use a simple pre-test/post-test design, you will have no way of telling whether the children would not have made those gains anyway, unless they are really spectacular. Some form of 'control' group would be ideal, but an adequate matched or randomised control group is difficult to establish in a natural setting. A 'comparison' group of self-selected non-participants might have to suffice. If there is previous information on the project children's reading progress, it is possible to compare their progress in the year(s) before the project to their rate of progress during the project. If this is possible for a comparison group as well, so much the better. Very often relevant information is collected anyway as part of a school's routine monitoring, so only a little extra time is involved in further numerical analysis. More complex evaluation designs are described in Topping (1984a) and Cook and Campbell (1979).

The next problem is finding reliable, valid and relevant measures which generate data which are readily analysable. A deluge of impressionistic opinion may be fascinating, but is unlikely to facilitate the formation of clear conclusions. Standardised reading tests, either group or individual, may be used, but all those currently available have at least one major disadvantage, if only that they are time-consuming to administer. Criterion-referenced reading tests may be more valid and relevant, but not necessarily, and results are then not easily compared between projects. 'Diagnostic' tests are largely irrelevant and often very time-consuming. Structured feedback from the participants (children, parents, teachers) is always valuable, but it does need to be structured. Questionnaires, structured interviews, and recorded group feedback meetings are three obvious possibilities here.

Once the data are gathered, analysis of them need not be excessively complex, so long as it is thorough. Statistical procedures, if utilised, should complement common sense rather than replace it. Readers will by now be aware that if a parental involvement project for a reasonably broad target population yields ratio gains of markedly *less* than twice normal rates of progress, the project organisers should ask themselves some searching questions. As the state of knowledge in the field improves, the standard expectation should rise even higher.

The Future

Much remains to be done. Experimentation and expansion with various techniques at the upper and lower ends of the age spectrum is an obvious area for development. This also applies to the ability spectrum. For many of the techniques, there is a need to articulate structured guidelines for parental involvement beyond simple oral reading (precision teaching and direct instruction already encompass this). Beyond oral reading, there will be yet more complex difficulties in evaluating the effects of a project, unless precision teaching or direct instruction formats are used. Careful exploration of the effects of more than one technique used concurrently or consecutively is essential. And, of course, much straightforward replication of the seminal work reported in this book is necessary, as is further work on long-term duration and generalisation of gains.

Another fruitful field of enquiry will be the social and organisational psychology of project establishment and maintenance. It is interesting, for instance, that many children (particularly boys) involved in small-scale parental involvement in reading projects report that they have tried hard to keep this fact secret from their playmates, despite there being little evidence that their friends would be anything other than eager to join in. The development among all pupils and teachers in a school of a positive, high-status ethos for such projects would seem to be a desirable objective. As data accumulate, the relative effectiveness of a variety of organisational structures for training and follow-up procedures in relation to different target populations should also become calculable.

Speculation about the long-term future of the parental involvement in reading movement is equally fascinating. Although considerably better researched and evaluated than many innovative educational developments, it remains to be seen whether evidence of effectiveness is sufficient by itself to sustain the relevant teacher behaviour. How crucial might be the catalytic role of the support service or agency from outside the school, in introducing innovation and in sustaining the nexus of agency supporting school to support parents to support child? Three-quarters of the contributors to this book have a professional base outside of schools, and have clearly played a major part in disseminating innovation, but are they now dispensable?

Will all schools eventually have a parental involvement in reading programme? If not, why not? Doubtless there is a danger of a residual minority of schools feeling under pressure to mount a project, and blundering half-heartedly into setting up some feeble token gesture, thereby bringing the whole movement into disrepute. To date, the good results have been achieved with schools which were well motivated. Fortunately, the parental involvement in reading movement has many of the qualities necessary for long-term survival, and it seems most unlikely that it will fade away like many other educational innovations, to be reborn in a different guise in another 25 years.

While children undoubtedly gain a great deal from parental involvement projects, and parents often derive considerable personal benefit, what do the schools gain? More insecure members of the teaching profession may feel anxious about 'giving away' some of their mystical, esoteric techniques. In fact, such projects often free teachers from the impossible burden of trying to give children adequate reading practice in school. Teachers will still 'hear children read' for assessment and diagnostic purposes, but much less frequently than before. Professional time can be freed for a whole range of other initiatives — for instance, conscious changes in the teaching of reading in school, which could, and arguably should, become considerably more sophisticated and technical.

Schools are already looking at parental involvement projects in curriculum areas other than reading. Indeed, the PAIRS project (see Chapter 21) already incorporates work in spelling, and reports of parental involvement in writing and number work are beginning to appear.

In view of the demonstrated effectiveness of parental involvement techniques, and the accumulating evidence of long-term duration of gains (see Chapters 4 and 16 in particular), which compare favourably to the long-term effectiveness of provision of extra and more expensive professional teaching resources, prescription of availability of a parent involvement project in some form is increasingly likely to be a feature of 'Statements of Special Educational Need' resulting from assessments under the 1981 Education Act (or 'Individual Educational Programmes' under PL 94–142 in the USA). For some children, access to parent involvement projects will become mandatory. It is hoped that this does not rob these projects of their essential vitality.

References

Bandura, A. (1977), *Social Learning Theory*, Prentice-Hall, Englewood Cliffs, New Jersey

Bronfenbrenner, U. (1970), *Two Worlds of Childhood: US and USSR*, Russell Sage Foundation, New York

Clarke-Stewart, K.A. (1978), 'Evaluating Parental Effects on Child Development', in L. Schulman (ed.), *Review of Research in Education*, F.E. Peacock Publishers Inc., Itasca, Illinois

Cook, T.D. and Campbell, D.T. (1979), *Quasi-experimental Design and Analysis Issues for Field Settings*, Rand McNally, Chicago

Haskett, G.J. and Lenfestey, W. (1974), 'Reading-related Behaviour in an Open Classroom: Effects of Novelty and Modelling on Preschoolers', *Journal of Applied Behaviour Analysis*, vol. 7, no. 2, 233–41

Topping, K.J. (1983), *Educational Systems for Disruptive Adolescents*, Croom Helm, London

Topping, K.J. (1984a), *Paired Reading Training Pack*, Kirklees Psychological Service, Huddersfield

Topping, K.J. (1984b), 'Kirklees Psychological Service Paired Reading Project: First Annual Report', unpublished document, Kirklees Psychological Service, Huddersfield

32 PLANNING PARENTAL INVOLVEMENT IN READING

Sheila Wolfendale

Introduction

The aim of this chapter is to provide the elements of planning a parental involvement in reading programme and to equip intending participants, particularly teachers, with the means of carrying it out. We would like readers to benefit from the considerable collective experience which is represented in this book, and to use work reported here as a starting-point for their initiatives.

Some readers may wish to replicate a project; others may have plans for advancing upon ideas explored in a particular study; yet others may want to build upon their own existing work and may find inspiration from the examples of others.

What comes across from the accounts in this book is the paramount importance of prior planning and of the need to establish at the outset the key components — identifying aims, purpose, objectives, the mechanics of execution and the means of evaluation. Each description testifies to a commitment to prior planning and the carefully thought-through inclusion of these components, irrespective of project scale.

Chapter 33 gives examples and details of resources which could be useful, even essential, for those wishing to be active in the area.

We should like to spell out in some detail requisites for a successful parental involvement in reading programme. The main ones were briefly listed as 'planning guidelines' in Chapter 3 and it is our intention to amplify and expand upon this *aide memoire* in this chapter.

It is important to make it clear that as co-editors we do not wish to impose any particularly conceptual framework upon the reader. An *à la carte* rather than a *prix fixe* approach characterises the purpose of this book. The reader is encouraged (to mix metaphors) to regard the book as a pot pourri of 'good things' to dip into and take from whatever best suits him/her and his/her work settings.

Thus a variety of models is presented, within the framework of a rationale for the whole area of parental involvement (Chapter 1), and of the teaching and learning of reading and the place of parents in these processes (Chapter 2).

So the planning guidelines which constitute this chapter represent a roof beneath which a range of models can be housed. We can present the guidelines as a task analysis, and we try in this chapter to give as much detail and specificity to the tasks as is possible within the confines of one chapter. What is ultimately each reader's own decision is how to translate and apply these. As this book is not a 'how to' instructional manual in a step-by-step prescriptive sense, readers wishing to pursue a particular model or method will need to go to source to find out the minutiae of practice derived from a particular theory, and training instructions.

The way in which we present planning guidelines is not in an invariable order nor do we wish to think that *all* components must be adopted. It may be helpful at this point to distinguish between a 'minimal' and a 'maximal' approach. The reader will have noticed that the projects range in complexity, with the most elaborate undoubtedly qualifying for the status of research and the least elaborate representing routine school provision. This range can be represented on a continuum thus:

on which each type of approach can be plotted accordingly.

Minimal approaches are and should be characterised by the same degree of prior planning and consultation that characterises a maximal approach. In other words, parental involvement in reading is an innovation which requires a considerable amount of preliminary organisation and the consideration, if not adoption, of all possible components. Again, each reader will decide how far to go, which components to take on board.

Structure of the Chapter

A working conceptualisation has been adopted which clusters the planning guidelines and points of action into a series of five stages. Each stage comprises a abstract–practical mix and each stage with its main elements (as signposts) is presented in a box as a summary to each stage. The suggestions and questions contained at each stage cannot be exhaustive and we hope they will trigger and generate others relevant to readers' own settings.

The suggestions-and-questions format has been adopted to avoid the temptation and pointlessness of providing a long, tedious checklist. We aim at a judicious mix of asking salient questions which will be pertinent to individual schools for different reasons and providing suggestions where we hope readers are looking for practical guidance. Occasionally we resort to 'comments' if there seems to be the need to elaborate. This format and the details contained at each stage are intended to be applicable to all schools. How the scheme is adopted and executed for different ages and target populations of children will be up to teachers. The 'stage' categories are inevitably not discrete and exclusive of one another; although each stage dovetails into the next, a little overlap is inevitable and some cross-referencing is essential and has been explicitly built in. As a shorthand, the abbreviations PIR (for parental involvement in reading) are used throughout this chapter, and provided at the end is a short list of further reading texts which will be useful for planning purposes.

As an advance organiser, the five stages are:

Stage I:	Starting-points and First Considerations
Stage II:	Planning
Stage III:	Action
Stage IV:	Maintaining and Monitoring
Stage V:	Measurement and Evaluation

Stage I: Starting-points and First Considerations

Objectives: to review the school's current policies and provisions and to clarify aims.

Current Policy on Parent–School Relations

Questions.

How are parents involved with the school?
Is there a PTA?
Do parents come into school to hear reading, help with activities?
What format is there for parent–teacher meetings?
Do children already take reading books home?
Does the school have a community focus and community links?
Is there a parents' or community room in school?

What plans are there, other than PIR, to extend parental involvement?
How do parent governors work with the school and how best can they represent parents?

School Factors

Suggestions.

(i) Take into account at this stage factors about numbers on roll, class size, staff–pupil ratio, deployment of staff.
(ii) Consider the school's catchment area and any areas of special circumstance, special needs, etc., such as: (a) ethnic composition and the needs of parents and children whose first language is not English, bilingual representation in the school; (b) socio-economic background of intake and the extent to which this will have a bearing on the project; (c) proportion of children in school who have designated special educational needs and how the project can benefit them.
(iii) Consider current school resources, their sufficiency for the project, and estimate what further resources might be required.

Current Curriculum Policies

Questions.

What is the policy on the teaching of reading and what reading schemes are in use?
What is the system (and organisation) for teaching reading and allied subjects (e.g. literacy, language development)?
Does the organisation include whole class, small-group teaching?
Do 'special interest', 'special need' groups exist?
What is the policy on special needs?
What is the policy on multicultural education and its bearing on the proposed project?
If relevant to consider, what is the policy and practice on integration of children with special educational needs?

Other Current Initiatives/Commitments

Comment. It is important to take into account curricular or other initiatives with which the school is currently involved, in order to estimate the availability of time and energy of staff to take on board a PIR programme. Take into account curriculum innovation as well as staff attendance at in-service courses.

Interest and Availability of Personnel

Questions.

(i) Teaching Staff. What is the expressed interest and enthusiasm of staff in participating in a PIR programme?
Can individual staff members be identified who would be willing to be involved in a project?
What preliminary groundwork has been undertaken to date, in the way of attendance at INSET, staff discussion, examination of materials?

(ii) *Parents*
What is the likely response of parents? (Use current parental involvement as a base-line.)
What preparation needs to be undertaken to establish and foster parental interest?

(iii) *Out-of-school Personnel*
Has the potential interest of the educational psychologist, adviser, advisory (remedial, resource) teachers been canvassed, as well as their availability in participating and supporting?
Has the role of teaching staff with a home-contact brief (home–school liaison, outreach teacher) been considered to be part of a PIR project?

Costing

Questions.

Have these likely costs been taken into account — book purchases, buying other materials, duplicating and photocopying, video-hire, assessment and record-keeping forms, postage, equipment (e.g. for storage, shelving), etc.?
Are there other resource implications (e.g. travel claims)?

Clarification of Aims

Questions.

Why is a PIR project under consideration?
What is wanted from it?
What is its envisaged scope? (Cf. latter part of Chapter 1.)

Stage I: Summary

Starting-points and First Considerations

Objectives
Current Policy on Parent–School Relations
School Factors
Current Curriculum Policies
Other Current Initiatives/Commitments
Interest and Availability of Personnel
Costing
Clarification of Aims

Stage II: Planning

Objectives: to list and to detail all the intended components of the PIR programme.

Target Children

Questions.

What is to be the composition of the children involved? A preliminary breakdown might be useful, such as: Age Range/Class(es)/Numbers/Current Reading Level(s).
Is the programme to be geared to children initially learning to read, to those with reading difficulties? (Cf. Clarification of Aims, Stage I.)
Is the programme to be angled at children with communication needs (children and/or parents who first language is not English, and those who would respond to a bilingual approach)?

Compatibility with Existing Provision

Questions.

How will the plans fit in with present policies (see Stage I)?
Will existing resources be sufficient?
What extra resources and materials will be needed (see below)?
What additional organisational factors need to be considered?
What will staff responsibilities be (see below)?

Reading Method

Comments. As this book illustrates, there are a number of possibilities:

parent listening, behavioural approaches, Paired Reading, and combinations and variations of these including Shared Reading, the linguistic/language experience approach, children listening, family reading groups, family book reviews.

Suggestions.

(i) Consider the features of each method before deciding on the appropriateness for the project.
(ii) Criteria for choice will include: proven effectiveness, compatibility with current teaching methods, popularity rating (extent to which teachers and parents will enjoy using a method), and whether or not the goal is to compare methods.
(iii) Before embarking on a chosen method, ensure that participants will have adequate knowledge of the technique, its rationale, and understanding of ways in which it will be applied, and how people will be trained in its use.

Materials

Suggestions for Reading Material.

(a) Existing reading material — includes the reading scheme, books from class and school libraries, school bookshop.
(b) Borrowed or purchased material — includes school/public library, teachers' class library, resource centre loan, visiting book bus, LEA special fund allowance, books and papers from home.
(c) 'New' materials — includes 'take home' sheets for child and parent use, which may parallel and augment a reading scheme; especially prepared sheets with reading games and activities; material prepared by teacher–parent groups, e.g. 'find out' exercises, stories, poems.

Suggestions for Training Materials.

(a) Handout or booklet for parents — in practice, these cover project aims, scope, 'do's and don'ts', and other points of guidance and support. The booklets are either designed to back-up reference material or as training manuals, in which case they need to be rather more elaborated, but still well organised and expressed with clarity.
(b) Audio-visual aids — planners need to decide whether to obtain,

hire, etc., available resources (Chapter 33), and consider whether home-made or local material is more suitable.

(c) Training packs — these consist of (a) and (b) above, as well as other instructional and practice materials (for example, a step-by-step sequence for parents who are learning to apply a particular technique).

Recording Material. See below.

Project Personnel

Questions

(i) *Teaching Staff*
Who is to be project leader/co-ordinator?
Who will be responsible for and involved in training?
Who will take on responsibility for daily, weekly running?
Who will be involved in the project, i.e. whose children will participate?

(ii) *Parents*
What will be the means of contacting parents?
How will they be initially briefed?
What will be the best form of parental training (see below and Stage I)?
How will they be guided and supported through the project?
What feedback and lines of communication to parents will be inbuilt?

(iii) *Out-of-school Personnel*
Are identified persons involved in initiating the project?
How can they help in the design, running and monitoring?
How can they support the project?
Are there other people who could participate, such as other family members, friends, adult volunteers, schoolfriends, peers?

(iv) *The Children*
How will they be initially briefed?
How will they be prepared to participate?
What means will there be to keep them informed?

Assessing, Measuring, Evaluation

Comments. The reader is advised at this point to cross-refer to Stage V. Decisions about the place of testing, assessment and measurement in a broader sense and the purpose and form of evaluation are central and crucial. Then return to this stage.

Record-keeping

Suggestions. School-based records of:

(a) Work covered at home and in parallel at school.
(b) Materials sent home and returned.
(c) Completed and returned parents' record card (see below).
(d) Test results, other assessment if applicable.
(e) Dates, content of home visits, meetings at school.

Another useful item is the parents' record card. In general, parents record date, time, material covered, method(s), and under 'Comments' they note child's responsiveness, errors (if required to do so), and their own reactions and observations.

Training

Cross-refer to Stage III for elaboration of training approaches.

Time-scale

Suggestions. There are a number of possibilities and permutations, such as

Open-ended routine provision of a PIR programme for target children with the possibility of later inclusion of other children or other classes (a rolling, cumulative programme).
Routine, low-key provision but 'experimental' in being of a 'try out' finite nature, e.g. a six-week burst, followed by short programme repeats over the school year, or adoption of an open-ended programme, or a repeat or revised version.
Hypothesis-testing, 'one off' experiment, short-term (a few weeks) or longitudinal study (may be paralleled by concurrent studies in other schools).

Maintaining and Monitoring

Cross refer to Stage IV.

Stage II: Summary

Planning

Objectives
Target Children
Compatibility with Existing Provision
Reading Method
Materials
Project Personnel
Assessing, Measuring, Evaluation (Stage V)
Record-keeping
Training (Stage III)
Time-scale
Maintaining and Monitoring (Stage IV)

Stage III: Action

Objectives: to introduce the project to parents and children, to carry out training and organisational procedures.

Approaching Parents

Suggestions. Use existing arrangements for parent–school contact as the context for deciding the most appropriate way of introducing the plans to parents and of gaining their support and involvement. Options include:

Letter home, explaining the project, asking for volunteers and suggesting a meeting.
Letter home, explaining the project, outlining target classes and groups, asking for parental endorsement and participation; suggest a meeting.
Call initial open meeting, explain, describe, illustrate PIR (via role play done by teachers or children — the latter, preferably — slides, OHP, video, demonstration of materials and examples) and ask for volunteers.
As above, with pre-selected parents.
Small group meeting, in classes, tutor group, remedial/special needs department; outline project, with components of above, and ask for participation.
Home visiting (preferably from member of staff, educational psychologist, etc., experienced in this area) to parents of target children. An initial telephone call to arrange is a common sense courtesy.

Publicity via posters, advertisements, announcement in local press, noticeboards — these approaches are supplementary to those above.

Considerations in Approaching Parents

Suggestions.

(i) Timing of meeting, visits: make provision for working parents and time meetings to accommodate their needs, even if this means repeat performances.
(ii) 'Hard to reach', 'stay away' parents: small group meetings, home visits may be effective means of establishing personal contact. But it may be that under-confident parents may be drawn in by the success of the project when under way, so be patient and continue to bridge-build.

Preparing Children

Suggestions. Taking age-related factors into account:

Discuss reading and reading progress with children, individually or in small groups.
Describe schemes and approaches and their success, stressing that children's interest and co-operation are essential requisites.
Outline project plans and the part they and their parents can play.
Enlist children's help, where appropriate in: preparing and illustrating booklets, role-play exercises as part of training.
Train children in the chosen method(s): see below.

Note: consider including children in meetings held for parents.

Preparing Resources

Questions.

Are there enough supplies of in-school books?
Have adequate stocks of borrowed or purchased material been ordered?
Is there enough extra, supplementary material for the duration of the project?
Have enough record forms been duplicated, printed?
Are there enough parents' booklets, training materials?
Have audio-visual aids been ordered in enough time?
How will the children transport their reading materials to and from home (plastic wallets or bags, specially sewn bags, folders)?

Where will reading materials be kept and displayed and record cards stored? Consider use of filing cabinets, tall cupboards, shelving, racking, Lawcoboxes, and their accessibility to parents and teachers.

Testing (Pre-project and Base-line Attainment Measures)

Comments. Cross-refer to Stage V and return to this point.

Training

Suggestions. Although this section refers to parents, the content and 'teaching procedures' are applicable to those teachers who will need training. Below are suggestions for the structure and content of training.

(1) Planning points. Venue of meeting(s); teachers to be present; areas of responsibility (who will make tea/coffee, who will introduce, work the video, guide the participating children, etc.)? Will a crèche be available?

(2) Setting and location of the meeting(s). At the risk of making a perhaps obvious point, it should be borne in mind that outside a PTA context, parents and teachers do not often meet in conducive and congenial circumstances, and that parents in particular need to feel welcome and relaxed when in school. Seating arrangements and availability of refreshments are important features of the setting.

(3) Number of meetings. One training meeting may be enough, though perhaps one follow-up and consolidation session will be necessary, depending upon the complexity of the training and time needed for parents to practise and acquire the required skills. Some projects find a 'one off' session sufficient, others have utilised a several-session intensive instructional workshop format.

(4) Format. As discussed above in 'Approaching Parents', a large or small group format will be chosen, and what follows under 'Content' and 'Procedure' will need to be modified to match with the chosen format.

(5) Content. A list of the 'universals' (included in all projects to a greater or less extent) that need to be covered includes the following:

Description of PIR and other reported ventures (deal with who and what are involved, success rates).
Aims, purpose of the project *per se*, and in relation to aims, policies and current school practice.
Introduction to the method(s) to be used.
The daily/nightly (or several times a week) routine of the 10–15 minute meetings at home and the requisite conditions, often summarised in

the form of: the 'do's and don'ts' sheet (i.e. an outline of favourable/unfavourable home conditions in which the reading session takes place, and the 'common-sense' way of creating and maintaining conducive conditions).
The parents' record form, the purposes and benefits of record-keeping and mechanics of doing so.
Contact and review points: teachers to outline to parents what periodic points of contact, consultation, discussion, support and review are built into the programme (see Stage IV).

(6) Procedure. There will be permutations on what is presented below and the ordering will vary to suit the circumstance but basically the options are as follows:

Initial talk/lecture.
Use of video and/or role play by adults or children to demonstrate: (a) chosen method(s); (b) do's and dont's.
Any other aid, such as overhead projector.
Talk and demonstration of materials, record-keeping, give out parents' booklet.
Display of books, other materials.

(7) Specific instruction. As hinted above, it may well be a prime requisite to guarantee success of one or more methods for parents to master and feel at home with the method, teaching/recording procedures, and any error analysis, observation and recording approaches. Whether or not a specifically behavioural approach is the framework, parents will need instruction in principles of consistent reinforcement and accuracy of observation and recording. To incorporate these 'teaching points', training sessions need to include opportunity for practice and rehearsal, feedback and 'knowledge of results', participant modelling and role-play exercises in duo.

NB. It is worth pointing out that a considerable number of primary schools hold occasional sessions for parents on the teaching of reading and numbers, and do their best to acquaint parents on current approaches. If such provision has not existed, it may be advisable to include these elements as part of a workshop approach.

Terms of the Agreement

Suggestions. Planners may wish to build in explicit terms, in order to accommodate all participants and to reduce the possibility of later misunderstandings. This can be done in the form of a written 'contract' which briefly sets out what each participant has agreed to do for the duration of the project and which can be signed by all parties.

Stage III: Summary

Action

Objectives Approaching Parents Considerations in Approaching Parents Preparing Children Preparing Resources Training Terms of the Agreement

Stage IV: Maintaining and Monitoring

Objectives: to ensure smooth operation by listing and carrying out routine checks, and to carry out monitoring procedures that form part of the assessment and evaluation.

Checking on the Practicalities

Questions.

Are the stocks of books and materials regularly and routinely renewed?
Are the storage facilities adequate for display and access by teachers, parents, children?
Are the mechanics for distribution and collection of material flowing between school and home proving effective?
Are the designated times for contact between teachers and parents proving to be the best times?

Monitoring Progress

Record-keeping: Questions.

Are parents' record cards completed?
Are parents' record cards returned regularly?
Do teachers read these and make their comments?

Feedback: Questions.

What mechanism is there for feedback from participating teachers?
How is feedback from children ensured?

Meetings: Questions.

Are there review/support meetings between teachers, parents and other participants?
Are these one-to-one, small/large group?
What is the purpose of meetings and how are the records of meetings used?
Is it necessary to have 'retraining', refresher sessions?

Home Visiting: Suggestions. As stressed above, home visiting should be undertaken by teachers and others with experience in this area. Home visiting during a PIR programme can serve any one or more of these functions:

To reach parents who cannot attend scheduled school meetings and to offer guidance and support.
To review progress, clarify concerns, problem solve.
To check upon the consistency of application of the method(s) and redirect if necessary.
As a researcher, carry out observation and home-based measurement on, for example, parent–child interaction, influence of family members and domestic factors on the programme, effectiveness of parent as teacher, reading rate, error rate, error type.

Assessment: Questions.

What is the format for reviewing children's reading progress (a) routinely, (b) as part of the programme?
At what point during the project is the suitability of the material that is sent home reviewed?
What types of continuing or periodic observation and/or assessment are most applicable to the programme? (Now cross-refer to stage V).

Stage IV: Summary

Maintaining and Monitoring

Objectives
Checking on the Practicalities
Monitoring Progress
- Record-keeping
- Feedback
- Meetings
- Home Visiting
- Assessment (Stage V)

Stage V: Measurement and Evaluation

Objectives: to select appropriate design and measurement techniques and to carry out project evaluation and review.

Scope

Comments. Refer to Stage I for 'Aims'. It will be clear by now that we are advocates of building in means by which planners can gauge effectiveness and 'worthwhileness'.

(1) Minimal approaches: criteria of success may include these — intrinsic enthusiasm and enjoyment on the part of all; workability and smooth running of a scheme that builds in record-keeping but nothing more and a school policy that positively encourages parents to be involved in this way. For a 'minimal' approach several planning guidelines in Stages I–IV will be relevant.

(2) Towards a 'maximal' approach: scope is limitless, here are some possibilities, all demonstrated throughout this book:

To gauge reading progress over time, hypothesising that parental involvement with accelerate performance.

To measure the effects of a particular method within PIR, perhaps to compare with another method on a different group of (matched?) children.

Introduce PIR for children with reading difficulties or 'slow learners' as 'remedial' intervention.

To research the parameters of 'parents as teachers', 'parents as behaviour technicians' — that is, go beyond crude reading-attainment

measures to analysing subtle interactive effects, parents as models, as instructors, the learning potential of the home, and so on.
Explore and exploit the potential of parent and teacher working together.

Design and Methodology

Consider these dimensions:

Selection of Children: Questions.

Will control groups be desirable or possible?
Would an alternative be the use of comparison groups?
Will numbers of children be chosen for convenience (i.e. a whole class, an age group), for guaranteeing statistical significance, and/or on educational criteria (children in 'need', other categories)?

Role of Planners. Questions. (These apply to in- or out-of-school personnel.)

Will the planner be an organiser and liaison person?
Will the planner be a participant (as a teacher)?
Will the planner be an objective researcher (involved in pre- and post-testing data collection)?
Will the planner be a participant researcher (in addition to testing and data collection, visiting and supporting parents and teachers)?
Will the planner be the 'agent of change'/enthuser/animateur/catalyst/facilitator, in also influencing directions and outcomes?

Other Design Considerations

Questions.

Would a short, small-scale exploratory study be desirable to pilot materials (record cards, questionnaires), to explore attitudes, establish the feasibility of the project?
In the envisaged time-scale, will allowance be made for examinations, holidays, inspections, other school events?
Can planners ensure that there will be uniformity of training and instruction given to groups on successive occasions?
Can planners ensure that there will be uniformity and consistency of checking and monitoring procedures such as home visits or retraining?
Can planners ensure that there will be no deviations from agreed procedure and timings and no randomness in the number and timing of

meetings for example?
Will it be sensible to anticipate and take account of possible sample attrition?
Could there be Hawthorne effects which need taking into account?

Measurement Techniques

Comments. Consider these requirements for any measure used: cost-effectiveness of materials and time in administration and scoring; reliability; validity; relevance to the project; analysable data. If planners are going to compile their own instruments in addition to or instead of standardised tests they will need to pilot these (e.g. for questionnaires, surveys, interview frames and items), obtaining co-rater agreements (for coding frames, categories, items, for observation and recording), trying out informal reading inventories.

Suggestions: Pre- and Post-measures.

Reading Tests
Standardised tests (e.g. Graded Word Recognition, Sentence Reading, Comprehension, Cloze).
Non-standardised (e.g., Cloze, Informal Reading Inventory, Word Recognition Lists from project material). (More suitable for monitoring.)
'Diagnostic', especially tests which are aimed at or include miscue/error analysis. (More suitable for monitoring.)
Progress through graded reading scheme, pre- and post. (More suitable for monitoring.)

See reference list, for Raban, Topping (for time-series designs), Vincent *et al.*; also recommended are the test catalogues produced by the National Foundation for Educational Research and other publishers. Also, the appendix to this chapter gives an alphabetically arranged list of standardised tests which have been used in PIR. This gives no indication of frequency nor of 'best buys', but conveys a flavour of what people have used.

Attitudes
(a) Attitudes to reading of children pre- and post-project.
(b) Change of attitude to PIR by parents, children, teachers pre- and post-project.
(c) Views and feedback on the progress and outcomes.

Suggested measures are:

Interview — individual or group, structured or not.
Questionnaire — oral individual; oral group (with taped group discussion); sent (survey type) to participate, with no face-to-face contact.

Behaviour Change on the Part of Children, vis-à-vis
(a) motivation;
(b) attention to task;
(c) self-image.

These would not only apply to the PIR, but also to generalised effects in other learning situations, where change might be ascribed to the PIR. Suggested measures are:

questionnaire;
inventory (such as self-concept);
observation (base-line, post-base-line, set above under 'Comments'), re-establishment of co-rater agreement, etc.; also consider type of observation.

Teaching/Learning Skills. Suggested measures are:

observation, including use of video for frame-by-frame and micro-analysis;
audiotape feedback.

Suggestions: Monitoring. (Assessing progress during the project; build in appropriate time-intervals.)

Reading
Standardised tests.
Non-standardised tests (see above).
Parents and teachers to record errors on a 'Reading Behaviour Chart' (construct and pilot?)
Probes (cf. PAIRS, Chapter 21).
Targets achieved daily/weekly.
Check on prompts and correction procedures and teaching style.
Progress through reading scheme.

Behaviour Change. Observation at home and in school (time- and event-sampling, diary-keeping). On the last, note that while impressionistic, qualitative data have their place, such data should not appear as a 'stream of consciousness', but be recorded under categories and/or sequentially in diary form and serve a purpose. Such information may illuminate and enrich the 'hard' data. Examples include case studies, users' impressions, accounts of events, unexpected influences upon the programme.

Teaching/Learning (Periodic Checks)
Observation, including video.
Audiotape — of reading behaviour, teaching instruction, error analysis.

Attitudes and Responsiveness
Record forms;
meetings;
home visits (see Stage IV).

Evaluation

Comments. All the planning stages constitute, *in toto*, the evaluation of PIR, and the success or failure of a project will rest on the care and tightness of a design that takes into account a significant number of the planning components. No project can be evaluated on the basis of *post hoc* decisions. So planners will now refer back to the original aims, to the criteria of success that were inbuilt, to the appropriateness of the measures used as well as their results.

Types of Evaluation

Comments. There are two main types of evaluation, 'process' (or formative) evaluation and 'product' (or summative) evaluation. Summative evaluation looks at the end-product of a project, without looking closely at how effective each of the various aspects of the organisation and methods of the project were in achieving this goal. These latter questions are the focus of formative evaluation, so named because the data gathered enable planners to re-form a better project next time, to adjust the current one. Above, we detailed a considerable number of formative and summative measures to use.

Treatment of Results

Suggestions.

Examine results of pre- and post-test measures and analyse them for significance.
Examine outcomes of other pre- and post-measures and analyse.

Examine data from monitoring procedures and analyse.
Appraise these results against aims.
Match the outcomes against the criteria for success.

Aftermath

Suggestions.

Decide whether or not the project should repeat, unchanged.
Decide whether or not the project should repeat with modifications.
Decide if it is to be renewed as part of home–school policy (i.e. becomes routinely available provision).
If so, decide what maintenance and support structures need to be built in.
Share the results and decision-making with all the participants.

Finally, incorporate continued PIR into school policy, and over time consider its status in relation to curriculum, school organisation, areas of staff responsibility and school management structure.

Stage V: Summary

Measurement and Evaluation

Objectives Scope Design and Methodology Measurement Techniques Evaluation Types of Evaluation Treatment of Results Aftermath

Running Workshops

Suggestions. The outline of Stages I to V has inevitably been school-focused, since most projects originate within individual schools. These planning guidelines, however, would be easily suited for use in centrally based in-service training workshops, where one major aim might be to 'train trainers'. In this way, too, workshops can provide the source and inspiration for dissemination.

Chapter 10 in this book described a six-week workshop. The teachers attending it had pre-contracted to initiate a programme after the cessation of the course and the three co-ordinators who ran it likewise pre-contracted to offer assistance to those schools (eight in all) in setting up and monitoring their project.

This model of INSET in PIR offers more to course members if they can be actively involved during the course with activity, so that learning is participant and theory and practice can inform each other. For example, tasks that participants can undertake during the course with colleagues in school can be those in Stage I and some of those in Stage II. It is suggested that a support and information network of first and successive wave PIR workers could be one constructive offshoot of centrally or regionally organised INSET. In that way, experienced first-wave participants can instruct and demonstrate on later workshops, which can extend, as time goes by, to deal with the evaluation of local projects. This local expertise can be shared among and between schools.

Appendix: List of Reading Tests used in PIR Projects

Burt Graded Word Recognition Test
Caerleon Assessment of Phonic Skills
Carver Word Recognition Test
Daniels and Diack Standard Reading Test
Dolch List of 89 commonly occurring words
English/British Picture Vocabulary Test
Jackson Phonic Sheets
London Reading Test
Neale Analysis of Reading Ability
NFER Tests, A, B, C, and D
Primary Reading Test
Southgate Group Reading Test
Spooner Group Reading Test
Young Group Reading Test

Further Reading

The texts on this list offer useful information on some of the planning elements dealt within this chapter.

Brigham Young University Press editors (1982), *How to Involve Parents in Early Childhood Education*, Brigham Young University Press, Utah. Overview of parental involvement and specific suggestions for approaching parents, setting up programmes in various areas

Carr, J. (1980), *Helping Your Handicapped Child*, Penguin, Harmondsworth. Uses behaviour-modification techniques for teachers and parents to achieve behaviour change

Gipps, C., Steadman, S., Blackstone, T. and Stierer, B. (1983), *Testing Children: Standardised Testing in LEAs and Schools*, Heinemann Educational Books, London. On the basis of their research, the authors offer a critique of LEA testing and summarise pros and cons of assessing reading in particular

Griffiths, A. and Hamilton, D. (1984), *Parent, Teacher, Child*, Methuen, London. General details of how to set up PIR, including use and examples of record cards

Laishley, J. (1983), *Working with Young Children*, Edward Arnold, London. Helpful on observation approaches

Newson, E. and Hipgrave, T. (1982), *Getting Through to Your Handicapped Child*, Cambridge University Press, Cambridge. Introduces a behavioural framework for identifying and observing behaviour and drawing up 'treatment' plans

Raban, B. (1983), *Guides to Assessment: Reading*, Macmillan, London. Discursive, informative review of purposes and many techniques of assessment

Reading: Involving Parents, Coventry Community Education Development Centre, Briton Road, Coventry. Includes sections on parents helping at home and in school, home visiting, and parents who do not speak English

Shearer, M.S. and Shearer, D.E. (1977), 'Parental Involvement', in Jordan, J.B., Hayden, A.H., Karnes, K. and Wood, M.M. (eds), *Early Childhood Education for Exceptional Children*, Council for Exceptional Children, Reston, VA. Delineates and illustrates types of parental involvement and gives examples of materials used in training parents

Topping, K. (1984), *Paired Reading Training Pack*, Kirklees Paired Reading Project, Huddersfield. Includes planning *proforma* and handout on evaluation

Vincent, D., Green, L., Francis, J. and Powney, J. (1983), *A Review of Reading Tests*, NFER-Nelson, Windsor. Compendium and comprehensive review of reading tests

Westmacott, E.V.S and Cameron, R.J. (1981), *Behaviour Can Change*, Globe Education, Basingstoke. Covers observations, data collection, planning a teaching programme

Wyckoff, J. (1980), 'Parent Education Programmes: Ready, Set, Go', in Fine, M.J. (ed.), *Handbook on Parent Education*, Academic Press, New York. Chapter deals with the issues of how to organise and teach parenting skills to groups of parents

33 RESOURCES: EXAMPLES AND DETAILS

Sheila Wolfendale and Keith Topping

Readers will appreciate that this chapter could have constituted a whole book by itself. The co-editors have personal collections of resource materials which are very large indeed, although many such materials have overlapping content. Within the space available to us here, we can merely list some of the more central resource materials, giving details of their availability. Within the chapter, the organisational structure of categorisation under the headings of 'Parent Listening', 'Paired Reading', 'Behavioural Methods' and 'Variations' is again followed.

Parent Listening

Baker, C. (1980), *Reading Through Play*, MacDonald Education, London

Bennett, Jill (1982), *A Choice of Stories*. (A select and annotated bibliography for the under-twelves, published at £1.80 by the School Library Association, Victoria House, 29–31 George Street, Oxford OX1 2AY).

CAPER (Children and Parents Enjoy Reading). A tape/slide presentation and a series of booklets and workbooks is available, including material for work with 'pre-readers'. Further details from: Peter Branston, Educational Psychologist, Education Department, County Hall, Swansea SA1 35N, West Glamorgan.

The Community Education Development Centre, Briton Road, Coventry, CV2 4LF, has a wide variety of resource materials available.

At one extreme, this includes a £1,500 in-service package for LEAs, comprising ten one-day sessions, a variety of paper materials, visits and evaluative meetings.

A recent (1984) wide-ranging booklet is titled *Reading: Involving Parents*. Previous booklets have included:

Reading: What Every Parent Should Know (1978)
Beginning Reading: A Book for Parents
Improving Reading: A Book for Parents
Put Yourself in Their Place: Reading
Lend an Ear

Also available via the CEDC is a video entitled *Who's Your Teacher Mum?* (25 mins.) depicting a home-reading scheme, reading workshops and parents helping in classrooms at Breckfield Infants' School, Liverpool.

Doncaster MBC Teaching Support Service has available a particularly well-produced booklet entitled: *Helping Your Child to Read* available from: Teaching Support Centre, Sandringham Road, Doncaster DN2 5LS, South Yorkshire.

A very wide-ranging collection of information, usefully summarised, will be found in: Elden, Y., Gregory, E. and Wolfendale, S. (1983), *Parents and Community in Education*, available from Sheila Wolfendale, Psychology Department, North East London Polytechnic.

Friedlander, J. (1981), *Early Reading Development: a Bibliography*, Harper & Row, London has a useful 'Parent Involvement: Bibliography' section, giving annotated references mainly to work in the USA (pp. 194–9).

Hannon, P., Long, R., Weinberger, J. and Whitehurst, L. (1985), *Involving Parents in the Teaching of Reading: Some Key Sources*. An annotated bibliography of 100+ international references, mainly about 'Parent Listening', available from the Division of Education, University of Sheffield.

Jackson, A. and Hannon, P. (1981), *The Belfield Reading Project*, Belfield Community Council, Rochdale. A substantial booklet with plenty of practical detail: £1 including postage and packing (discount on bulk orders) from The Treasurer, Belfield Community Council, Samson Street, Rochdale, OL16 2XW.

Jeffs, A. *Children and Parents Reading*, 80p from National Committee of Parent–Teacher Associations Publications, 43 Stonebridge Road, Northfleet, Gravesend, Kent.

Mackay, D. and Sims, J. (1976), *Help Your Child to Read and Write More*, Penguin Books, Harmondsworth.

The National Book League (Book House, 45 East Hill, Wandsworth, London SW18 2QZ) produce: *Children's Books — an Information Guide* (£1.78).

The National Committee of Parent–Teacher Associations have commissioned *Children, Parents and Books*, a 14-minute 16 mm film about the value of reading at home, which is available from Concord Films, 201 Felixstowe Road, Ipswich, Suffolk (tel. 0473 76012).

PACT. A Handbook for Teachers is available from: Pitfield Project, Hackney Teachers' Centre, Digby Road, London E9. A video is also available: Unit A: *Bringing Home and School Together to Develop Reading* (58 minutes: VHS £35, Betamax £38, Umatic £45, notes £3, VAT extra). Available from CLF Vision, Chalfont Grove, Gerrards Cross, Buckinghamshire (tel. 02407 4433). Unit B is expected to be available in mid-1985. A straightforward description of the project is available in Griffiths, A. and Hamilton, D. (1984), *Parent, Teacher, Child*, Methuen, London.

Peake, A. (1984), *Hearing Your Child Read at Home — Suggestions for Parents* is available from the Family, Child and Education Advisory Centre, 6 Chatsworth Street, Liverpool L7 6PT (tel. 051 709 6664).

The Portsmouth Film and Video Co-operative, Hornpipe Arts Centre, Kingston Road, Portsmouth (tel 0705 861551); has two relevant videos available: *Reading Together* (1984 — VHS or Betamax, 25 mins; about parental involvement in reading schemes at two schools in Hampshire) and *Parents, Children and Teachers — A Working Partnership* (1983 — VHS, 22 mins; showing parental involvement with parents working in school, including parental teaching of pre-reading skills).

The Centre for the Teaching of Reading (Director: Betty Root), School of Education, University of Reading, 29 Eastern Avenue, Reading RG1 5RU, Berkshire; tel. Reading 62662/3; produces a series of useful booklets:

Parental Involvement in Reading (checklists for parents and teachers)
Stories for Reading Aloud to Children (3–7 years) by Cliff Moon
Children Learning to Read — What Parents Can Do to Help
Guidelines for Those Who Hear Children Read

These will be found to be clear, thorough and sensible. A video is also available: *Crossfire*, which shows parents, teachers and children working together in Campsbourne Infant School in Haringey, particularly with reference to children and their reading. (Hire £10, purchase £30, both plus VAT and postage and packing).

A tape/slide presentation is also available, entitled *Helping Your Child to Read*. This is in two parts, each based on 12 slides and expected to last for 12 minutes, the first part focusing on preschool and the second on reading and school.

Thatcher, J. (1984), *Teaching Reading to Mentally Handicapped Children*, Croom Helm, London.

Townsend, D. (1982), *Reading: The School and Parents* (55p); Townsend, D. (1982), *Reading: How Can I Help My Child?* (available in English, Punjabi, Hindi, Gujarati, Vietnamese, Cantonese). Both from: Reading and Language Development Centre, Nene College (Park Campus), Broughton Green Road, Northampton NN2 7AL.

Trelease, J. (1984), *The Read-Aloud Handbook*, Penguin Books, Harmondsworth. Includes an extensive annotated bibliography of 'recommended' reading material.

Warlow, A. *et al*. (1979), *Read! Read! Read! Some Advice on How You Can Help Your Child*, 3rd edn. Available from: ILEA Centre for Language in Primary Education, Ebury Teachers' Centre, Sutherland Street, London SW1V 4LH.

Paired Reading

A very simple introduction to the area is provided in two articles:
K.J. Topping (1984), 'Paired Reading', *Child Education*, vol. 61, no. 12, 10–11.
K.J. Topping (1985), 'Paired Reading: Setting up a School-based Project', *Child Education*, vol. 62, no. 1, 10–11.

Roger Morgan's original article is worth consulting in detail, to see where it all began:
Morgan, R.T.T. (1976), ' "Paired Reading" Tuition: A Preliminary Report on a Technique for Cases of Reading Deficit', *Child Care, Health and Development*, vol. 2, 13–28.

The other papers cited in Chapter 11 ('An Introduction to Paired Reading') are also worth following up for those interested in Paired Reading with specific populations (Asians, non-readers, ESN(M) pupils, 'dyslexics', etc.). Not all of these are easy to acquire, however.

The most comprehensive collection of resource materials available to date is Topping's *Paired Reading Training Pack* (1984). This includes sets of paper materials to structure and facilitate planning, running and evaluating a Paired Reading project. A video for modelling at initial training meetings is incorporated. Details below:

Paired-reading Training Pack

A. *Preparation and Planning*

1. Leaflet: 'Setting Up a School-based PR Project'
2. Planning Information Proforma
3. PR Bibliography

B. *Training*

4. Training Video (55 mins)
5. Training Video Instructions
6. Parent's Leaflet: 'How to Do It'
7. Home Reading Record Sheet
8. PR Checklist on Method
9. Handout: 'PR — What are the Advantages?'
10. PR Evaluation Results Summary Chart

C. *Evaluation and Follow-up*

11. Leaflet: 'Evaluating PR Projects'
12. Follow-up Questionnaire (Parents and Children)
13. Teacher Evaluative Checklist
14. Parent Evaluative Checklist
15. Reading Interest Scale
16. Handout: 'Beyond Paired Reading'

A training pamphlet for peer or cross-age tutor Paired Reading projects is also available, as are training pamphlets for Asian parents in Punjabi, Bengali, Hindi and Urdu. All items are copyright.

Further details are available from: Paired Reading Project, Psychological Service, Directorate of Educational Services, Oldgate

House, 2 Oldgate, Huddersfield HD1 6QW, West Yorkshire (tel. 0484 37399 ext. 291).

Many other LEA Psychological Services or Reading Advisory Services will be able to provide guidance and (at least) training leaflets.

The Leeds Psychological Service uses a particularly simple pamphlet. The Ashfield Schools Psychological Centre (Nottinghamshire) produces a well-designed handbook for parents and a more substantial handbook for schools. This is backed up by a training video, checklists of technique and diary sheets. Doubtless other services have made efforts in similar directions.

Behavioural Methods

Reinforcement

Staats, A.W., Van Mondfrans, A.P. and Minke, K.A. (1967), *Manual of Administration and Recording Procedure for the Staats 'Motivated Learning' Reading Procedure*, Wisconsin Research and Development Centre for Cognitive Learning, Madison, Wisconsin. There are numerous other 'how-to-do-it' books for parents explaining the principles of behaviour modification, but few relating only to reading.

Pause, Prompt and Praise

T. Glynn *et al.* (1979), *Remedial Reading at Home: Helping You to Help Your Child*, New Zealand Council for Educational Research, Wellington (a manual for parents). Also four video films, also by Ted Glynn *et al.* (1979), series titled, *Helping You to Help Your Child*, (screened by South Pacific Television in 1979). Can be hired from NZCER Test and Book Sales Service, PO Box 3237, Wellington, New Zealand.

Precision Teaching

A very simple expository article is:
Muncey, J. and Williams, H. (1981), 'Daily Evaluation in the Classroom', *Special Education: Forward Trends*, vol. 8, no. 3, 31–4.

Less simple is:
Williams, H., Muncey, J., Winteringham, D. and Duffy, M. (1980), *Precision Teaching: A Classroom Manual*, 2nd edn, Coventry Psychological Service.

A classic, but technical, text is:
Formentin, P. and Csapo, M. (1980), *Precision Teaching*, Centre for Human Development and Research, Vancouver.

The Walsall PAIRS Project (see Chapter 21) is largely based on precision teaching methodology, which is simply explained in the PAIRS booklets for parents. These are:

1. *Getting Ready to Read*
2. *Reading to Your Child*
3. *Listening to Your Child Read*
4. *Teaching Words*
5. *Teaching Sounds*
6. *Teaching Spelling*
7. *Checking for Understanding*
8. *Checking for Progress — Words and Sounds*
9. *Checking for Progress — Listening to Your Child Read*
10. *Checking for Progress — Spelling*

These booklets may be available from: Principal Educational Psychologist, Child Guidance Service, Littleton Street West, Walsall WS2 8EN, West Midlands. (The booklets may be contracted out for publication by a commercial concern, but the Psychological Service at Walsall will advise on the current position).

Direct Instruction

The classic text is:
Carnine, D.W. and Silbert, J. (1979), *Direct Instruction Reading*, Charles E. Merrill, Columbus, Ohio.

A technical and sweeping discussion of the principles of Direct Instruction will be found in:
Engelmann, S. and Carnine, D.W. (1982), *Theory of Instruction*, Ervington, New York.

Another useful source of reference is:
Fabre, T. (1982), *The Application of Direct Instruction in Special Education: An Annotated Bibliography*, University of Oregon, Eugene, Oregon.

Engelmann and his associates have produced a *Direct Instruction Reading Manual for Parents* taken from the 'DISTAR' fast cycle, but this is not

easy to obtain in the UK as yet:
Engelmann, S., Haddox, P. and Bruner, E. (1983), *Teach Your Child to Read in 100 Easy Lessons*, Simon & Schuster, New York.

Other useful literature in the field is referred to in Chapter 18, 'An Introduction to Behavioural Methods'.

Commercial packs of materials based on Direct Instruction principles are available from:

DISTAR READING, READING MASTERY AND CORRECTIVE READING
Science Research Associates
Newtown Road
Henley-on-Thames
Oxfordshire RG9 1EN

METRA
Henley Marketing Services
102 Greys Hill
Henley-on-Thames
Oxfordshire RG9 1SL

who will be pleased to supply information on request.

Variations

Buckley, S. (1984), *Reading and Language Development in Children with Down's Syndrome: A Guide for Parents and Teachers*. Video: *Reading Skills in Pre-school Children with Down's Syndrome* (35 mins, VHS or Betamax £15, Umatic extra). Details: Department of Psychology, Portsmouth Polytechnic, King Charles Street, Portsmouth P01 2ER, Hants.

Fox Hill (see Chapter 28): *Have You A Minute? The Fox Hill Reading Project*, by H. Smith and M. Marsh. A booklet with a wealth of descriptive material about the project, available from the authors at Fox Hill First and Nursery School, Keats Road, Sheffield S6 1AZ.
Also see: Weinberger, J. (1983), *Fox Hill Reading Workshop*. (Another substantial pamphlet, available from Family Service Units, 207 Old Marylebone Road, London NW1 5QP).

W.E.C. Gillham (1974), *Teaching a Child to Read*, University of London Press, London. A slim paperback which is clear and thorough and has not been bettered since, as an attempt to transmit a curriculum-based approach to parents.

Mary Greening and Jean Spenceley (see Chapter 24) have pamphlets and video available to transmit their concept of 'Shared Reading'. Contact via the County Psychological Service, 5 Turner Street, Redcar TS10 1AY, Cleveland (tel. Redcar 485610).

C. Milburn is the author of: *The Children's Home Reading Course* (two packs available at £12 each, published by Blackie).

Obrist, C. (1978) (see Chapter 24), *How to Run Family Reading Groups*, Occasional Publication, United Kingdom Reading Association. A useful how-to-do-it booklet.

McNicholas, J. and McEntee, J. (1973), *Games to Develop Reading Skills*, 2nd edn, National Association for Remedial Education, Stafford.

'Hip Pocket' Booklets (1978): (1) *Reading Games* (2) *Spelling Games* (3) *Maths Games*, Harcourt, Brace, Jovanovich, Sydney.

Wade, B. (1984), *Story at Home and School*, Education Review, Occasional Publication no. 10, University of Birmingham.

Wood, A. and Simpkins, L. (1982), *Involving Parents in the Curriculum*, 3rd edn, Home and School Council, 43 Stonebridge Road, Northfleet, Gravesend, Kent.

LIST OF CONTRIBUTORS

Trevor Bryans Senior Educational Psychologist, London Borough of Brent (formerly Birmingham)

Sue Buckley Senior Lecturer, Department of Psychology, Portsmouth Polytechnic

Avril Bush Head of Special Needs Department, Deighton Junior School, Huddersfield, West Yorkshire

Roger Bushell Educational Psychologist, Tameside, Greater Manchester

Leslie Carrick-Smith Psychologist in private practice, Sheffield

Tessa Cooknell Educational Psychologist, Gloucestershire (formerly Birmingham)

Lyn Fry Senior Educational Psychologist, London Borough of Waltham Forest

Ted Glynn Professor Education, University of Otago, Dunedin, New Zealand

Alex Griffiths Principal Educational Psychologist, Calderdale, West Yorkshire (formerly ILEA)

Peter Hannon Lecturer, Division of Education, University of Sheffield

Alan Heath Educational Psychologist, ILEA

Jenny Hewison Lecturer, Department of Psychology, University of Leeds

Pauline Holdsworth Deputy Headteacher, Mowbray School, Bedale, North Yorkshire

Angela Jackson Community Teacher, Kirkholt Centre, Rochdale

Greta Jungnitz Head Teacher, Ash Tree Infant School, Halifax, West Yorkshire

Ann Kidd Educational Psychologist, Birmingham

Alastair King Educational Psychologist, ILEA

David Knapman Senior Educational Psychologist, Somerset

Marie Levey Educational Psychologist, Devon (formerly Birmingham)

Flora McLeod Community Education Development Centre, Coventry

Margaret Marsh Head Teacher, Fox Hill First and Nursery School, Sheffield

Andy Miller Lecturer, Child Development Research Unit, University of Nottingham

Roger Morgan Deputy Director of Social Services, Oxfordshire

Beryl Page Community Teacher, Belfield Community School, Rochdale

Chris Reeve Principal Educational Psychologist, Walsall, West Midlands

Mary Robertson Educational Psychologist, London Borough of Bromley

David Robson Senior Educational Psychologist, High Peak, Derbyshire

Hilda Smith Teacher, Fox Hill First and Nursery School, Sheffield

Jonathan Solity Lecturer, Education Department, University of Warwick

Jeremy Swinson Senior Educational Psychologist, Liverpool

Colin Tyre Chief Educational Psychologist, South Glamorgan

Lorraine Wareing Educational Psychologist, London Borough of Brent

Paul Widlake Community Education Development Centre, Coventry

Sam Winter Lecturer, Department of Education, University of Hong Kong

Peter Young Previously Senior Inspector, South Glamorgan; tutor, Cambridge Institute of Education

INDEX